This book is due on the last date stamped below.
Failure to return books on the date due may result
in assessment of overdue fees.

TAX REFORM

Selected Titles in ABC-CLIO's
CONTEMPORARY
WORLD ISSUES
Series

For a complete list of titles in this series, please visit
www.abc-clio.com.

Books in the Contemporary World Issues series address vital issues in today's society, such as genetic engineering, pollution, and biodiversity. Written by professional writers, scholars, and nonacademic experts, these books are authoritative, clearly written, up to date, and objective. They provide a good starting point for research by high school and college students, scholars, and general readers as well as by legislators, businesspeople, activists, and others.

Each book, carefully organized and easy to use, contains an overview of the subject, a detailed chronology, biographical sketches, facts and data and/or documents and other primary-source material, a directory of organizations and agencies, annotated lists of print and nonprint resources, and an index.

Readers of books in the Contemporary World Issues series will find the information they need to have a better understanding of the social, political, environmental, and economic issues facing the world today.

TAX REFORM

A Reference Handbook

Second Edition

James John Jurinski

**CONTEMPORARY
WORLD ISSUES**

ABC-CLIO

Santa Barbara, California • Denver, Colorado • Oxford, England

Library of Congress Cataloging-in-Publication Data

Jurinski, James.
  Tax reform : a reference handbook / James John Jurinski. — 2nd ed.
    p. cm. — (Contemporary world issues)
  Includes bibliographical references and index.
  ISBN 978-1-59884-322-4 (hardback) — ISBN 978-1-59884-323-1
(ebook)   1. Taxation—Law and legislation—United States.   I. Title.
  KF6289.J87   2012
  343.7304—dc23   2011053033

ISBN: 978-1-59884-322-4
EISBN: 978-1-59884-323-1

16 15 14 13 12   1 2 3 4 5

This book is also available on the World Wide Web as an eBook.
Visit www.abc-clio.com for details.

ABC-CLIO, LLC
130 Cremona Drive, P.O. Box 1911
Santa Barbara, California 93116-1911

This book is printed on acid-free paper ∞

Manufactured in the United States of America

Contents

Preface

In the first edition of this book your author predicted that "tax reform will continue to be a major policy debate in the first decade of the twenty-first century." A dozen years later this prediction has proved true. Although nearly everyone agrees that the U.S. tax system is in need of reform, the agreement ends there. One of the great debates of the next decade will be not only the design of the U.S. tax system but also the appropriate size of the government and the amount of wealth that the government will take from citizens in the form of taxes. Accordingly, the tax reform debate is also a debate about the role of government and individualism in American life. When the government funds programs like national defense, Social Security, subsidized school lunches, and federally subsidized student loans, the money come from citizens' taxes. Tax reductions will reduce these government programs as well as others, so many people have a personal stake in this debate.

The American Revolution started as a tax revolt. In the memorable Boston Tea Party, colonists angry about the rise in tea taxes imposed unilaterally by England dumped imported tea from ships into the Boston Harbor. This event popularized the cry of "No taxation without representation" and helped galvanize revolutionary fervor in the colonies. Displeasure with high taxes remains a contemporary issue. However, complaints about the tax amounts themselves are less frequent than complaints about the complexity and difficulty of complying with the tax rules. Congressional hearings castigating the Internal Revenue Service (IRS) for harassing taxpayers illustrate the widespread displeasure among Americans with the current U.S. tax system. This prevalent dissatisfaction suggests that one of the plans being considered to simplify or modify the present system may be adopted.

Tax reform has become a major issue for presidential candidates. Various candidates have campaigned to replace the current federal income tax system with a "flat tax," while others have proposed a national sales tax or a value-added tax that would harmonize the U.S. tax system with the systems of our major trading partners overseas. The debate about the future of "entitlements"—including Social Security, Medicare, and President Obama's health care program—continues. Although it is not clear whether any tax reform proposals will be adopted, it is clear that informed citizens need to understand how the tax system works and the key issues that need to be addressed and decided.

The need for tax reform is not only a federal issue. On the state and local levels a growing number of senior citizens resent paying higher taxes to support the public school systems and an ever-growing range of government social services. In many states, groups have "frozen" property taxes, resulting in underfunded schools and social programs. Also, states that are attempting to tax mail order and Internet sales are facing possible limitations on that power placed by the federal government. As more and more people use the Internet to buy goods and services, new taxes cannot be far behind.

Although there is not much agreement about the design of a reformed tax system, there is general agreement on goals. Most commentators agree that any reform proposal must promote simplicity. Even advocates of the current income tax agree that the tax code is in need of radical simplification. Another goal is fairness, not only for individuals but also for businesses. The current system undertaxes some taxpayers while overtaxing others. Finally, commentators agree that a reformed tax system must increase U.S. competitiveness in the global business environment and must also promote domestic job growth.

High taxes and complexity are not the only impetus for tax reform. Many reformers want to make the system "fairer," although there is little agreement about exactly what a "fair" tax system would look like. Others are concerned with modifying the current tax system to more evenly tax mail order sales and electronic commerce on the Internet. In addition, several groups want the tax system to influence Americans' behavior in certain ways, a not uncommon goal of taxation. Since World War II, Congress has used the tax system not only to raise revenues but also to control inflation, stimulate the economy, redistribute income, and encourage good behavior and discourage bad. Business advocates want the tax system designed to encourage investment. Environmentalists want the tax system designed to encourage citizens to make decisions that enhance the environment. Any discussion of tax reform must take into account these more complex policy matters.

Although this book discusses many complex tax issues, the text is written for laymen and students, with a minimum of legal and accounting jargon. The book stresses the political aspects of the debate rather than the technical aspects.

Chapter 1, "Background and History," provides a brief historical overview of different types of taxes, including tariffs, income taxes, death taxes, social security taxes, sales taxes, and property taxes. The chapter also contains a fairly detailed discussion of the U.S. income tax system as well as a look at tax equity issues. Finally the chapter discusses some of the better-known tax reform proposals.

Chapter 2, "Problems, Controversies, and Solutions," includes an overview of the U.S. tax system, tax policy, and proposals for tax reform. The chapter begins with a discussion of "fairness" (equity) issues. It concludes with an examination of several current tax reform proposals.

Chapter 3, "Special U.S. Issues," includes a discussion of a few special tax issues. The chapter looks at tax reform proposals involving "green" or "eco" taxes, including a discussion of "carbon taxes," which have been imposed in some other countries. The chapter next examines a number of problems with state and local taxation, with emphasis on multistate taxation issues. Finally, the chapter examines the legal and practical problem of taxing Internet sales.

Chapter 4, "Chronology," contains a timeline of tax highlights from 1620 to 2011.

Chapter 5, "Biographical Sketches," contains biographical sketches of individuals, some current some historical, who have made an impact on the issue of tax reform.

Chapter 6, "Data and Documents," presents an assortment of unbiased government documents and reports that contain detailed facts and statistics on taxes and commentary on various tax reform proposals.

Chapter 7, "Directory of Organizations and Associations," contains names, contact information, web addresses, and brief descriptions of organizations and associations interested in taxation and tax reform.

Chapter 8, "Resources," includes an annotated bibliography of printed books, scholarly and popular articles, and nonprint materials, including a list of Internet sites dedicated to tax reform.

Finally, the book contains a glossary of technical and non-technical tax terms that are useful in understanding the material in this book and other tax materials. The language of taxation is a bit like a foreign language, even to accountants and lawyers. Terms like *capital asset* often have a meaning in tax law that is different from their usual meaning in business. Even a slight change in terms and phrases can make large changes in meaning. Readers are encouraged to use the glossary as a resource when reading tax materials.

Readers need to be careful in relying on specific tax rules stated in the book. The tax rules change rapidly even when no major tax legislation is passed. Tax rates and amounts differ from year to year. This manuscript was prepared in the fall of 2011. By the time you read this book, several of the rules will have changed; so use the information with care. When in doubt, double check the rules on the web sites listed in chapter 8.

Although tax reform groups typically have political agendas, your author has striven to prepare a book for students and lay-people that presents both sides of the tax debate. Readers should examine the arguments and come to their own informed conclusions. Any errors you find in the book are my own.

This book has been written to teach citizens and students about tax reform and to provide a reference handbook to enable them to pursue the topic. Without the participation of informed citizens, tax reform will never come about.

1

Background and History

U nderstanding tax reform options requires a basic understanding of taxes in general and the U.S. tax system in particular. This chapter presents an overview of taxes, including the nature and goals of taxation and an overview of various kinds of taxes, including tariffs, income taxes, death taxes, Social Security taxes, sales taxes, and property taxes. The chapter also contains a fairly detailed discussion of the history of the U.S. income tax system.

Understanding Taxes

Nature of Taxation: What Is a Tax?

Any study of tax reform requires a general knowledge of taxation. A good place to start is with a definition of a tax. Paraphrasing a definition formulated by the late Professor Ray A. Sommerfeld of the University of Texas, a tax is a nonpenal but compulsory transfer from the private sector to the public sector levied without receipt of a specific benefit.

Taxes are not generally designed to punish taxpayers, although taxpayers often complain about punishing tax rates. In contrast, a traffic fine, which is also a transfer to the public sector, is penal in nature—it is meant to punish as well as raise revenue. In some cases, levies are designed as "sin taxes" with the goal of discouraging specific behavior. For example, alcohol and tobacco are often singled out as "vices" to which taxes should apply. Proponents of these taxes argue that the taxes will help push rational individuals to end their sinful habits. Little evidence supports this view. In fact, it is probably safe to assume that such taxes result in two undesirable outcomes: First, they encourage a black market of untaxed alcohol and tobacco products. Second, they impose an undue burden on poorer taxpayers, who continue consuming alcohol and tobacco products but have less money to support themselves and their families after paying the tax.

Taxes must also be differentiated from user fees—an increasingly popular moniker. A user fee is a government fee assessed only on people using a particular government service. Highway tolls, postage stamps, and entry fees to parks are examples of user fees; although they are compulsory and nonpenal, they apply only to individuals who are using the service. Hence a user fee is not strictly a tax. At first blush, user fees seem like a rational alternative to taxes because only those who use the service or facility are required to pay. However, the rationality and wisdom of user fees is also subject to debate. For example, the U.S. National Park Service is experimenting with collecting user fees at national parks and monuments. Although these fees help defray part of the parks' cost of upkeep, they can also be regressive because the rich and poor pay exactly the same fee. Governments also use taxes to regulate behavior. The most obvious example is a "sin tax" designed to discourage bad behavior, as described earlier. Taxes can also be used to encourage exemplary behavior. For example, the federal income tax law provides a tax deduction for qualifying individuals who make charitable contributions. In the hope of encouraging taxpayers to support their favorite charities, the government forgoes tax revenues because the tax deduction lowers the income amount on which the income tax is computed. This measure is highly effective in encouraging charitable contributions.

Goals of Taxation

Raising Revenue

The primary goal of taxation from biblical times to our own has been to raise revenue for the government. Although a tax may be enacted to encourage or discourage certain behavior, a "tax" must be primarily for revenue raising. Taxes also differ from user fees, from which the payer receives a direct benefit. In some cases certain taxes do benefit users. For example, the revenues from gasoline taxes are typically dedicated to highway maintenance and improvements. Drivers who pay the tax when they purchase gas receive a benefit, whereas nondrivers are not asked to pay and receive no direct benefit. Most taxes are not so earmarked. In the U.S. government, spending and revenue raising are normally not linked. With the exception of earmarked taxes like the gasoline tax, Congress does not directly link tax increases to increased costs in particular bills. The government spends income tax revenues on "public" goods and services, such as national defense, infrastructure, public education, and the national park system. It would be difficult to apportion user fees for these objectives.

Control of the Economy

Economists have long recognized that taxation can be used to influence a nation's economy. The history of taxation often parallels the history of wars. Governments need huge amounts of revenue to fund wars. Although they can rely on the printing press to merely print more paper money, the result would be runaway inflation. The government would spend the money to buy increasingly scarce goods and services, driving up prices in the process. The reduced purchasing power of the currency would spur the government to print even more money. Conversely, if the government imposed higher taxes, it could purchase goods and services for the war effort without resorting to expanding the money supply. At the same time, higher taxes would lower private demand because the higher taxes would ensure that the public had less money to spend. The U.S. government successfully used this strategy during World War II. During the Vietnam War the president and Congress resisted new taxes and did not cut domestic spending, which led to inflationary pressure. Therefore governments must balance monetary and tax policy to manage the economy and minimize inflation.

Tax rules also influence businesses' investment decisions. In a global economy, companies locate manufacturing plants in low-cost countries; taxes are one of those costs. Accordingly, low businesses taxes generally encourage business investment. Tax rates are not the end of the story however, because even countries with relatively high taxes may craft specific tax breaks to encourage certain types of business investment. Because business investment also creates jobs and wealth, the design of business taxes affects job creation. A well-designed tax reform plan should address all of these issues.

Wealth Redistribution

Taxes can be used for wealth redistribution. Most western countries incorporate this goal into their tax systems. The government theoretically plays Robin Hood by imposing higher taxes on the wealthy and delivering benefits to the more needy within society. The "progressivity" of income tax rates—the degree to which the percentage tax rates rise with income—is an obvious means to achieve this goal. Others argue that the government should ensure equality of opportunity and not equality of results. They also argue that the progressive taxation penalizes hard work and success.

In some societies, taxes have operated to redistribute wealth from the bottom of society to the top. In prerevolutionary France the king nearly bankrupted the nation by creating a lavish lifestyle for the royal family and court. Faced with crushing taxes and the spectacle of a parasitic nobility, the citizens revolted and, in the ensuing revolution, reduced both the level of taxation and the physical stature of the king and many of the nobility.

Although it is frequently assumed that today's taxes effect a redistribution of wealth from the better off to those who are less well off, there is little evidence to support this view. The progressivity of tax rates means that middle- and upper-income taxpayers pay a higher proportion of the taxes that go toward services that benefit everyone (including people who pay no taxes at all), like defense spending at the federal level and police and schools at the local level. However, middle- and upper-income taxpayers also receive indirect government benefits. In fact, much government spending as well as specific tax rules are designed to help middle- and upper-income taxpayers. For example, although low-income taxpayers may avail themselves of the opportunity to earn a college degree at a tax-supported public university or to use the tax-subsidized local airport, in reality they are much less likely to do so than are their more prosperous fellows. Although many assume that government "benefits" are directed to the poor, many government subsidies tend to be of greater benefit to middle- and upper-income taxpayers.

Types of Taxes

A government can impose a variety of taxes. When Americans think about taxes, they normally think about individual income taxes. In fact, the various levels of government collect a wide variety of taxes. Any discussion of tax reform must consider alternatives to the present income tax system, of course; but a brief review of other taxes is in order first.

Head Taxes
A head tax is simply a flat tax assessed on every citizen. Each citizen is obligated to pay the same amount, no matter what his or her income level or wealth. With this relatively unsophisticated tax, the burden falls more heavily on the poor than the rich.

Poll Taxes
Similar to the head tax is the poll tax, which is a tax on the privilege of voting. In colonial times and the early U.S. republic, voting was limited to property owners, and the poll tax was a continuation of this qualification. The poll tax ensured that only those with enough wealth could vote. When enfranchisement was expanded, the poll tax remained. Poll taxes were eliminated in the United States in the 1960s because they were typically used to disenfranchise African Americans and other poor voters who lacked the money to pay the tax.

Wealth Taxes
One of the oldest types of taxes is a wealth tax. "Wealth" consists of property owned, whereas "income" consists of income earned and received. An individual could have a very high income but very little wealth. For example, if a person who has zero wealth earns a lot of income during the year but spends all that income, he or she will end the year with no wealth. If that person is subject to a tax system that taxes wealth but not income, the person will pay no taxes. If the system taxes income but not wealth, the same person would be heavily taxed. Consider a second example: a person who inherits wealth and hoards it but has no income. This person would be heavily taxed by a system that taxed wealth but not income but would escape taxation if the system taxed only income and not wealth.

Because wealth taxes target the well off, these are considered "progressive" taxes, taxing the rich far more heavily than the poor. As the previous examples illustrate, income taxes tax those who are earning income and creating wealth currently, whereas wealth taxes most heavily tax those who have received their wealth from gifts or inheritances. Accordingly, the income tax tends to heavily tax "new money," whereas wealth taxes tend to heavily tax "old money" in wealthy families. To tap both sources of revenue, one could combine a wealth tax with an income tax. An argument can be made, however, that such a combination is unfair because the wealth tax will be taxing property that has already been subject to the income tax. Although this argument is generally correct, double taxation is a common occurrence.

These two taxes also show a generational bias. In general, older individuals have more wealth in the form of homes, investments, pensions, and businesses. Younger people who are working often have little wealth and are relying on their income to build wealth. A system that taxes only income and not wealth makes it increasingly hard to become wealthy and perpetuates the existing division between the haves and have-nots. A system that taxes wealth more heavily should lead to greater social mobility as hard-working and capable individuals are able to earn income and then build wealth.

Wealth taxes have existed for centuries because they are simple to understand and relatively hard to evade. Wealth taxes generally apply to real estate, business property, and other "tangible items." They can also apply to bank accounts and other types of "intangible" assets, like stocks and bonds. Typical problems with enforcing wealth taxes on property include the difficulty of valuing the property. Because the taxes are typically a percentage of a property's value, the assessment of that value is always contentious. The states rely on both wealth and income taxes. Localities rely on property tax—a type of wealth tax. The federal government does impose one type of wealth tax—the federal estate and gift taxes, which are taxes imposed on the transfer of wealth. However, the national government relies most heavily on income taxes, as described in greater detail in the next section.

Income Taxes

The United States primarily uses revenues from income taxes to run the federal government. All but a handful of states also have an income tax. In fact, for fiscal year 2009, Americans paid $968 billion in individual federal income taxes and corporations paid an additional $174 billion. In relative terms, in fiscal 2007 the federal government relied on the following taxes: 44 percent individual income tax, 41 percent Social Security and other payroll taxes, 8 percent corporate income tax, and 7 percent all other taxes.

The government derives over 60 percent of its revenue from income taxes alone, and 85 percent of that comprises income and payroll taxes paid by individuals. The income tax is relatively new. It was developed in the late 1700s by the British, who needed a new source of revenue to fund their war efforts. As discussed in the following sections, although there was a temporary income tax during the Civil War individual taxpayers started paying income tax to the U.S. Treasury only in 1913.

Payroll Taxes

Payroll taxes include federal and state unemployment taxes and local payroll taxes used to fund various local services, such as public transit systems. The Social Security tax (Federal Insurance Contributions Act, or FICA) is the most important payroll tax in the U.S. tax landscape. Indeed, in 2010 Social Security taxes made up one third of all U.S. tax revenues. Social Security taxes are relatively high; for taxpayers earning less than $25,000, Social Security taxes are normally higher than their federal income taxes. Although Social Security taxes are used to fund the Social Security Trust Fund, it is not a trust fund in the conventional sense. The money is not stashed away and segregated for the retirees' use. The government uses the money raised through Social Security to buy government securities, and the income from these securities are used to finance Social Security retirement, disability, and death benefits.

Students of taxation must recognize that FICA is really a type of tax passed by Congress rather than a retirement annuity system. Whereas income tax rates generally declined between 1962 and 1993, Social Security taxes increased steeply. In fact, Social Security is really a type of flat tax. Currently, the employer and the employee each pay 7.65 percent of the employee's earned income. Typically, employers withhold the employee's part and pay the entire combined 15.3 percent to the U.S. Treasury. Self-employed individuals pay both halves (15.3 %). Because of the recession, the employees' share of Social Security payroll taxes (but not benefits) were temporarily reduced during 2011. President Obama proposed and the Congress agreed to extending the reduction into 2012 to stimulate consumer spending, which aimed at reviving the sputtering economy.

Social Security taxes have been on the rise for the last half century: as late as 1976, the combined tax rate was less than 12 percent and applied to about $30,000 of income, whereas 2012's tax of over 15 percent applies to just over $110,000 of earnings, although the limit does not apply to the Medicare portion. As noted previously, because the full tax is imposed on only approximately $110,000 of income, the tax is regressive—the rich pay a lower effective tax rate than do average citizens. If one thinks of Social Security taxes as a form of income tax—and a good argument can be made for this treatment—their flat-rate structure and regressive feature greatly diminish the progressivity of the federal tax system.

Taxes on Transactions

Another type of tax is a tax on particular transactions. Although the most important of these is the retail sales tax, other special transaction taxes include real estate transfer taxes, severance taxes, and taxes on gross receipts. Real estate transfer taxes impose a tax on sellers of real estate. Severance taxes—taxes on the separation of natural resources from the land—are important state taxes in the western United States. Several severance taxes are imposed on gas and oil, minerals, and timber. The government has also required special "stamps" to be affixed to various legal documents from time to time. The famous "stamp tax" that helped fuel revolutionary discontent in the 1770s was one of these special transaction taxes. Another type of transaction tax is a "gross receipts" tax—a business tax that resembles an income tax but is imposed on sales rather than profits. This type of tax, developed during the Great Depression of the 1930s, is imposed on businesses whether or not they make a profit.

The retail sales tax is the most important of the transaction taxes. All but a handful of states impose a retail sales tax, and many localities also impose a "piggyback" sales tax on transactions. Surprisingly, sales taxes are a fairly recent development, starting in the 1930s, when states needed new revenue bases. Retail sales taxes apply only to retail sales, where the "ultimate" consumer pays the tax. Wholesalers are given a "wholesale tax exemption," which avoids the pyramiding of tax.

Governments like retail sales taxes because sellers have to collect the tax at the cash register and are required to handle most of the paperwork. A major sales tax issue is the design of the tax base: that is, what sales are excluded from the base. In most but not all states, the tax applies to the retail sale of goods but not services. In these states the sale of a book would be subject to tax but the sale of a lawyer's services would not. Additionally, many states specifically exempt the sale of medicine and food. Exemptions can be rather arcane. For example, in one state the purchase of a frozen pizza in a grocery store is tax-exempt, whereas the purchase of a baked pizza in a restaurant or at a take-out counter is taxable. If the pizza store sells customers "bake-it-yourself" pizzas that are taken home unbaked, the pizza is untaxed food.

Although in-state transactions pose little theoretical difficulty, transactions over state lines create both theoretical and practical difficulties. States' sales taxes are "destination" taxes—the "destination" state's tax applies (the tax in the buyer's state). In fact, since the actual sales transaction occurs in the seller's state, the destination state actually imposes a "use tax" on the buyer. The use tax rate is identical to the state's sales tax rate. States have great difficulty in enforcing the use tax except when cars are bought out of state. In the case of autos, the state can withhold issuing license plates unless the use tax is paid. When consumers buy goods by mail order from out of state or over the Internet, buyers are theoretically responsible for paying their states' use tax on the purchases, but almost no taxpayers comply. Accordingly, states would like retail mail order and web-based sellers like Amazon.com to collect their use taxes. Currently, only sellers with a physical presence in a state are legally required to collect the use tax, but this limitation is about to change. This issue is described in more detail in chapter 3.

Retail sales taxes are often criticized because they are regressive by nature. The rich and poor pay sales taxes at the same rate. Because the poor have to consume their entire income rather than save or invest part of it, a far higher proportion of their income is subject to this tax than is the case for the rich. Proponents of a national sales tax to replace the current income tax argue that a "consumption tax" (a retail sales tax) would allow money invested by the rich to go untaxed, thereby encouraging increased investment, job growth, and prosperity for all. Although these goals might be recognized, it would come at the cost of sacrificing much of the progressivity of the current tax system.

Excise Taxes

Excise taxes are taxes imposed on the sale of certain commodities. Accordingly, excise taxes, for example, a retail sales tax, are a type of consumption tax. The current federal tax on airline tickets is an excise tax. Until the 1960s, excise taxes were an important source of revenue for the federal government. Like sales taxes, excise taxes are regressive because the poor spend more, if not all, of their income than the better off. Excise taxes have been imposed on a wide variety of goods and services. Examples of current excise taxes are federal gasoline taxes, tobacco taxes, airline ticket taxes, and taxes on tires. Telecommunication taxes imposed by both the federal and state governments are excise taxes. The federal telecommunications tax used to fund school Internet access is a type of excise tax. Although excise taxes are currently out of fashion, they may become a more important source of governmental revenue as electronic commerce becomes a larger part of the U.S. economy. At the time of this writing, Congress is wrestling with the issue of whether the Internet should be a "tax-free zone" or whether sellers on the Internet should bear their fair share of the tax burden.

Customs Duties

Traditionally, customs duties have been an important revenue base for the United States and other countries. In fact, until passage of the individual income tax in 1913, the federal government was primarily run with customs revenues from the tariff. During the first 150 years of U.S. history, the high tariff was used both to raise revenues to run the government and also to discourage foreign imports, thus encouraging domestic industry. In the last half of the 20th century there were worldwide reductions in customs. The North American Free Trade Act (NAFTA)—between the United States, Canada, and Mexico—went a long way toward creating a "free-trade zone" between the three North American trading partners. Similarly, the World Trade Organization continued the General Agreement on Tariffs and Trade (GATT), which lowered international trade barriers.

Value-Added Taxes

A major type of tax not currently imposed by the United States is the value-added tax (VAT). All major countries except the United States impose a value-added tax, such as the Canadian GST, the Goods and Services Tax. As the name suggests, a value-added tax requires producers to add a tax to a product as they add value. Accordingly, the tax is included in the price of the goods and ultimately paid by the consumer of the product. Governments like VAT taxes because they pull in huge amounts of revenue. From a theoretical standpoint, a VAT tax is less transparent than an income tax. With an individual income tax, citizens clearly see how much tax they are paying. With a VAT tax, this amount is hidden.

VAT taxes also give nations a competitive advantage in the global market because they apply to imports but not exports. A VAT is not imposed on exported goods. Accordingly, the price of a Japanese car sold in Japan includes their VAT tax, but the cost of the same model when exported to the United States does not. This helps explain the price difference between products sold overseas and in the United States. When U.S. car makers, who are required to pay U.S. income tax on profits earned on worldwide sales, sell cars outside the United States, they normally raise their prices to include an amount to pay the income tax on the profit. For example, assume that a U.S. manufacturer exports and sells a luxury sport utility vehicle in Japan and expects to earn a $10,000 profit. If the company is in the 35 percent tax bracket, the company will have to increase the price of the car by $3,500 to recoup the cost of the U.S. income tax ($10,000 profit × 35%). The higher cost to pay the income tax reduces the attractiveness of U.S. goods overseas. Proponents of a VAT argue that replacement of the income tax with a VAT would increase the attractiveness of U.S. products overseas.

Tax Base and Tax Rate

In any tax system, there is a "tax base" and a "tax rate." A tax base comprises the property, income, or actions that are liable to taxation. For example, in a property tax system, some property is typically "tax exempt," such as schools, churches, and government property. This property is outside the tax base and is not subject to taxation. In this example, the tax rate is the percentage that is used to tax the property. If a parcel of land is worth $100,000 and the tax rate is 5 percent, the tax on the property would be $5,000 ($100,000 × 0.05). A sales tax operates in a similar manner. Some items are typically exempt from tax—prescription medicine, for example. Sales that are taxed are within the tax base, and the tax percentage—say 7 percent—is the tax rate.

Income taxes also involve tax bases and tax rates. Income is the tax base, and the percentage applied to it is the tax rate. Income taxation tends to be more complicated than property tax or sales tax in this regard. First, there is the problem of defining the income that makes up the tax base. Generally it is net income rather than gross income, meaning, for example, that profits rather than revenues are taxed for a business. Businesses and individuals who sell items and investments for profit are taxed only on their profits, or gains. Congress also has exempted certain income from the tax base. For example, gifts, life insurance proceeds, and inheritances are outside the tax base and can be received free of income tax. Lottery winnings and prizes are within the tax base

and are subject to income tax. This distinction is a tax policy decision made by Congress.

Proportional, Progressive, and Regressive Rates and Bases

Tax rates are even more complex. Property taxes and sales taxes
normally have a single tax rate in a taxing jurisdiction, although
there may be special tax rates in some cases. It would be possible
to have a single-rate income tax—say 15 percent. This would be
a "flat tax." In tax terminology, rates can be proportional, progressive, or regressive. A flat tax is considered to be proportional
because taxpayers' tax bills vary in direct proportion to their incomes. If a system has a progressive tax rate, tax rates themselves
rise as income rises. If a tax system is regressive, tax rates are actually higher for low-income taxpayers. The United States has always had "progressive" income tax rates. The more a taxpayer
earns, the higher the income tax rate. As of 2011, tax rates for
individuals range from 10 to 35 percent. Corporations pay rates
between 15 and 35 percent. Although these rates may seem steep,
they are low compared with the rates of other western countries
and low by historical standards. As late as 1962, individuals faced
top individual income tax rates in the United States of approximately 90 percent.

The tax rate itself does not tell the whole story, however. The
tax base to which the tax rate is applied may determine whether
a tax is progressive, proportional, or regressive. If some items are
excluded from the tax base, the resulting nature of the tax could
change. Consider "dependency exemptions" and "standard deductions," which are a part of the U.S. income tax system. Both of
these provisions exempt income from income tax and, in the case
of low-income taxpayers, may completely eliminate the tax. Even
if the income tax were a flat tax, dependency exemptions and
the standard deduction would cause the tax to be "progressive,"
because those at the bottom of the income scale would have a
lower percentage of their income taxed. For example, assume that
a flat tax of 10 percent is in effect and the combined provisions
exempted $5,000 of income. A taxpayer with $10,000 of income
would pay a tax of $500 ($10,000–$5,000 = $5,000; $5,000 × 0.10 =
$500) and would pay an effective tax rate of only 5 percent ($500 ÷
$10,000 = 5%). A taxpayer earning $100,000 would pay a tax of
$9,500 ($100,000–$5,000 = $95,000; $95,000 × 0.10 = $9,500) and an
effective tax rate of 9.5 percent ($9,500 ÷ $100,000 = 9.5%), despite
the fact that the so-called flat-tax rate appears to be proportional.

Exempting income from taxation through deductions can also have a regressive effect. If upper-income taxpayers are allowed to exempt income through "excess itemized deductions" or can earn income subject to lower capital gains tax rates rather than normal tax rates, the seemingly progressive income tax rate structure is potentially regressive. If the Social Security tax is considered an income tax, it is regressive for this reason. Only a portion of a person's income is subject to the tax. In fact, only earned income (income from wages, salaries, etc.) and not investment income is subject to this tax. For example, for the year 2012 only the first $110,100 of income was subject to the tax. Accordingly, a plumber with $50,000 of earned income will have 100 percent of that income subject to the Social Security tax. A professional baseball player earning $1 million would have only about 11 percent of his income subject to the full tax.

A nominal tax rate is the official tax rate that applies to income. The effective tax rate is the tax rate that actually applies to all of the taxpayer's income. In the earlier example, we saw that a flat tax that had a flat nominal tax rate of 10 percent could actually result in a higher or lower effective tax rate if not all income was taxed. If income at the bottom is exempt from tax, the effective rate for low-income taxpayers would be lower than the nominal rate. If income at higher levels is effectively exempt (most probably by deductions claimed only by the wealthy), those taxpayers' effective rates might be lower than the nominal rates.

Average versus Marginal Tax Rates

It is also important to distinguish average tax rates from marginal tax rates. A marginal tax rate is the tax rate that applies to the last dollar of income, whereas an average tax rate is the effective average tax rate on a taxpayer's income. For example, consider a taxpayer in a hypothetical 40 percent income tax bracket. Although the taxpayer's marginal rate is 40 percent, not all the taxpayer's income is subject to this rate. The U.S. system requires only some of the income to be taxed at this rate; some of the taxpayer's income will be taxed at much lower rates and some will be tax-free. The taxpayer's effective rate, or average rate, may be less than 20 percent even though the marginal rate is 40 percent.

The distinction between average and marginal tax rates is an important one. The fact that only part of a taxpayer's income is subject to the highest rate explains a common fallacy of the uninformed, who sometimes comment that they actually lose money after receiving a pay raise because of being pushed into a higher income tax bracket. This is never the case, because only the additional income is taxed at the taxpayer's highest marginal tax rate. Uninformed taxpayers assume that after receiving a pay raise, all of their income would be subject to the higher tax rate rather than just the incremental increase in pay.

Marginal tax rates do determine the value of tax deductions. Assume that one taxpayer has a 15 percent marginal tax rate while another has a marginal tax rate of 40 percent. If each taxpayer claims an additional $100 of deduction, the deduction is worth $15 in saved taxes to the first but $40 to the second. The deduction is worth more than twice as much merely because of the difference in marginal tax rates.

Principles of Taxation

In 1776 Adam Smith set forth a number of rules for a rational system of taxation in his landmark *The Wealth of Nations* (New York: Dutton, 1919). Smith established four general canons of taxation: taxation must be based on an individual's ability to pay, and taxation should be certain, convenient, and economical. Although Smith's canons of taxation were conceived in the 18th century, Smith's insights are still valid. Before we consider Smith's canons in more detail, we should look at some additional goals of a tax system. That is, revenues should be stable and predictable, yet the tax system should be flexible enough to accommodate changes in the economy, which may cause a downturn in revenues, and flexible enough to increase revenues on relatively short notice to meet an emergency fiscal crisis, such as a war. Today, economic goals are equally important, and tax systems must be designed so that they encourage greater productivity and industrial output. Finally, efficient administration and compliance should always be goals.

Ability to Pay

"The subjects of every state ought to contribute towards the support of government, as nearly as possible, in proportion to their respective abilities; that is, in proportion to revenue which they respectively enjoyed under the protection of the state" (Smith, *Wealth of Nations*).

The first of Smith's canons concerned the ability to pay, often referred to as "equity." In Smith's view, the first requirement of a system is that it be fair. He thought the rich should bear a greater tax burden not only because they simply have more wealth but also because they also benefit more than the poor from having the government protect their interests. At the start of the 21st century, it is easy to lose sight of the fact that governments, through their systems of law and order, preserve property and wealth. Those with the greatest wealth derive the greatest benefit. Tax equity is discussed in more detail further on.

Certainty

"The tax which each individual is bound to pay ought to be certain, and not arbitrary. The time of payment, the manner of payment, the quantity to be paid, ought all to be clear and plain to the contributor, and to every other person" (Smith, *Wealth of Nations*). The certainty goal has a number of facets. Basic fairness requires that the tax system be designed so the tax is not an arbitrary amount fixed by the government. All taxpayers must be treated alike. Businesses operating in less developed countries frequently complain that tax administrators in some of these countries arbitrarily single out a company and force it to pay higher taxes. Additionally, because both individuals and businesses plan their transactions with tax consequences in mind, even across-the-board changes must be minimized. Although the U.S. tax system is not generally arbitrary, in the sense that all taxpayers are subject to the same rules, the rapid change in its tax rules suggests that the system does not always produce certainty. For example, in the last 25 years the United States has drastically changed its taxation of capital gains (profits from investments). Unpredictability of returns tends to discourage investors.

Convenience

"Every tax ought to be levied at the time, or in the manner in which it is most likely to be convenient for the contributor to pay" (Smith, *Wealth of Nations*). It is to the advantage of both the government and taxpayers to make taxpaying more convenient. The more inconvenient and cumbersome the tax, the more likely are taxpayers to avoid paying. Although the government can achieve more convenient taxation, a convenient system might also leave citizens with far less information about their tax burden. An example is gasoline taxes. Gas taxes are built into the price of gasoline, and few drivers notice that nearly half the cost of their gasoline bills is actually a variety of federal and state taxes.

Theoretically, all taxes could be collected using this system by hiding the tax in the cost of goods and services. Although this would be a convenient tax, the invisibility of the tax burden is contrary to the goals of a democracy. Cynical politicians might be attracted by this system, which would allow them to raise taxes with very little citizen scrutiny.

Economy

"Every tax ought to be so contrived as both to take out and keep out of the pockets of the people as little as possible over and above what it brings into the public treasury of the state" (Smith, *Wealth of Nations*).

Smith's fourth canon, economy, focuses on a benefit to the citizens rather than the government. A major criticism of the U.S. tax system is that the complexity of the system is a major burden on both individuals and businesses. The time spent in planning and complying with the tax laws decreases productivity and reduces national competitiveness. Much of the complexity in the current income tax system comes from trying to achieve economic goals and equity. The current tax code provides lower tax rates for capital gains than other types of income, and much of the tax code is concerned with limiting those benefits. Additionally, much of the tax code's complexity consists of elaborate rules to ensure that similarly situated taxpayers pay similar, if not identical, taxes.

Although many taxes in the United States are collected by third parties—gasoline taxes, sales taxes, and Social Security taxes on wages—its income tax system is largely a self-assessment system. Although employers deduct income taxes from the salaries and wages of workers, taxpayers themselves are responsible for computing the tax due, reporting to the government, and paying any amount owed or requesting a refund. The government could, in the name of convenience, compute taxes for everyone.

A Brief History of the U.S. Tax System

During the 19th century the federal government was much smaller than it is today. The familiar federal agencies were smaller or nonexistent, the military establishment was far smaller, and there were few federal entitlement programs that required large bureaucracies and revenues to run. Accordingly, during the

19th century the federal government was able to operate almost exclusively on revenues from customs duties. During the 1800s the tariff that applied to imported goods was a constant political issue. The tariff had two main goals, which were both equally important. First, the tariff raised revenues for the federal government. Second, by making foreign goods relatively more expensive to buy, the tariff gave an advantage to fledgling American manufacturers. The tariff was a contentious political issue throughout the 1800s because it favored geographic areas that had manufacturing. For example, some commentators have suggested that the tariff was one of the prime causes of the American Civil War. The high tariff greatly benefited the industrialized North, while it created high prices for citizens in the southern states, where there was little manufacturing. Even after the Civil War, the tariff remained a hot political issue in national politics and was often a prime issue in congressional and presidential elections. Even as late as the 1930s, the tariff still provided a significant part of the federal government's revenue.

The history of taxes is also the history of war, because governments have often developed new taxes to finance the massive funds needed to fight a war. In fact, the income tax was first used by the British to finance wars against Napoleon. The first use of the income tax in United States was during the American Civil War. Even prior to the Civil War, the U.S. secretary of the treasury had considered using an income tax during the War of 1812. During the Civil War, southern privateers disrupted shipping between northern cities and Europe. Because of this disruption, revenues from the tariff were unreliable, and the union government needed additional funds to finance the war effort. The Union government sold bonds and raised the tariff but needed still more funds, so it imposed the first U.S. income tax.

The original income tax was quite modest by today's standards. The first tax, a flat tax, was passed in 1861 but never actually went into effect. A second tax imposed in 1862 had graduated tax rates that ran from only 3 percent to 5 percent. The tax fell most heavily on the wealthy: 90 percent of Americans were exempt from paying any income tax at all during the war. As the war dragged on, Congress increased the tax rate until it reached 15 percent in 1864. During this time the government established the Bureau of Internal Revenues to collect the tax. Interestingly, compliance was good, and patriotic individuals paid the income tax to help fund the war effort.

After the Civil War the federal government needed additional revenues to finance reconstruction in the South and pacification of the Native American tribes in the West. Although the income tax was retained, it was reduced to a flat tax of 5 percent on incomes above $1,000 and 2.5 percent on incomes above $2,000. When trade increased after the war, collections from the tariff increased so rapidly that Congress paid off most of the war bonds. Congress allowed the first income tax to expire in 1872.

Interest in income taxes continued, however. Most of the manufacturing and wealth in the country was concentrated in the northeastern states. Citizens in the South and West were generally in favor of income tax because taxpayers in the northeastern states were far more likely to be paying it. In fact, this view was correct: during the Civil War, taxpayers in the northeastern states provided nearly three quarters of the income tax collections received by the federal government, a pattern that continued after the war's end. However, in the post–Civil War era, the tariff remained the chief tax issue. By the 1890s, interest in the income tax brought the issue to center stage. In 1892 the Democrat Grover Cleveland won the presidency, beating the Republican Benjamin Harrison by a wide margin. Cleveland had been beaten by Harrison in the presidential election 4 years earlier. In that election, Cleveland had campaigned for lowering the tariff. Cleveland now backed an income tax, recognizing that many of his supporters in the Southwest were also proponents of a federal income tax. Republicans and Democrats who lived in the wealthy and industrialized Northeast opposed an income tax for the logical reason that they would be the ones paying it.

Literally scores of income tax bills were proposed in Congress between the Civil War and 1894, supported by southern Democrats, westerners, and urban populists who wanted a fairer tax system. Republicans and northeastern Democrats who supported the high protective tariff opposed the income tax as a socialist abomination. However, in 1894, Congress enacted the first federal income tax since the Civil War. The tax was immediately challenged in court, and in 1895 the U.S. Supreme Court, in the landmark case *Pollack v. Farm Loan and Trust Co.*, decided that the 1894 income tax was unconstitutional. Curiously, the Supreme Court had upheld the constitutionality of the Civil War income tax just 20 years before. In the 1895 Pollack case, however, the Court reasoned that the income tax was unconstitutional because it violated the constitution's apportionment requirement.

During the first hundred years after the passage of the Constitution, a distinction was made between direct and indirect taxes. A direct tax was a tax on property, whereas an indirect tax was a tax unrelated to property. The tariff was considered an indirect tax. The Constitution requires that direct taxes be "apportioned"; this provision was included in the Constitution at the behest of the wealthier states to ensure that their citizens would not be made subject to onerous taxes by the national government. Apportionment requires that any direct tax be directly apportioned to the population of the state. In this way the citizens of each state pay no more than their fair share. If Virginia makes up 8 percent of the population, the Virginians will pay no more or less than 8 percent of the tax.

The Civil War tax was upheld by the Supreme Court because everyone assumed at the time that the tax was an indirect tax rather than a direct tax. Accordingly, there was no requirement that the tax be apportioned. In the 1895 Pollack case, however, the Court started with the premise that the new income tax was a direct tax. Therefore income tax collected in each state had to precisely correspond to the number of citizens in the state. The Court reached this conclusion by reasoning that because taxes on real estate are direct taxes, a tax on the income from real estate must also be a direct tax. After the Supreme Court ruled the tax unconstitutional, the government had to stop collecting income tax and went back to relying on the tariff. In 1896 Congress raised tariff rates to an all-time high.

Political support for a federal income tax did not end with the Pollack case, however. Citizens in the South and West continued to lobby for a federal income tax. In 1908 President Theodore (Teddy) Roosevelt endorsed the income tax. Although Roosevelt was a Republican—a party whose members normally opposed income taxes—and was from New York—a state where the tax was unpopular—much of his political support came from the West, where citizens were in favor of an income tax. In 1909 Republican senators from the western states joined Democrats in calling for a federal income tax, and President Taft joined them. Congress enacted a corporate income tax and called for the ratification of the 16th Amendment to the U.S. Constitution, which would lift the Pollack case's ban on individual income tax. In 1913 the 16th Amendment to the Constitution was formally certified, authorizing the individual income tax that had been declared unconstitutional 18 years earlier in the Pollack case.

The 1913 income tax signed by President Woodrow Wilson imposed a tax of only 1 percent on income above $3,000, a large amount in those days. An additional graduated rate schedule imposed an additional tax on higher incomes and a 6 percent rate on incomes above $500,000, which was a vast amount in 1913. Although opponents of the tax challenged the legality of the new income tax in court, after the 16th Amendment was enacted, the tax was here to stay.

Six years later Congress was able to use the newly enacted income tax to help pay for World War I. Tax rates were raised during the war, and an extra profits tax was imposed on corporations. Still, only the wealthy were subject to income tax: only about 5 percent of Americans actually had to pay the tax. The federal government relied primarily on tariffs and other miscellaneous revenues for its operation. During the economic boom years of the 1920s and also during the depression years of the 1930s, the federal income tax continued to be a tax imposed only on the wealthy. In 1942, however, the need to raise money for World War II changed forever the scope of the tax and the tax environment in United States.

The Revenue Act of 1942 greatly expanded the number of Americans required to pay income tax. Prior to this act, only 4 million Americans, less than 4 percent of the U.S. population, were subject to the federal income tax. After the passage of this act, 50 million in Americans—half the U.S. population—were required to file returns and pay the tax. Tax rates also greatly increased. The initial tax rate was 23 percent, and those earning over $14,000 had to pay at the rate of 50 percent. A corporate income tax rate was set at 40 percent, with an additional excess profits tax imposed at 89.5 percent.

Interestingly, these higher rates had two purposes. First, the government needed the revenues to finance the war effort. Second, the high tax rates were imposed in order to control inflation during the war. With consumer goods scarce, the government was rightly concerned that without high tax rates the country would suffer from runaway inflation. An equally significant development occurred in the following year. Congress passed the Current Tax Payment Act of 1943. This law established the "pay-as-you-go" system, a term invented by a Macy's department store executive, which set up the familiar income tax based on withholding specified amounts from employees' wages. Self-employed individuals were still required to pay their income tax by making quarterly estimated tax payments. The withholding system offers three main benefits to the government: First, it ensures that the tax is collected. Payment is far more certain when the tax is deducted from employees' paychecks by their employers than when employees submit their tax on April 15. Some employees would simply not have the money to send in. Second, the government enjoys the use of the money as soon as it receives it from the employer. Third, the government has to deal with only about 1 million employers sending in checks for taxes rather than 50 million individuals. This system greatly reduces the government's workload as well as potential errors. Withholding, a wartime measure, is still one of the most important features of the tax system.

This period also introduced income tax features that we now take for granted. At one time, no joint tax returns were allowed for married couples. Joint returns were introduced in 1948. During the next 10 years the government created additional filings statuses, including head of household, single, and married filing separately, which have all become fixtures in the tax code.

One major change in the tax code between 1960 and 2000 was the decrease in the progressivity of the tax rates. During the 1950s, top tax rates for individuals ranged up to 92 percent. President John F. Kennedy, a Democrat, proposed a major tax cut, which when enacted by Congress reduced the top individual tax rate to 50 percent on earned income and 70 percent on unearned income (generally investment income). These tax rates continued until 1980. Kennedy reasoned that although the wealthy would benefit more greatly from the tax cuts, "a rising tide raises all ships." Kennedy reasoned that by returning more money to the private sector, all Americans would benefit from increased investment and increased business activity. The same "trickle down" theory was adopted by President Ronald Reagan, a Republican, about 20 years later. The Kennedy tax cut also benefited low-income taxpayers: The standard deduction was raised so that many low-income individuals would not be subject to federal income tax at all. Additionally, corporate tax rates were reduced to a maximum of 48 percent.

President Kennedy was also one of the first presidents to use the tax system to control the economy. Kennedy and his advisers included tax provisions like the Investment Tax Credit (ITC) to stimulate the economy to lift it out of a recession. Generally, recessions end either because businesses invest in the economy or consumer confidence rises and consumers spend the country out of the recession. Kennedy reasoned that tax provisions that would encourage businesses to invest in new equipment could be used to jump start the economy, and this belief proved correct. After 1962 it became accepted that the income tax system could be used to manage the economy.

The 1969 Tax Reform Act initiated a 30-year period of nearly constant change in the tax laws. The velocity of the changes was unprecedented in the history the nation. Tax law had not essentially changed from 1945 to 1969. Although a number of deductions were added or eliminated over the years, tax law stayed essentially stable. The 1969 act, however, included several reforms aimed at increasing the fairness of the tax system, including passage of the alternative minimum tax (AMT) to ensure that all wealthy Americans would pay some tax despite legal tax planning that reduced their tax bills to zero.

Tax reform was again an issue in the election of 1980. Former Governor Ronald Reagan of California ran against Democrat Jimmy Carter, the incumbent president. The economy was in the doldrums, hit by high interest rates and high oil prices induced by the OPEC oil embargo. Americans were growing increasingly alarmed that U.S. industry was no longer competitive with Japanese and European competitors. Low U.S. productivity and the need to replace outmoded and inefficient factories in the American rust belt was a familiar theme in the business press. Business leaders blamed government policy—especially high taxes—for the decline of American manufacturing.

Inflation and attendant high interest rates also played a role in tax reform during this period. During the last half of the 1970s the U.S. inflation rate was in the double digits while productivity lagged, leading to the term *stagflation*. This combination adversely affected individual taxpayers: if their incomes merely rose with inflation, their buying power remained constant but their income was taxed at higher and higher levels because of the progressive tax rates. This phenomenon was termed "bracket creep" and was eventually ameliorated by indexing, or adjusting the personal exemption and standard deduction—both of which exempt income from taxation—to the inflation rate. Investors and corporate taxpayers both complained that they were paying taxes on "inflationary gains."

Reagan had championed tax reform during his election campaign, and he carried out his promises once in office. Reagan embraced Representative Jack Kemp's call for a major tax cut. The original Kemp-Roth tax cut proposal had suggested a 33 percent reduction in individual tax rates. President Reagan's proposals were somewhat more modest. The final legislation, the Economic Recovery Tax Act of 1981 (ERTA), slashed individual income tax rates by 23 percent, with rate reductions of 5, 10, and 10 percent over 3 years (the full reduction was never realized because of subsequent changes in the law). The act also included most of the 10-5-3 depreciation proposal, added a number of new or expanded deductions, and started the indexing of the personal exemption and standard deduction amounts. All of these were revenue losers.

Although private economists and economists at the Congressional Budget Office had projected that the act would create serious revenue shortfalls, the administration's own economists believed that slashing tax rates would create additional business activity, which would actually generate additional tax revenues. In fact, the shortfalls exceeded even the dire predictions of the private economists. Although tax revenues had increased when tax rates were cut in 1964–1965, after the 1981 tax cuts, the anticipated revenues failed to materialize. As Herbert Stein, a the former chairman of the Council of Economic Advisers under Presidents Nixon and Ford, pointed out, the supply-side tax plan allowed the deficit to balloon while the savings rate shrank and no significant improvement was made in U.S. productivity. In fairness, ERTA was a failure in part because the Democrat-controlled Congress would not enact cuts to help stem the growing federal deficits, as President Reagan had hoped. The result was unprecedented federal deficits that prompted a quick change in fiscal direction.

Alarmed at the revenue free fall that resulted from the 1981 tax act, Congress passed the Tax Equality and Fiscal Responsibility Act of 1982 (TEFRA), which contained a number of business tax increases, to attempt to slow the mounting budget deficit. By 1985 Congress had passed the emergency Deficit Control Act of 1985 (the Gramm-Rudman Act), which set specific deficit targets for the years 1987–1993. The importance of this particular piece of legislation for U.S. tax policy can hardly be overstated. Because Congress was unable to stop itself from overspending, Congress enacted Gramm-Rudman to act as an automatic brake. As specified by the act, the Office of Management and Budget (OMB) was required to forecast whether the target deficits would be reached. If the forecast was more than $10 billion off, the president was required to initiate across-the-board spending cuts. Under this system, any tax act had to be carefully devised either to be revenue-neutral or to increase tax revenues. The Omnibus Budget Reconciliation Act of 1990 replaced the deficit targets with spending targets and revamped the act's mandatory sequestration provisions.

The wariness of deficit spending reappeared in 1986, when the Congress considered the Tax Reform Act of 1986. From the start, congressional leaders agreed that any new tax act should be revenue-neutral—roughly the same number of tax dollars would be collected under the revised law as were collected under the prior law. With legislators sobered by the mounting deficits, by the mid-1980s there was no call for reducing the amount of federal revenues.

The 1986 Tax Reform Act created the most comprehensive overhaul of the federal tax code in 30 years. Although some so-called tax reform acts have had little to do with actual reform, the 1986 act was very much a reform measure and was ultimately embraced by politicians from both major political parties. Although the law was enacted during the Reagan administration, the act began life in 1977 as the Bradley-Gephardt bill, named after its two Democratic cosponsors. The bill essentially reduced tax rates but kept tax revenues "neutral" by eliminating many tax deductions. The bill also eliminated the special low tax rate for capital gains, which had been a feature of the tax code since 1922. The act reversed many of the tax breaks given to the real estate industry in 1981 and contained serious anti–tax shelter rules. The 1986 act not only reduced top tax rates but also raised the amount of income that could be earned tax-free, exempting an estimated 6 million poor families from paying any federal income taxes. Politically acceptable to conservatives because it decreased tax rates, the act was also acceptable to liberals because it eliminated many tax breaks for the wealthy. The 1986 act can be characterized as a true reform measure because it embraced the idea that lowering tax rates and broadening the tax base (the items subject to tax) would be fairer for all taxpayers. By 1990 the reform fervor had cooled, along with the economy. With a recession looming, Congress enacted the Deficit Reduction Act, which included increases in gasoline taxes, "sin taxes" on liquor and tobacco products, a luxury tax on expensive consumer goods, and modest income tax rate increases. Although the act did increase federal revenues, reforms were conspicuously missing.

During the late 1980s, further tax rate cuts became unpalatable to the public. President George H. Bush and the Congress were able to raise revenues without raising taxes by limiting the use of deductions, adding surtaxes, and imposing the 1990 excise tax on luxury goods. Finally, when Democrat William J. Clinton came to office, enough Republicans in Congress, alarmed once more at the growing federal deficit, joined with the Democrats to pass a fairly major tax increase for both individuals and corporations. With a top individual tax rate of 39.6 percent, the 1993 tax act restored a good deal of progressivity to the tax rates but little else that could be termed a "reform." A booming economy until the end of the century created a windfall for the U.S. Treasury. Although small deficits had been predicted, the federal government earned a modest annual surplus by 1998. Because of increased tax collections thanks to the robust economy, Congress decided that there was no need to enact major tax increases for the last 7 years of the century. In the year 2000, a presidential election year, the healthy U.S. economy continued to generate small budget surpluses. In the first half of the year, the Republican-controlled House of Representatives and Senate both voted to phase out the federal estate tax completely. In its place the Congress would enact a system of taxing certain capital gains at the time of a taxpayer's death. President Bill Clinton, in his last year of office, vetoed the measure, arguing that any surplus should be used to stabilize the Social Security system and to reduce the national debt.

President George W. Bush came into office with a pledge to cut taxes. At that time Bush believed that the federal government would continue to enjoy small surpluses. Rather than use the surpluses to reduce the debt, Bush wanted the money back in the hands of citizens. Accordingly he proposed a major income tax cut that would be phased in between 2001 and 2003. All individual tax rates dropped: the lowest rate dropped from 15 to 10 percent while the highest rate dropped from 39.6 to 35 percent. Bush also provided the middle class with a major new benefit by increasing the child tax credit from $500 to $1,000. This tax credit offset tax dollar for dollar. Accordingly a qualifying family with three children could reduce their taxes by $3,000 ($1,000 × 3) rather than $1,500 ($500 × 3). Because the credit phases out for upper-income taxpayers, the rich did not benefit from the increased credit. However, many of the poor, who paid only Social Security taxes, got no benefit either. Even if a poor family had three children, they got no benefit, because if they did not pay any income tax, they had no tax to offset. The federal estate tax was to be phased out between 2002 and 2009 and would disappear completely in 2010 but would reappear in 2011 unless Congress eliminated it completely in the decade before 2010. A revised estate tax did reappear in 2011, but the first $5 million in an estate escapes the tax.

Because these tax cuts were part of the annual congressional budget resolution, which is not subject to filibusters or amendments, it had to include a sunset clause. Accordingly the Bush tax cuts were set to expire automatically at the end of 2010. Extension of all or some of these cuts then became a major political issue.

The federal surpluses envisioned by George W. Bush never materialized; in fact, the federal government experienced a solid decade of large deficits. A number of events contributed to the deficit, including an economic slowdown in the aftermath of the terrorist attack on New York City's World Trade Center and the costly wars in Afghanistan and Iraq. Starting in 2007, the real estate market started to collapse, and it soon became clear that the nation's real estate "boom" was really a real estate "bubble." This collapse threatened a number of major financial institutions, leading the federal government to finance a costly Wall Street bailout. The real estate collapse also triggered a serious economic recession. With businesses' profits plunging and millions of workers unemployed, tax collections declined as government spending increased. The government resorted to borrowing at levels unheard of in peacetime. The result was a major increase in the national debt, and projections suggested that unless spending was slashed or taxes were increased, these deficits would only grow.

The 2001 Bush tax cuts were designed to expire in 2010. Although many assumed that Congress would act before 2010 to extend or repeal the cuts and certainly to prevent the estate tax from expiring before 2010, Congress let the federal estate tax expire for the year 2010 and did not take action on the Bush income tax cuts. President Obama reached a compromise with Republicans in Congress: the Bush income tax cuts were extended for 2 years and the estate tax was reenacted, but at a lower tax rate. Despite calls for bipartisan tax reform to help defray the cost of the mounting budget deficit, partisan bickering between the Republicans and Democrats prevented any progress. The success of the Tea Party movement caused Republicans to strengthen their stand against any new taxes despite the looming federal deficits. Democrats were reluctant to cut "entitlements" like Social Security and Medicare. Although there was little legislative progress, the looming federal deficit triggered a great deal of interest in fundamental tax reform. By 2011 leaders from both political parties realized that tinkering with the tax code would be insufficient to solve the deficit issue. Although politicians and citizens with different political views wanted tax reform, they did not agree on what shape it should take. A few of these proposals are discussed in chapter 2, "Problems, Controversies, and Solutions."

2

Problems, Controversies, and Solutions

This chapter presents an overview of the U.S. tax system, tax policy, and proposals for tax reform. The chapter begins with a discussion of fairness (equity) issues. The chapter concludes with an examination of the goals of tax reform and several current tax reform proposals.

Equity Issues (Fairness)

A basic tenet of any tax system is fairness. Adam Smith's canons of taxation, discussed in chapter 1, refer to this concept as "equity." Smith argued that a "good" tax must also be equitable. Indeed, much of tax reform is directed at introducing more equity and fairness into the tax system. Unfortunately equity often comes at the cost of complexity. Much of the complexity in the current Internal Revenue Code, for example, is in place to ensure that similarly situated taxpayers are treated alike.

A more troubling issue is that fairness is often in the eye of the beholder. Reformers differ in their perception of what is fair. Some argue that fairness requires that the rich pay more tax than the poor. This argument is made not only for the very practical reason that the rich have the resources to pay but also because the rich benefit more from a stable governmental system. Although hardly anyone would disagree with the view that the rich should pay more than the poor, there is little agreement about how much more they should pay. A bit of history is illustrative. The top U.S. individual income tax rate has varied over the last 75 years from 92 percent in the 1950s and early 1960s to 31 percent after 1982 and to slightly less than 40 percent since 1993. Some tax reformers argue that the current maximum income tax rates are far too high, whereas others protest that they are far too low.

Put in a slightly different perspective, the current maximum individual income tax rate is one of the lowest in all western countries. Indeed, tax rates for Americans of all income levels are close to their lowest since World War II. However, at the same time, the Social Security tax—a regressive "flat tax"—has been continually rising since 1969. Although American taxpayers may have been enjoying their income tax cuts, they were apparently unmindful of the steep increases in payroll taxes that snatched back the benefit of any income tax cuts. In assessing the equity of the current system, students of tax reform must assess the combined income and payroll taxes paid from taxpayers' paychecks rather than focusing just on the income tax. The total amount coming out of workers' paychecks is what really counts.

In examining equity it is helpful to distinguish vertical equity from horizontal equity. *Vertical equity* refers to the fairness of the tax system vis-à-vis taxpayers with different patterns of income. For example, a salaried taxpayer may have relatively stable income year to year, whereas a commissioned sales representative may have dramatic income swings year to year. If, on average, they make the same income over a period of years, they should be paying roughly the same tax. *Horizontal equity* refers to the extent to which taxpayers with similar incomes pay roughly the same tax. Even among those who disagree about what burden various economic segments should shoulder, few if any argue that two taxpayers in the same economic position should pay significantly different tax bills. In the current tax system there is a good possibility that similarly situated taxpayers may pay far different amounts of federal income tax.

For example, assume that two managers working at a company earn the same salary. One manager is single and rents an apartment. The other manager is married, his spouse stays at home to take care of their two young children, and he owns his own home. The second manager may well pay far lower taxes than the first manager. Although taxes are generally imposed equally on all taxpayers, Congress has allowed deductions to encourage certain behavior. For example, to encourage homeownership, the tax code includes deductions for home mortgage interest and real estate taxes. Once this taxpayer has itemized deductions in excess of the standard deduction, the taxpayer can claim other deductions, such as charitable deductions. Additionally, the second manager can also reduce his or her income subject to tax by claiming four dependency exceptions instead of the one available to the single taxpayer. In short, relief and reform measures in the tax code frequently operate against horizontal equity.

Problems with horizontal equity also apply to businesses as well as individuals. When the 1986 Tax Reform Act was passed, Congress tried to reduce the tax disparity between corporations. Prior to the 1986 act, corporations engaged in manufacturing were paying far lower tax rates than corporations engaged in retail or service businesses. The disparity arose in the late 1970s and early 1980s, when Congress attempted to use the tax code to assist what were then viewed as ailing industries with factories in the rust belt. Although the relief measures may have been well-meaning, they also greatly reduced horizontal equity.

The U.S. Tax System

The first thing to keep in mind in thinking about the U.S. tax system is that it comprises multiple tax systems. In our federalist form of government, which distributes power amongst national, state, and local governments, each level has the power to levy its own taxes. Although we take this system for granted, it is easy to envision a system in which only the national government would collect taxes and distribute a share in the form of revenue-sharing to the states and localities. Of course, this does happen when the federal government assists states and cities with building highways and other public improvements. All levels of government not only levy taxes but also borrow funds for long-term uses by issuing bonds. In the U.S. system, the interest on state and local bonds is generally not taxed for federal income tax purposes, which makes the bonds relatively more attractive as investments. The concept of dividing money-raising responsibility among the three levels of government is referred to as fiscal federalism. Having many tax systems instead of one creates complexity and compliance problems for taxpayers. Businesses that operate in a number of states and cities rightly complain that they spend as much money trying to comply with the tax laws as they spend paying the taxes. As the United States enters the 21st century, the federal government's tax system is heavily reliant on income and payroll taxes. States typically use a combination of individual

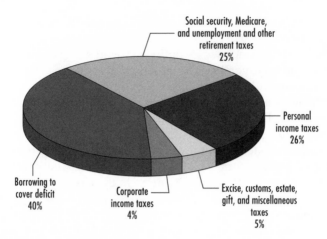

FIGURE 2.1 Federal income for the fiscal year 2009 (Form 1040 Instructions, 2010. Department of the Treasury, Internal Revenue Service.)

income taxes and business taxes, whereas localities generally rely on property taxes. State and local taxes are discussed in more detail further on. The federal government (see Figure 2.1) funds nearly half its revenue needs through the individual income tax. Nearly that much comes from various payroll taxes that are earmarked for Social Security, Medicare, and unemployment. Normally, the corporate income tax provides 10 percent of the federal government's revenue needs—a percentage that has varied by only a percent or so over the last few decades. Various excise taxes, customs duties, and the estate and gift taxes make up the remaining 5 percent. In absolute terms, in 2009, individuals paid $968 billion in income taxes and an additional $891 billion in payroll taxes.

Sources of Tax Law

The United States has many sources of tax law. As in other areas of the law, certain sources have greater authority than others, creating a hierarchy of sources. In the United States the highest authorities are laws of Congress (statutes), court cases, and treaties with foreign nations. The Treasury Department issues both regulations and rulings interpreting the tax laws. Although these do not have the same force as statutes, they must be followed unless taxpayers wish to challenge their validity. Approximately one regulation is thrown out by the courts each year because it is found to be contrary to the tax code or another law of Congress.

In the U.S. legal system, private agreements may not violate a law. Accordingly, private parties may not agree between themselves about the ultimate tax consequences of a transaction; the government's tax law controls. Laws of Congress or the states cannot contradict the U.S. Constitution. In the very earliest years of the republic, the Supreme Court established itself as the arbiter of power in the federal system: by long-standing tradition, the Supreme Court has the power to declare laws of Congress unconstitutional and null and void. Interestingly, the Supreme Court established this power in a court case in which a state attempted to tax national bank notes. The federal courts have the power to declare Treasury regulations and even sections of the Internal Revenue Code unconstitutional.

In practice, the Court accepts few federal tax cases and allows Congress wide latitude in deciding how Americans should be taxed. The Supreme Court is far more active in hearing state tax cases. Taxpayers often allege that state taxes are discriminatory or unfair, and the Court acts as umpire in the federal system.

National Tax Policy

Although it may seem that the U.S. tax system is put together haphazardly, there are policy considerations underlying the system. First, taxes are in place primarily to provide sufficient and reliable revenue to fund the government's programs. Figure 2.2 illustrates that in 2009 Social Security, Medicare, and Medicaid require 34 percent of the outlays, and various social programs consume another 21 percent. National defense takes another 22 percent, though even fairly recently it consumed a larger percentage. Currently the interest on the national debt is close to 8 percent—a number that is projected to rise in the near future.

Although revenue raising is the primary objective of the tax system, regulating the economy and redistributing wealth are also aims of basic tax policy. Many provisions in the tax code are in place to encourage individual taxpayers to modify their behavior or to assist taxpayers in meeting certain goals that are good not only for the individuals but for the country as well. For example, the tax code allows individuals to deduct amounts contributed to charity. By allowing the deduction, the government forgoes

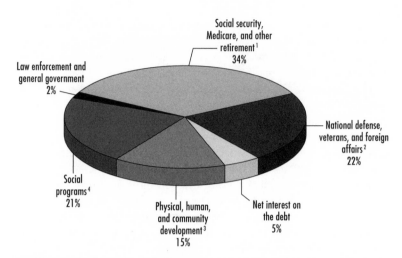

FIGURE 2.2 Federal outlays for the fiscal year 2009. (Form 1040 Instructions, 2010. Department of the Treasury, Internal Revenue Service.)*

*The percentages for outlays do not total 100 percent due to rounding.

1. Social Security, Medicare, and other entitlements. These programs provide income support for the retired and disabled and medical care for the elderly.

2. National defense, veterans, and foreign affairs: About 22 percent of outlays were to equip, modernize, and pay our armed forces and to fund national defense activities; about 3 percent were for veterans' benefits and services; and about 1 percent were for international activities, including military and economic assistance to foreign countries and the maintenance of U.S. embassies abroad.

3. Physical, human, and community development: These outlays were for agriculture; natural resources; environment; transportation; aid for elementary and secondary education and direct assistance to college students; job training; deposit insurance, commerce, housing credit, and community development; and space, energy, and general science programs.

4. Social programs: About 13 percent of total outlays were for Medicaid, food stamps, temporary assistance for needy families, supplemental security income, and related programs; the remaining outlays were for health research and public health programs, unemployment compensation, assisted housing, and social services.

collecting the tax. For example, suppose that a taxpayer whose marginal tax bracket is 28 percent contributed $1 to a charity. If the taxpayer is able to deduct that amount, he will have his tax reduced by 28 cents. This amounts to a government subsidy designed to encourage individual behavior. Note that a taxpayer who is in the 35 percent marginal tax bracket will get a 35 cents advantage, whereas a low-income taxpayer in the 15 percent bracket will enjoy only a 15 cent reduction in tax. By their nature, deductions are more beneficial to the wealthy.

Another example is the deduction for home mortgage interest. Businesses may deduct their interest expense without question. In fact, a business may deduct all of its expenses because the tax is levied on the firm's profits after costs have been deducted. An individual cannot generally deduct interest. For example, interest on a car loan or a loan to finance a vacation is not deductible. Congress has enacted a special provision that allows an individual to deduct the interest on a home mortgage, subject to some limitations. Because home buyers can deduct the interest, the government is providing them with a subsidy to buy the home. In fact, many, if not most, home buyers are able to buy more expensive homes because of the tax deduction for home mortgage interest. Home sellers, home builders, real estate agents, hardware makers, and even lumberjacks are indirect beneficiaries of this deduction because it increases the number of homes sold and built. Many millions of Americans have a vested interest in keeping this deduction a part of the tax code. The real estate and timber industries are two vocal supporters of the home mortgage interest deduction.

The revenue the government forgoes by allowing a deduction is known as a tax expenditure, a concept first recognized by Stanley Surrey, a tax expert who worked at the Treasury Department and later became a professor at Harvard Law School. Tax expenditures have become institutionalized in the Treasury Department's Tax Expenditure Budget.

The Tax Expenditure Budget is in effect a "reverse budget" because it shows the lost revenue to the government resulting from each tax deduction. Leading the pack are retirement benefits, which are deductible to employers, and medical deductions, with the home mortgage interest deduction not far behind.

Although the use of tax expenditures to influence individual behavior at first seems clever, evidence suggests that it may be less effective than hoped. Encouraging behavior by offering tax deductions has several obvious drawbacks. First, there is no guarantee that taxpayers will be encouraged. The deduction may reward only taxpayers who would have taken the targeted action anyway. Also, it may be hard to draft a deduction that will be narrow enough to benefit a target. For example, if the government provides a generous deduction to encourage builders to build low-cost apartment houses, there is no guarantee that the units will be built where there is a shortage of such housing. In fact, the realities of the real estate market may dictate that the units be built elsewhere. Additionally, as just discussed, deductions benefit the wealthy far more than middle- and low-income taxpayers. If the government wants to encourage certain actions, it can subsidize the activities by direct grants or through loans that make the activity easier for taxpayers. For example, in addition to allowing students to deduct the cost of their college degrees and providing education tax credits, the government has also opted for a government-insured student loan program to encourage higher education.

The Political Process

In the United States, tax issues are an important part of the political landscape. Tax laws are enacted by Congress rather than by a nonpartisan federal agency. The content of the tax laws reflects the fact that they are a product of the often partisan political process. Taxpayers of all persuasions are free to suggest changes to the tax code to their elected representatives. Individuals, various special interest groups, public interest groups, businesses, and industry associations all actively lobby Congress to change the tax laws on their behalf. Even foreign businesses and governments try to influence the passage of U.S. tax laws that affect foreign trade or foreign investors in the United States. Because taxes are uniformly unpopular, politicians from both leading political parties often seize upon tax reform for their own political advantage. Politicians wishing to appeal to wealthier taxpayers or to taxpayers desiring a smaller government frequently promise to lower taxes. Politicians who wish to appeal to low- or middle-income taxpayers frequently propose programs to "soak the rich." Politicians from both parties often try to appeal to specific taxpayer groups, like senior citizens.

Many of the benefits in the tax code are designed to benefit both upper-income taxpayers and middle Americans. Wealthier taxpayers are the source of campaign contributions for those in Congress. Middle-income taxpayers make up a substantial voting bloc. Because these taxpayers are more likely to vote than low-income Americans, politicians spend a good deal of effort passing tax measures to benefit them. During the 1990s, Congress made the first $250,000 of profits ($500,000 for married couples filing jointly) from the sale of a family home tax-free. At the urging of the president, Congress also passed a number of tax breaks for families who are or will be sending their children to college. Irrespective of the merits of these provisions as tax laws, their passage with little debate illustrates that Congress is generally more interested in passing provisions benefiting voters than constituencies that tend not to vote. Senior citizens enjoy a number of benefits because senators and representatives are well aware that senior citizens are politically well informed and vote in large numbers.

Although the political process often results in better tax law because it exposes proposals to vigorous debate, this method of tax making also has its disadvantages over a nonpartisan approach. Tax measures often benefit narrow interests rather than the country as a whole. Frequently debates on taxes are undertaken for partisan reasons rather than to advance the best interests of the country. A typical ploy involves passing a large tax cut with full knowledge that it will be vetoed by the president and not overridden. The process is nearly risk-free, because constituents will appreciate the tax-cutting effort and members of Congress do not have to worry about being fiscally irresponsible because they know that the president will prevent disaster.

Under the U.S. Constitution, tax bills originate in the House of Representatives, although they may originate in the Senate when they are attached to riders or other bills. Generally, tax legislation starts in the House Ways and Means Committee. Once approved by the committee, the bill is referred to the full House for approval. If approved, the bill is sent to the Senate Finance Committee for consideration. That committee typically creates its own version of the bill, which it will send to the full Senate for passage. The two versions of the bill are then reconciled by a joint conference committee. Once the final version of the bill is created, it is resubmitted to both the full House of Representatives and the Senate for the final vote. This is not the last step, however, because the legislation must be signed or vetoed by the president. Even if the president vetoes the bill, Congress can override the veto by a two-thirds vote in favor.

Although Congress writes the tax code, the court system plays a large role in making tax law. Although the tax code is famous for its complexity and thoroughness, it can still be difficult to apply rules to specific situations. Taxpayers often find themselves at odds with the government about the proper tax treatment of a particular item. If a taxpayer's treatment of an item is questioned, she can always ask for a hearing to appeal the decision. If the taxpayer comes away unsatisfied, she can proceed to court. Even if the court's decision favors the government, the taxpayer is always able to appeal at least one more time to a higher court. Accordingly, the courts are the final arbiters of how the tax law is applied to a particular situation.

In the federal court system the taxpayer has a choice of forum. After going through the appeals process in the IRS, the taxpayer can proceed to the U.S. Tax Court, the U.S. District Court, or the U.S. Claims Court. The U.S. Tax Court, as the name implies, is a specialized court that hears only federal tax cases. The judges are tax experts, and the court sits without a jury. The primary advantage for taxpayers of going to the U.S. Tax Court is that the taxpayer does not have to pay the tax before proceeding to trial. However, the overwhelming majority of the decisions of this court favor the government. If a taxpayer does not wish to go to the U.S. Tax Court, he has the option of paying the disputed tax, requesting a refund that will be denied, and then suing the government for a refund in either the local U.S. District Court or the U.S. Claims Court in Washington, D.C. District courts are local trial courts, and the taxpayer may be able to get a sympathetic jury. If the taxpayer loses in any of these courts, he may appeal to the U.S. Circuit Court of Appeals. There is a circuit court of appeals in each of the 11 geographic circuits in the United States. Although a tax case can theoretically be appealed all the way to the U.S. Supreme Court, that court is not compelled to hear every case brought before it. The Supreme Court hears only a handful of cases each year and very few tax cases. Generally they will hear a case only if it affects a large number of taxpayers or is a type of case about which courts of appeal in different parts of the country have come to different conclusions.

Once a court has decided an issue, the case becomes precedent. All inferior courts must follow the decision. If a federal circuit court of appeals has decided an issue, all district courts within the geographic circuit must follow it, and the U.S. Tax Court now follows such precedents also. Courts in other judicial circuits will look to the decision as guidance but are not compelled to follow it. If a state or local tax issue is contested in the state court system, precedents operate in the same manner. If the case is decided by a state appeals court, all inferior courts in that state must follow it. However, the decision is not binding on courts of other states or even on federal courts within that state.

Tax Administration

Although Congress is responsible for writing the federal tax laws and the courts are responsible for interpreting them, the Treasury Department has responsibility for administering the laws. The

Internal Revenue Service is part of the Treasury and is charged with administering the tax laws. This administration has three major responsibilities. First, the IRS publishes guidance for taxpayers that fills in the gaps in the tax laws. Treasury regulations are written to parallel the tax law in the Internal Revenue Code. Additionally, the Treasury issues "Private Letter Rulings," which provide formal guidance to a taxpayer who asks about a technical tax issue. The IRS publishes "Revenue Rulings," which give generalized guidance to common questions. Second, the IRS creates forms and instructions, physically processes those forms, and collects the tax for employee withholdings and tax payments made to the Treasury. Finally, the IRS conducts audits of taxpayers' returns and operates a collection agency to recover unpaid taxes. The IRS has traditionally been an enforcement agency, much like a police department. Under the agency's new mission statement, the agency is striving to change its mission to one of taxpayer education. Congress authorized this change in focus after examining the results of IRS audit and collection activity. The IRS manages to find hundreds of thousands of taxpayers who, through ignorance, carelessness, or fraud, have underpaid their taxes. However, the IRS has been relatively ineffective in collecting much of the overdue tax. Taxpayers often simply do not have the money to pay, and although the goal is to make everyone pay his or her fair share, the old system did not always produce this result. Treasury management has concluded that the government could maximize the amount it collects by educating taxpayers to file and pay correctly at the outset rather than relying on the audit and collections department to collect later.

The Federal Income Tax

In most years the income taxes provide approximately half of the federal operating budget. When borrowing is subtracted from the total revenues received by the government, the income tax makes up more than half of all funds received by the federal government. Additionally, most knowledgeable tax experts believe that any tax reform during the next decade will most likely consist of reforms to the present federal income tax system rather than an abandonment of the system and adoption of an entirely different type of tax. Alternatives to the federal income tax system are discussed later in this chapter. Although it is not necessary to have a detailed knowledge of the tax rules to understand the issues behind tax reform, a basic working knowledge of the federal income tax is helpful in understanding how the present system can be reformed. This overview presents an examination of how the income tax is applied to both individuals and businesses in the United States.

Income and Exclusions

The Gross Income Concept

In the United States, "income" is defined quite broadly. This concept is important because calculation of the income tax begins with determining gross income: what income is subject to tax and what is excluded. The Internal Revenue Code defines gross income as "all income from whatever source derived, including (but not limited to) the following items." The code section goes on to list 15 examples. The key word is *examples*; the U.S. tax law defines potentially anything as income unless it includes a specific exception. These exceptions are called *exemptions*. For example, the tax code specifically exempts gifts. Accordingly, a person could receive $1 million in cash or property as a gift and the amount would not be subject to income tax, although the donor might be subject to a federal gift tax on the transfer.

The substance rather than the label the parties use controls the taxability of the transaction. Although gifts are nontaxable, labeling a transfer as a gift is not enough—the transfer must actually be a gift, which is normally understood to be a "gratuitous" transfer. Even within a family, a brother could not make a gift of corporate stock to his sister, receiving in turn a gift of $2,000 of cash from her. However, if both siblings knew the stock was really worth $3,000, the transaction would be part gift, part sale. Furthermore, a gift is understood to be a transfer for less than fair market value with no expectation of a return.

A 1960 Supreme Court case helped define the simple word *gift* for tax purposes. One businessman, a Mr. Berman, called another, Mr. Duperstein, who was in the same business, asking if Duperstein knew of any potential customers for some of Berman's products. Duperstein provided Berman with some names of potential customers. The names proved useful, and Berman called back telling Duperstein that he wanted to give him a present: a new Cadillac. Duperstein protested, saying he really didn't expect anything in return and he already had both a Cadillac and an Oldsmobile. Berman was insistent, and Duperstein accepted the car. Duperstein's tax return was audited, and the IRS insisted that he should include the value of the gift on his tax return and pay tax on it. Duperstein protested and fought the case all the way to the Supreme Court. Although the justices agreed that the facts were mixed, they also agreed with the IRS that this was not a nontaxable gift but either payment for Duperstein's past services or an inducement for him to be of service in the future. Even something as simple as a gift can cause problems in tax law.

The current income tax system generally relies on the realization concept: income is not taxable income unless the taxpayer has a realization event, which occurs when a taxpayer converts property to cash or, less commonly, to other property. For example, when a taxpayer sells stock that has increased in value and receives cash, this is a realization event. In contrast, when the taxpayer's stock goes up in value but the taxpayer holds the stock rather than selling it, the taxpayer is better off because the value of the stock has risen but there is no realization event. Accordingly, the tax code does not impose an income tax when property rises in value. Economists take a broader view of income. For example, if a taxpayer holds stock that increases in value during the year but the taxpayer decides not to sell, an economist would argue that the taxpayer has income because there has been an accretion to wealth. For tax purposes, no tax would be collected because there has been no realization event. Tax would be imposed only when the taxpayer sold the stock.

Similarly, some economists argue that homeowners should be taxed on the rental value of their homes. For example, assume that taxpayer A invests $100,000 in a home and lives in it. The taxpayer sells the home a year later, making a profit of $10,000. If the taxpayer financed the transaction, the mortgage interest would be deductible, and the profit on the sale would be tax-exempt because profits from personal home sales are tax-exempt up to $250,000 for a single person and up to $500,000 for a married couple filing a joint return. Taxpayer B invests $100,000 in an identical home but rents out the property, receiving $12,000 of rental income. Taxpayer B can deduct his interest cost, if any, because the house is an investment property, and he can also claim some tax-free return of his investment in the form of a depreciation deduction. Taxpayer B himself lives in an apartment and pays nondeductible rent of $12,000. Taxpayer B must pay taxes on the net rental income. Economists argue that to be equitable, Taxpayer

A should also have to pay a tax on the "imputed rental value" of her home. This would remove some but not all of the tax advantage Taxpayer A enjoys over Taxpayer B. Homeowners would of course rise up in alarm if this proposal ever left academia. In fact, tax breaks for homeowners are well entrenched and benefit not only homeowners but also the real estate, building, and home mortgage industries, to name only a few.

Statutory Exclusions

Because of the tax code's broad definition of *income*, many types of inflows are potentially taxable. Congress has specifically exempted many of these, which are known as exclusions. Some of the more common exclusions include loans, gifts, inheritances, life insurance proceeds, damage proceeds, and tax-exempt interest. However, some of these items may be subject to either the federal gift tax or the estate tax before the recipient receives them.

Although some countries exempt lottery winnings, they are taxable in the United States. Similarly, although college scholarships were once totally tax exempt, only the amount that covers tuition, books, and supplies is now exempt, and amounts for room and board are potentially taxable. However, in practical terms, many scholarship recipients' income is so low that even adding in the nonexempt portion of scholarships would not force them to pay income tax.

Treatment of Individuals

With the exception of the joint filing status for married couples, each individual is treated as a separate taxable entity for reporting purposes. The creation of joint returns was discussed earlier in this chapter. The four familiar filing statuses—single, joint, head of household, and married filing separately—have now been part of the tax code for over 50 years. Individuals can claim an exemption to shelter income from taxation for themselves, their spouses, and any dependents.

Deductions

As mentioned earlier, deductions are a matter of legislative grace and may be granted or taken away as Congress sees fit. Generally no deduction is allowed for personal, family, or household expenses. Since these are not related to business or investment, they are simply not deductible. Expenses that are business- or invest-ment-related generally are deductible but may be subject to dollar limitations. In addition to general rules to encourage certain kinds of behavior or to grant relief to taxpayers, Congress has enacted a number of deductions that are really personal in nature. These include medical deductions, home mortgage interest, charitable deductions, and interest and taxes on the family home.

Business Taxation

Corporations are viewed as separate taxable entities and pay a separate corporate tax ranging between 15 and 35 percent. One distinguishing feature of the income taxation of corporations is the double tax on dividends. Because corporations receive no deduction when they pay shareholders a dividend, any profits distributed as dividends are taxed once to the corporation and then again when received by shareholders. This double taxation encourages companies that need to raise money to borrow funds rather than issue stock. The tax code also contains another strong incentive for such behavior: the interest on debt is deductible. In a period of low interest rates and modest inflation, the after-tax cost of borrowing money becomes very low. Economists argue that this government subsidy for borrowing creates distortions in behavior.

One reform measure that has frequently been suggested is the integration of individual and corporate taxes. Economists some-times argue that little or no tax is actually paid by corporations, who are able to pass along the cost of the tax in their products and services. The net result is extra compliance costs and economic distortions as corporations structure transactions for tax reasons rather than rational business reasons. Because corporations ulti-mately do not pay much tax after passing the cost on to consum-ers, economists argue that eliminating the corporate tax would make economic sense. In practical terms, such a change would be difficult politically because corporations don't vote but individu-als do. Many would be incensed at this type of change.

Corporations are not the only type of business entity; smaller businesses are run as sole proprietorships, partnerships, and lim-ited liability companies. All of these entities enjoy single-level in-come taxation at the owner rather than the entity level, although they do have to pay payroll taxes on behalf of their employees. In contrast, corporations pay income tax on their profits, and corporate shareholders are also taxed when those profits are distributed to shareholders as dividends.

Businesses may generally deduct all their expenses as long as they are "ordinary and necessary." Such expenses include deductions for depreciation (tax-free recovery of business investment) and deductions for entertainment expenses, subject to percentage limitations. The most significant business deductions are deductions for contributions to employee medical insurance and retirement and pension plans.

Taxation of Investment Income

As mentioned earlier, for most of the century the tax code has contained a preference for the taxation of capital gains. These gains are taxed far more lightly than "ordinary income." The 1986 tax bill had eliminated the preference, but since 1990 the capital gains tax break has been repeatedly expanded. Because the wealthy receive the bulk of this benefit, this change has helped enlarge the gulf between the wealthy and the middle class in America.

Federal Tax Reform

Criticisms of the Current Tax System

The current U.S. tax system has been criticized from both sides of the political spectrum. Not surprisingly, these criticisms often center on who should be responsible for paying the bulk of the tax. The well to do argue that they bear an unwarranted share of the tax burden. Advocates for low-income taxpayers argue that the tax code should be more aggressive in redistributing income from the haves to the have-nots in society. These positions represent a basic disagreement not only about the role and scope of government but also about the basic structure of society, which is really a separate issue from the size of government. On the one hand, some argue that the tax system should foster a more egalitarian society with less extremes of wealth. The United States is notable among developed nations for its great disparities of wealth. The United States more closely resembles a third-world economy in its wealth distribution patterns. Others argue that government should have no role in wealth distribution, and the tax system should merely exist to fund basic services and national defense and no more. President Ronald Reagan shared this view, arguing that the tax code was no place for social engineering.

Students of taxation need to keep in mind that although the individual income tax is by far the most significant U.S. tax at the start of the 21st century, it is not the only tax. For low-income taxpayers, federal payroll taxes are a larger expense. Although Social Security taxes are regressive and have become more so over the years, few tax critics focus on the costs of these taxes to low-income Americans. This part of tax reform remains largely unnoticed.

There have been a number of proposals to allow the complete or partial "privatization" of Social Security. In his 2006 State of the Union address, President George W. Bush warned that the Social Security system was "bankrupt" and urged Congress to pass a partial privatization of the retirement system. The proposal would have diverted a part of Social Security taxes to private accounts. President Bush's proposal never became law. Currently Social Security funds are invested in government securities, which provide a modest but guaranteed return. Payments are not dependent on market forces but are established by Congress. The current system pays retirement benefits based on a worker's length of service and pay at the end of his or her career. The system is weighted to provide some modest income redistribution. Lower- and middle-income workers receive payments that more closely resemble their former paychecks as compared with higher-income workers. From time to time, Congress increases payments to account for inflation, but the payments do not rise and fall depending on the stock market.

If Social Security were fully or partially privatized, all or some of the Social Security funds would be invested in the stock market. Some plans would allow retirees some choice in what sort of investments—and how much risk—they would like to take on in funding their accounts. If Social Security is privatized, retirees' retirement benefits would be linked in whole or part to the market. Based on past history, retirees might be better off because common stocks have provided a better return than fixed investments over the long run. If a retiree retires during a market downturn, however, benefits might be lower than what would have been payable under the nonmarket Social Security system. Proponents argue that giving workers freedom of choice would be a good idea and could greatly enhance their retirement incomes. Opponents argue that Social Security should be seen as a safety net that guarantees retirement income. Under some proposals, re-tirees would be allowed to redirect only a portion of their Social Security payments to private investments. This type of proposal is probably the most likely to be enacted. This is the type of proposal that President George W, Bush offered in 2006.

A more pressing issue for Social Security may be the system's long-term fiscal viability. Actuaries monitor the amounts collected in Social Security taxes and predict whether those amounts will be sufficient to fund future benefits. In the 1980s the system was so poorly funded that Congress raised payroll taxes. During the 1990s the robust economy generated huge surpluses and post-poned the projected shortfall far into the future. The deep reces-sion in 2009 and 2010 resulted in more benefits being paid out than taxes paid in. If the economy does not recover, the system may face a crisis similar to the one seen in the 1980s. On the other hand, if the economy rebounds and more Social Security taxes are collected during the next decade, any shortfall in the system may be far in the future. Whatever the future of the economy, the deficit in the federal Medicare program is a much larger problem than the Social Security deficit. For the wealthy, the federal es-tate and gift taxes are the main threat. Although the amount of revenue brought in by the federal estate tax is relatively small, the tax bills—ranging between 37 and 55 percent—for individual families are huge. These tax rates were reduced to a maximum of 35 percent, but just for 2011 and 2012. Owners of smaller busi-nesses and family farms and ranches are often hard pressed to find the cash to pay these taxes. In some cases the family business must be sold to pay the tax. Although some would argue that the tax is a small price to pay for success, others argue that the estate and gift taxes are inherently unfair because the wealth is being taxed twice. Although proposals to repeal the estate tax have attracted support and the tax disappeared for the year 2010, a revised ver-sion of the tax remained in place for the years 2011 and 2012.

Another frequent complaint about the current tax code is its complexity. Few would argue that the code is not remarkably com-plex. Much of the current complexity stems from the distinction between capital gains and ordinary income, a distinction added in 1921. Certainly, many business provisions in the tax code are in place to counter taxpayer transactions that attempt to get favor-able capital gains treatment. Although the elimination of the pref-erence for capital gains would go a long way toward eliminating complexity, those who benefit from the capital gains rate are un-likely to champion this change because it would be against their economic interest. In addition, they argue that lower capital gains rates are a basic part of the tax code and are in place to encourage investment and thus strengthen the economy.

Much of the complexity in the code is in place to ensure equitable treatment for taxpayers. Because taxpayers earn their income in different ways but must report on the same tax forms, the tax code must provide complex mechanisms to ensure that similarly situated taxpayers pay an equivalent tax. Other complex rules are in place to provide tax relief in specific situations. Although tax is normally imposed when a taxpayer disposes of property, the code incorporates the "wherewithal to pay" concept, which provides tax deferral when the taxpayer's transactions do not produce cash. For example, real estate investors who exchange rather than sell their property may defer paying tax until they are "cashed out." Taxpayers rely on this type of treatment. Beginning in January 2000, accrual-basis business owners were no longer able to defer tax on gains when they sold their businesses, even if the sales price was not immediately received. Business owners and their lobbyists immediately beseeched lawmakers to reinstitute the "installment sale election" so that these business owners could be taxed more fairly. However, tax relief comes at the price of more complexity in the tax rules.

Perhaps a more serious and fundamental question concerning the present system is the fact that it distorts behavior. Critics argue that an income tax tends to discourage savings and investment because interest and dividends are taxed. They argue that a consumption tax—either a flat tax that exempts interest, dividends, and capital gains—or a retail sales tax would provide no such disincentives. Admittedly, the U.S. savings rate is one of the lowest in the world: At times, the savings rate is actually negative. However, there is no accurate way to predict whether changes in the tax system would have the expected effect on savings. Other economists have argued that because Americans are typically "target savers" rather than "systematic savers," the expected decrease in consumption and increase in savings may not materialize.

Difficulties in Implementing Tax Reform

Although nearly everyone agrees that tax reform is needed, implementing tax reform can be extremely difficult. The difficulty has a number of distinct causes. First, gaining consensus about the nature of the reform can be difficult. The discussion earlier about the fairness of a flat-rate versus a progressive income tax is a case in point. Although a higher-earning taxpayer will pay more than a lower-earning taxpayer under both systems, the progressive rate will force the higher-earning individual to pay far higher taxes than he or she would under the flat-tax rate. Many informed people will disagree about the inherent fairness of either of these tax structures. There is even more controversy when reform proposals involve major changes—such as abandoning the current income tax system in favor of a value-added tax (VAT) or a consumption tax, like a national sales tax.

Changing from a system that taxes income to one that taxes consumption or wealth necessarily involves value judgments about what type of tax is in the national interest and who should bear the brunt of the tax burden. In reality, taxpayers normally feel that the best tax is a tax someone else will pay. Gaining consensus can be difficult because of the uncertain consequences that may result from tax reform. In fact, it can be very difficult to predict, much less quantify, the results of tax law changes. Changes in tax rules, of course, affect both the government and taxpayers. Although the Treasury tries to predict the results of tax reform changes, those predictions are not always accurate. It can be extremely difficult to predict human motivation. Taxpayers themselves are even worse predictors than the Treasury Department. When Congress lowered the business tax deduction for business meals and entertainment from 80 to 50 percent, restaurant operators and others in the hospitality industry predicted a rash of restaurant failures because taxpayers would shun their establishments. In fact, no such calamity took place. One problem with tax law changes is that taxpayers who have planned their transactions under the prior rules may be upset with the changes. In many cases the tax law changes will make transactions less profitable. Taxpayers have argued that these changes should be illegal because of their retroactive effect. However, the courts uniformly hold that Congress may change the tax rules as it sees fit to do so and that the government makes no explicit or implied promise that the expected tax results will materialize in the future. For example, landowners who sell their property and agree to receive payments from the buyers over a number of years can use the "installment sale method" to report their gain. Instead of recognizing all their gain (profit) in the year of sale, the sellers can recognize a proportionate amount of the gain in the years in which the sales proceeds are actually received. In most cases, this method allows taxpayers to spread their gains over several years. This can often push the income into lower tax brackets. In any event, it allows the taxpayer to postpone payment of the tax until later years. Under the "present value concept," the taxpayer has a huge financial advantage by postponing payment of the tax until later years. Present value is essentially the reverse of interest. An individual is better off receiving a sum today than at a later date and better off paying a tax later than paying it today. An example will illustrate the point.

In 1986, Congress decided to change the capital gain rules. For years prior to 1987, long-term capital gains were taxed at a maximum of 20 percent and often at rates far lower. For years starting in 1987, the capital gains tax preference was repealed, requiring taxpayers to pay tax rates of up to 31 percent on the gain. Taxpayers who had sold their property in earlier years—1984, for example—argued that they should be allowed to use the 20 percent tax rate to payments received later. The taxpayers argued that the application of the higher rate to a transaction that was planned years before was an illegal retroactive change in the law. The courts, however, agreed with the IRS that although the taxpayers had not foreseen that Congress would repeal the favorable capital gains tax preference, the taxpayers' "expectancy" that the future rates would be the same was just that—an expectancy, not a guarantee. Sometimes taxpayers benefit from tax reform changes and sometimes they suffer.

One criticism of the U.S. tax system is the velocity of changes in the tax code, and many of these changes can only vaguely be described as real reforms. Compared with other countries, the U.S. tax rules are seen as fluid and unpredictable. Foreign investors sometimes complain that the uncertainty over tax law changes makes it difficult to quantify expected returns from U.S. business investments.

Tax Reform Lessons: The Marriage Penalty

Even tax reform measures backfire over time. One well-known embarrassment is the joint return. It, allowing a husband and wife to combine their incomes and file a single Form 1040, was introduced into the tax code in 1948. Prior to that date, individual taxpayers filed individual tax returns. A husband and wife who each had income to report would each file their own returns. In eight western community property states—Arizona, California, Idaho, Louisiana, New Mexico, Nevada, Texas, and Washington (Wisconsin has since joined the ranks of community property states), husbands and wives have a legal right to one half of their spouse's income. The federal courts decided that in those eight states, when a married couple had income from only one spouse (which was often the case in 1948), they had the option of reporting the income on one tax return or splitting the income and reporting each half on two separate tax returns. Filing two tax returns generally allowed the couple to pay significantly lower taxes than their counterparts in the other 40 states. In response, a number of those other states attempted to become community property states so as to allow their residents to avail themselves of this tax break.

Responding to this problem, Congress enacted legislation creating the joint return for 1948. At the time, the joint return was viewed as an important tax reform that solved a serious inequity problem. The joint return allowed spouses to combine their income and pay a low tax rate (before 1948 there was only one tax filing status and only one tax rate). In the community property states, a married couple could still file two tax returns, but if they did they would be forced to use the "married filing separately" tax rates (still available as of 2000), which would force them to pay higher combined taxes. Couples in all states opted to file the new joint return. Initially this provided a real tax break for married couples because it allowed spouses with different incomes to average their tax rates and pay lower taxes.

Because of social biases, in 1948 and for the next 20 years it was very common for wives to receive much lower wages and salaries than their husbands. Additionally, many more women in that period did not work outside the home and reported no wages or salaries of their own. In this environment the joint return and joint tax rates were real boons to families. However, time changed this windfall into a penalty.

As more women entered the workforce and demanded pay equality, women's compensation grew much closer to that of their husbands on average. In fact, in many urban areas, wives typically out earn their husbands. However, the joint return and tax rates devised in 1969 produced an unforeseen result: instead of providing these married couples with a tax break, it created a "marriage penalty." This penalty resulted because the tax assessed on the joint return when husbands and wives report relatively equal compensation actually exceeds the amount of tax that would be reported if the couple were single and reporting using the single rates. Before 1969 a married couple's income was essentially divided in half, and each spouse was taxed as an individual. Accordingly, a married couple making $100,000 would be taxed as two taxpayers making $50,000 each. Because in 1969 single people making $100,000 were taxed at much higher rates, the new 1969 tax tables taxed two married individuals at a higher rate than two single people with the same income. The idea was to make things fairer for single taxpayers, but the change created the marriage penalty for married couples. Now they were paying more taxes than unmarried couples with the same income. A married couple's only other option, other than using the joint return, was to use the married-but-filing-separately rates, which normally produce an even higher tax bill. The 1948 tax reform—the joint return—had become a tax penalty in 1969.

Congress was not unsympathetic to the plight of this constituency. For a time the tax code allowed a deduction equal to half the lower-earning spouse's income to redress the marriage penalty. When tax writers enacted the 1986 Tax Reform Act, however, they eliminated this deduction because the tax writers were under pressure to keep the new measure revenue-neutral (not a tax increase or decrease as compared with the pre-1986 rules). Accordingly, the reform deduction designed to preserve the intention of the original reform expired. The Bush tax cuts tried to eliminate the marriage penalty for at least middle-class taxpayers. The tax tables were reconfigured in 2003 to equalize the tax brackets of married couples and single taxpayers. The rate penalty still applies to higher-income taxpayers, however. The 2003 reform also changed the standard deduction. Before 2003, single taxpayers' standard deductions were more than twice as high as those of married couples. Since 2003, a married couple has gotten the same standard deduction as two single filers.

Eliminating the joint return altogether might solve the marriage penalty problem for everyone. In today's economy, both spouses usually work. Couples in the community property states would receive only a small benefit by splitting their income over one another's returns. This loss of tax revenue would probably be a good price to pay for eliminating the marriage penalty, which at the time of this writing affected married couples in all 50 states.

Federal Tax Reform Options

As mentioned above, although nearly everyone believes that tax reform is necessary, there is little agreement about the design of the reformed system. The following sections discuss several of these options.

Incremental versus Fundamental Tax Reform

As discussed earlier in this chapter, it is helpful to distinguish the incremental tax reform of the present system from fundamental tax reform. Many Americans have come to believe that our present system of taxation, which relies most heavily on the federal income tax, is overly complex, anticompetitive, or both. Although many agree that the present system has serious shortcomings, there is far less agreement on exactly what sort of replacement would be in the best interests of the country. This final section of the chapter briefly discusses a number of the major alternatives to the present federal income tax. At the outset, students must distinguish between two types of tax reform: incremental tax reform, which strives to fine-tune the present system, and fundamental tax reform, which strives to replace the current system based on the income tax and payroll taxes with a new tax system. The last 40 years of the 20th century were characterized by incremental tax reform as Congress spent considerable energy fine-tuning the tax rules to encourage economic growth, to cut taxes, or to discourage certain kinds of behavior.

Although Americans from many walks of life have articulated the shortcomings of the present system and have called for fundamental tax reform, there has not been a political groundswell of discontent to propel Congress to replace the current system. Undoubtedly fear of the unknown is a factor. During prosperous times, citizens and politicians alike are reluctant to tinker with the tax system because they are fearful that the changes may disrupt the economy. Likewise, during recessions, politicians are reluctant to undertake major changes because the changes may result in severe and unexpected revenue shortfalls. Such shortfalls could cause the government to grind to a halt and leave government employees, bondholders, and eventually Social Security recipients unpaid.

Goals of Reform

Although many Americans agree that reform is a good idea, there is far less agreement on exactly what the word *reform* means. For most Americans the disagreement centers on two fundamental and interrelated questions: What type of tax or taxes is most appropriate? And how much should the rich pay? At the heart of tax reform is another question: How much of the tax burden should fall on the rich, the middle class, and the poor in society? This issue has no "correct" answer. Although many Americans feel that the tax system should be used only to raise revenue and not to reengineer society, many others strongly believe that the tax system should be used for income redistribution so that society is not made up of only the very rich and the poor. Issues about simplicity and ease of administration are really questions about the type of tax. No one would argue that simplicity is an attribute of the present system. Many of the "simple" systems—such as a flat tax or a national sales tax—are predicted to radically shift tax burdens to low-income taxpayers. Again, the degree to which the tax system should "soak the rich" is a basic issue in designing the tax system.

Another basic goal of most tax reform is revenue neutrality. Because spending bills and taxing bills are not directly linked, Congress must pass tax laws to raise enough revenue to cover the expenses of running the government. Accordingly, because tax bills have no provision for cutting spending, any new tax system must be revenue-neutral—the new tax scheme must bring in as much revenue as the old one. In practical terms, the more radical the tax reform proposal, the more uncertain the consequences and the greater the risk of a shortfall.

From an economist's point of view, a tax system should also be judged on its promotion of economic efficiency: the tax system should not alter or distort incentives to work, consume, or save. Economists also insist that the merit of any particular tax reform proposal must be judged with reference to tax incidence as well as tax excellence. *Tax incidence* refers to the party that bears the ultimate cost of the tax. For example, when a corporation pays a corporate income tax on its products, it may be able to pass along the tax to its customers in the form of higher prices—if consumers are willing to pay the higher prices. The ultimate incidence of the tax falls not on the corporation but on its customers. The market's structure and forces within it play a large role in determining to what extent a company can shift its tax burden. Although economists have spent a good deal of time studying the incidence of the corporate income tax, it is generally beyond the scope of this book.

Economists are interested in how the tax system can be designed to enhance the operation of the economy. Many economists would argue that although the government could entirely finance its operations through borrowing, it should use taxes to regulate private spending on goods and services to prevent inflation, excessive imbalance of payments, and unemployment. Some economists argue for "tax minimization"—setting the tax at the lowest possible level to restrain private spending to the desired level.

In addition, economists argue that the system should promote "tax neutrality"—taxpayers should not be encouraged to make decisions for tax reasons. For example, the current income tax system has been criticized for its encouragement of corporate debt over equity. Because interest payments are deductible but dividend payments are not, there is an inherent bias in favor of using debt. Although a completely neutral system may be desirable, it may be hard to design in practice.

Economists desire a tax system that will maximize national income—the after-tax income received by all taxpayers. This requires taxing some activities to subsidize others. For example, the government currently uses the tax system to indirectly subsidize low-income housing. Problems with the "tax expenditure" concept were noted earlier in the chapter. Finally, economists are also concerned with "benefit taxation"—matching tax burdens with government benefits. Economists argue that to the extent possible, taxpayers should pay taxes in proportion to the benefits they receive from the government. This goal runs counter to another goal of taxation: taxing according to people's ability to pay. Designing a tax system that taxes those with the most wealth is appealing not only from an equity (fairness) standpoint but also from a practical one. Benefit taxation aside, it is almost always easier to collect a tax from someone who can pay it than from someone who cannot.

Replacing personal and corporate income taxes with a consumption tax has the potential to improve America's competitiveness because it would encourage greater savings and investment. Proponents of a consumption tax argue that the change would increase an investor's after-tax return on investments, eliminating what they consider a bias against capital formation in the current income tax system. Others argue that there is no guarantee that a change in the tax system will increase the private savings rate. Proponents of a consumption tax also argue that it should help our competitiveness in foreign trade. Because the tax will encourage savings and discourage consumption, the change should help the U.S. balance of trade.

From the government's standpoint, simplicity and ease of administration are just as important as equity and economic efficiency. Of course, these goals are often in conflict. When the government creates a targeted tax benefit to make the tax system "fairer" for low-income taxpayers, simplicity and ease of administration suffer. What is clear is that a shift to a consumption tax of some sort would greatly simplify tax rules. Even if Congress were to include many targeted relief provisions, the system would still be far simpler than the current system. For example, if Congress were to enact a national retail sales tax, it would most likely exempt many categories of transactions to minimize the regressiveness of the tax. Twenty-nine of the states with sales taxes currently exempt purchases of food for this reason. Determining exactly what is "exempt food" will add complexity to the rules, but hardly as much as in the current system. Another important issue in reforming the current system is how to handle the transition to a new system. Without special transition rules, many taxpayers would be hit with large tax bills in the year of the change. If the law granted special relief to these taxpayers, there would be a large revenue shortfall. The costs associated with the costs of the 2009 Wall Street bailout and President Obama's health care reforms make passage of one of these alternatives more likely.

Incremental Tax Reform

Over the years numerous incremental reform proposals have been advanced. Most of these have attempted to create a fairer and simpler system the by lowering rates and eliminating "loopholes" that either provide tax deductions or allow certain kinds of income to escape taxation or to receive favorable capital gains treatment. At the time of this writing, the most recent proposal is the tax fairness and simplification bill of 2010.

This bill, a broad tax reform proposal similar to the 1986 reforms, was announced on February 23, 2010, by Senate Finance Committee members Ron Wyden, D-Ore., and Judd Gregg, R-N.H. Its stated goals are to implement a simpler and fairer tax system by lowering tax rates and eliminating narrow tax breaks that benefit special interests. One highlight of the plan is a simplified one-page Form 1040s for individual filers. This legislation would reduce the number of income tax brackets from six to three, triple the amount of the standard deduction, eliminate the alternative minimum tax, but retain an exclusion for capital gains and the deduction for residential mortgages. It would also lower the corporate income tax rate to a flat 24 percent and eliminate many loopholes, which Senators Wyden and Gregg termed "corporate welfare." The Wyden-Gregg proposal represents a generally mild reform of the current system; it is actually less comprehensive than the 1986 reforms, which actually abolished the capital gains break.

Alternatives to the Income Tax

There are four primary alternatives to the current income tax system. The first is a national retail sales tax collected by businesses on retail sales to customers. The second is a VAT like those used in almost every other western country. The third alternative is a flat tax—somewhat similar to the current income tax but without many of the deductions in the current system. The last alternative is a personal consumption tax, which would also resemble the current income tax system. One type of consumption tax is the proposed United Savings Allowance (USA) tax.

National Retail Sales Tax

A national retail sales tax would be an additional tax on retail purchases—similar to the sales tax now imposed in most states. Supporters of a national retail sales tax argue that although a high sales tax would cause some hardships, on balance the change would be worth it because individuals would no longer have to file any tax returns. Merchants would collect the tax and send the money along with forms to the federal government. Although this would shift the compliance burden to businesses, businesses are already set up to comply with such a tax in the 45 states with state retail sales taxes.

A national retail sales tax would differ from a VAT in that it would be collected on the final sale of goods (and perhaps services) to the retail consumer. The retailer collects the tax from the ultimate consumer and not from businesses that have added value to the product, as would be the case with a VAT.

One of the primary problems with a national sales tax is that it would be regressive—lower-income taxpayers would be facing a higher tax burden and higher-income taxpayers a lower tax burden. Most proposals include some form of tax rebate designed to mitigate the regressivity of the tax. This might take the form of a rebate equal to the tax rate times the official poverty level. The rebate would attempt to ensure that lower-income taxpayers would be reimbursed for many of the national sales taxes they would pay. Experts have variously estimated that the tax would have to be in the range of 15 to 33 percent to be revenue-neutral. Such a high rate could cause major disruptions. For example, consider a consumer who lived in a state with a 5 percent sales tax and a hypothetical 20 percent national sales tax. If the taxpayer bought a $20,000 car, the combined state and national sales taxes would be an additional $5,000, bringing the after-tax price of the car to $25,000. This level of taxation would discourage the purchase of big-ticket items. Additionally, it would encourage cheating. The car buyer might try to persuade the seller to illegally give a receipt for a lower amount to minimize the sales tax due. Experience with state sales taxes suggests that taxpayers do not change their behavior on account of sales taxes unless they are making large purchases, in which cases tax evasion becomes attractive. If the sales tax rate were 17 percent or above, evasion might become more common. Sales taxes can be evaded by bartering or by asking the seller to misstate the price of the goods sold. From an administrative viewpoint, a national retail sales tax would be easier to administer than a value-added tax for the simple reason that only retailers—not all businesses—would be required to collect and remit the tax.

During the 2008 Republican presidential primaries, former Arkansas Governor Mike Huckabee proposed a national retail sales tax that he called the "Fair Tax." The tax, with a basic 30 percent rate, would apply not only to sales of goods but also sales of services. Huckabee argued that the rate was really 23 percent because when 30 cents is added to a dollar purchase, the 30-cent tax represents only 23 percent of the $1.30 spent. Huckabee promised that the new tax would replace not only the federal income tax but also all other federal taxes, including Medicare, Social Security, and personal and corporate income taxes. Additionally, he promised to eliminate the Internal Revenue Service (IRS). John McCain, who did not support the Fair Tax, went on to win the Republican nomination. Like the flat tax (discussed further on), the Fair Tax stands a reasonable chance of being seriously considered as a replacement for the current income tax system.

Value-Added Tax

A VAT is a business-level tax on the sale of goods and services. VATs generally work like a sales tax at the seller's level. However, the tax is "invisible" to consumers because it gets built into the price of the goods. The tax is imposed on the value added at each level in the production of an item. Because the tax is ultimately reflected in the sales price of products, the VAT is a consumption tax, not an income tax. The VAT is widely used internationally; if adopted, therefore, it would more closely match the U.S. tax system with those of the nation's trading partners. All types of businesses, not just retail sellers, would be subject to a VAT.

One of the problems with the VAT is its complexity for sellers. In practical terms, the "value added for each business is the difference between the value of a business's sales and its purchases from other businesses. Accordingly, the tax is on the value added to the goods and services purchased during a given period. There are actually two systems for assessing VATs. The most common—and the type used in Europe—is the "credit invoice" VAT. These taxes require companies to maintain detailed records of all their sales and purchases. The other type is known as the subtraction system. Businesses could use their current financial books and records, so that this type would be far simpler and less costly to implement.

Adoption of a VAT would harmonize the U.S. tax system with those of its trading partners—a real goal now that the United States is increasingly dependent on foreign trade. A VAT would favor U.S. exports because it is only imposed on imports and goods sold in the United States. U.S. products would be relatively cheaper to buy overseas. Currently U.S. sellers increase their sales prices to recoup the cost of the federal income tax. In other words, sellers increase their prices by their estimated federal income tax burden to try to shift the tax to customers.

The VAT has the advantage of being able to pull in large amounts of revenue. Because it is a business-level tax, it would eliminate the need for individuals to file any tax returns— assuming that the tax rate was high enough to replace the revenue provided by both the current individual and corporate federal income taxes. The cost of the tax would be reflected in higher prices charged for goods. The tax would not be "transparent" because it would be hidden in the price of the goods—somewhat similar to the cost of the federal and state gas taxes that are hidden in the price of gasoline sold at the pump.

Flat Tax

Of all the major tax reform proposals, the flat tax has received the most publicity and also the most public support. Flat tax proposals envision replacing the current multirate income tax with a single rate system that is also highly simplified compared with the current income tax system. Several formerly communist eastern European countries have adopted flat rate income taxes, in contrast to western European countries, which typically employ individual income taxes with steeply progressive rates.

Although most of the publicity for the flat tax centered on Steve Forbes's 17 percent individual flat tax proposal when he ran for president in 1996, most flat tax proposals actually impose a flat tax on both individuals and businesses. Originally championed in the 1996 Kemp Commission on overhauling the federal tax system, the flat tax has enjoyed a number of influential supporters over the years, including Representative Dick Armey (R., Tex.). Representative Armey's proposal in the year 2000 envisioned about a 17 percent tax on wages, salaries, and pension income. Passive income like interest, dividends, and capital gains would be received tax-free. Few if any deductions would be allowed, although specific flat plans differ on this detail.

On the face of it, such plans seem unfair, but proponents counter with an exemption that would create a large floor of income that would go completely untaxed. For a family of four, only income above $31,000 would be taxed, and the excess would be taxed at only 17 percent. In fact, this provision would mean that many low- and middle-income families would no longer have to pay income tax (although they would still have to pay Social Security taxes on their earnings).

Other politicians have also offered their own flat tax proposals, and some of these have included certain deductions that many taxpayers have come to expect, including the home mortgage interest deduction and the charitable contribution deduction. Charities and other nonprofits are concerned that without such a deduction charitable giving would fall precipitously, just at a time when the government is handing more responsibility for caring for the needy over to such groups. The real estate industry, including mortgage lenders, is generally opposed to the flat tax because of the elimination of the home mortgage deduction. This elimination could serve to decrease home prices because housing would be less affordable. Although this change would benefit first-time home buyers, it does not benefit the tens of millions of existing homeowners who may stand to lose tens of thousands of dollars in home value if prices do in fact drop. However, retaining the home mortgage deduction under a flat tax plan leads to troubling details: if interest is not taxed but a home mortgage deduction is allowed, a homeowner could merely take out an extra-large mortgage or a home equity loan, invest the money, deduct the interest on the mortgage, and receive the investment interest tax-free.

The major advantage of the flat tax is its simplicity. In an era when fewer and fewer taxpayers are able to complete and file their own tax returns, many voters would be supporters of the flat tax idea. Some other flat tax plans do not exclude investment income.

The business flat tax would be imposed on revenues less wages paid and purchases made from other businesses. Additionally, the entire cost of new equipment and buildings could be deducted in the year of purchase.

The main criticism of the flat tax concerns revenue neutrality. Many experts believe that the tax rate would have to be far higher than 17 percent to be revenue-neutral. Proponents argue that progressive tax rates discourage people from working harder. There are few data to show that higher tax rates encourage people to stay home and remain idle. In fact, one could suggest that they might work even harder knowing that they would also have to pay the higher taxes. It is likely that taxes would discourage effort only when the rates were very high—much higher than the current maximum. What is more likely is that successful individuals would minimize the amounts they received as salary and maximize the amounts they received as stock, which, when sold, would be taxed at capital gains rates. Under the current flat tax proposals, capital gains would be subject to no tax. For example, the billions of dollars earned by Bill Gates, the cofounder of Microsoft, are actually represented by his stockholdings. Under a flat tax system, which also contemplates the repeal of the federal estate and gift taxes, this wealth would go completely untaxed. This result would probably be politically unacceptable. Proponents argue that a flat tax is fairer because progressive rates penalize hard work and success. Whether or not a flat tax or progressive tax is "fairer" must remain a matter of personal opinion—there is no "right answer."

Personal Consumption Tax

A personal consumption tax would resemble the current income tax in many respects because individuals would continue to pay taxes on wages and salaries and—unlike the flat tax—on interest and dividends. However, borrowed funds would also be included in the amount subject to tax. The tax would work as a consumption tax because any funds saved or invested during the year would be deducted. The tax would be imposed only on income consumed (spent) during the year. In most proposals the personal consumption tax has been supplemented by a business tax to ensure that business purchases of goods and services for consumption were taxed.

An example of a personal consumption tax is the Unlimited Savings Allowance (USA) tax plan advanced by Senators Nunn (D., Ga.) and Domenici (R., N.Mex.). It would be similar to the current income tax but would exempt new savings and investment. However, it would impose higher tax rates than the current federal income tax. The plan would include versions of the current earned income credit (which refunds money to the working poor), graduated rates, and a personal exemption creating a "zero bracket" for low-income taxpayers.

Although it is the most complicated proposal, a personal consumption tax may have the best chance of being implemented simply because it preserves many of the features of the current tax system. Tax reform is a political process, and special interest groups will want to preserve their established tax breaks. A personal consumption tax is the best vehicle to continue these breaks because it most closely resembles the current tax system.

How to Judge the Alternatives

Any reform proposal must be judged with reference to the differences in design between the taxes and how the alternatives affect a taxpayer's burden of complying with the tax laws and the government's ability to administer those laws. In terms of design, the proposals differ in the type of taxpayer affected, the preferential treatment given to certain types of income or transactions, and whether graduated rate structures are involved. Compliance by taxpayers and ease of administration by the government also differ. Proposals that tax only businesses are obviously attractive from a compliance standpoint. Although replacing the graduated rates with a flat tax implies a simplification, in fact the percentage calculation is actually a very small part of the complexity problem inherent in the present system. The problems stem from defining taxable and exempt income and determining eligibility for deductions. Consumption tax systems that require individuals to report information about their savings and investments so that these will not be subject to tax are potentially even more complicated than the present system.

Although the flat tax has garnered the bulk of the attention, this fact does not necessarily mean that it is more likely to be adopted than any of the other proposals. Although the flat tax is intrinsically appealing because it eliminates complexity, the proposal has not yet had to withstand a rigorous public debate comparing its numerous disadvantages in relation to its obvious simplicity of design.

Although public opinion does matter, tax reform in the United States is ultimately driven more by pragmatic realities. All of these tax reform proposals must be judged by their impact on economic efficiency, equity, simplicity for taxpayers, ease of administration for the government, and revenue-generating capacity. In the current pay-as-you-go fiscal environment, the first prerequisite is for a reliable and predicable source of revenue. From a less pragmatic perspective, economists generally favor a switch to a consumption tax—such as the national retail sales tax, VAT, flat tax, or personal consumption tax—to improve economic efficiency and make the tax system more neutral. One problem with the current tax system is that it discourages savings because income that is earned and saved is taxed. A tax designed as a consumption tax would provide that any income that is saved is tax-exempt—hence the tax is on income that is consumed (spent).

However, economic efficiency and bolstering the U.S. savings rate are not the only factors to be considered in evaluating the proposals.

A primary difference in the proposals involves who would be subject to the tax. Taxes can be levied on businesses, consumers, or both, as under the present system. In one sense, under a national retail sales tax or value-added tax, only businesses would be paying the tax. Whereas all businesses would be subject to the VAT, only businesses that sell to consumers would be subject to the national sales tax. In another sense, consumers would be paying because retailers would be collecting the additional national retail sales tax at the point of sale. In the case of the VAT, the purchase price would in many, if not most, cases include a value-added tax.

The promises of simplicity and ease of administration are obviously high on the list of reasons to abandon the current tax system. Generally a tax system that is relatively easy for taxpayers to comply with will be easy for the government to administer. This point argues for either the VAT or the national retail sales tax, because both of these systems would eliminate the need for individuals to file tax returns. The flat tax, with few if any deductions and only one tax rate, appears to be simple, although it would still require individuals to file returns unless they fell under its exemption limits. Despite the attractions of simplicity and administrative ease, equity (fairness) remains a major issue. The switch to consumption taxes may come at the price of radically shifting the burden of taxpaying down to middle- and low-income taxpayers. With a society that is increasingly stratified between the haves and have-nots, it may not be wise to change to a tax system that would accelerate this trend. The current system does promote income redistribution, and the amount of income redistribution, if any, that should be retained in a reformed tax system is a question that must be addressed. This issue is a political and social one rather than a purely economic one.

Policymakers and citizens must recognize that changes in the tax system may have a major impact on the quality of life of many poor and elderly Americans. Under the current income tax system, the poor pay no income tax and the working poor may actually receive money from the government by electing to claim the earned income credit, a type of "negative income tax." Without some kind of structural relief built into a national retail sales tax or VAT system, the poor may be forced to pay tax when they purchase goods. Although most tax reform proposals feature some device to exempt the poor, policymakers must closely examine whether the device will work as promised.

Finally, there must be reasonable assurance that any tax reform measure will also be revenue-neutral. This last requirement may be the most daunting and, in practical terms, may ensure that the United States continues its policy of adopting incremental rather than fundamental tax reform during the next quarter century. The readings in chapter 6 provide a more detailed analysis of some of these specific tax reform proposals.

2012 Tax Reform Proposals

By 2012 there was a broad nonpartisan consensus that tax reform would have to be part of any solution to reducing the growing federal budget deficit. Spending had exceeded tax revenues by alarming amounts. Whereas conservative leaders supported changes to the system, they stood fast on opposing "new" taxes. Liberals would not accept program cuts without additional taxes on the wealthy. In this environment several detailed tax proposals emerged. Some proposed simplifying the current income tax system, while other advocated scrapping the present income tax and replacing it with a VAT or a consumption tax (retail sales tax).

Bowles-Simpson
The National Commission on Fiscal Responsibility and Reform (often called Bowles-Simpson or Simpson-Bowles) was a 2010 bipartisan presidential commission created to identify "policies to improve the fiscal situation in the medium term and to achieve fiscal sustainability over the long run." The commission's tax reform plan—which was not initially approved by Congress—called for across-the-board tax rate reductions for individual taxpayers. The plan would eliminate many tax deductions but preserve the deduction for home mortgage interest. The plan would tax long-term capital gains as ordinary income.

The plan broadens the corporate tax base by eliminating deductions, and it also lowers corporate tax rates. The plan also increases the gasoline tax to help close the government's tax gap.

BPC Plan
The Bipartisan Policy Center's (BPC) Debt Reduction Task Force created a tax reform plan aimed at reducing the national debt. Cochaired by former Senate Budget Committee Chairman Pete Do-

menici (R-N.M.) and Alice Rivlin, Budget Director under former President Bill Clinton, Director of the Congressional Budget Office, and Vice Chair of the Federal Reserve, the BPC plan called for two individual tax rates, 15 and 27 percent. The plan eliminates the alternative minimum tax as well as many deductions, including state and local taxes. The home mortgage interest deduction would be replaced by a tax credit. The corporate tax rate would be reduced to 27 percent. The estate tax would be retained at a 45 percent tax rate on wealth over $3.5 million. The plan would also enact a new 6.5 percent national sales tax targeted to reduce the national debt and would expand alcohol taxes to help close the tax gap.

Fair Tax Act

The Fair Tax Act of 2011, introduced by Representative Rob Woodall (R-Ga.) and Senator Saxby Chambliss (R-Ga.), repeals the individual income tax, the corporate income tax, all payroll taxes, the self-employment tax, and the estate and gift taxes. All of those taxes are replaced by a 23 percent national retail sales tax. The tax-inclusive retail sales tax would equal 23 percent of the sum of the sales price of an item and the amount of the retail sales tax. Every family would receive a rebate of the sales tax on spending amounts up to the federal poverty level.

Freedom Flat Tax Act

Introduced by Representative Michael Burgess (R-Tx), this plan authorizes an individual to make an irrevocable election to be subject to a flat tax (in lieu of the existing tax provisions). The flat tax was based on the concepts of the Hall-Rabushka flat tax proposal. It would also repeal the estate and gift taxes. The initial tax rate for individuals not engaged in business activity who selected the flat tax would be 19 percent; but after 2 years this rate would decline to 17 percent. The individual flat tax would be levied on all wages, retirement distributions, and unemployment compensation. The flat tax would have "standard deductions" that would equal the sum of the "basic standard deduction" which would depend on filing status, and the "additional standard deduction," equal to $6,530 for each dependent of the taxpayer.

Ryan Plan

Representative Paul Ryan's (R-Wi.) plan gives individual taxpayers a choice of how to pay their taxes—through existing law or through a highly simplified code with a return that fits on a post-card: a flat tax with almost no special tax deductions, credits, or exclusions (except the health care tax credit). The plan has two tax rates, 10 and 25 percent. It eliminates both the alternative minimum tax and the estate tax. The plan eliminates all taxes on interest, capital gains, and dividends and replaces the corporate income tax with a value added tax.

Wyden Greg Plan

The bipartisan plan lowers the number of individual tax brackets from six to three and eliminates the Alternative Minimum Tax. The plan triples the standard deduction, but all miscellaneous itemized deductions are eliminated. The first 35 percent of capital gains would not be taxed with the excess taxed as ordinary income. The corporate tax rates would be replaced with a 24 percent flat tax.

Other Tax Plans

President Obama's modest tax reform proposals included letting the 2001 "Bush tax cuts" expire for single individuals with incomes above $200,000 ($250,000 if married filing jointly). Obama also suggested patching but not eliminating the Alternative Minimum Tax, and capping the benefit of itemized deductions at 28 percent. Obama also proposed a reduction in the corporate tax rate and an elimination of corporate loopholes. Although the broad outline of the plan is known, specifics are missing. Candidates challenging President Obama have also suggested tax reform proposals. The best known of these is Herman Cain's "9-9-9" plan, which calls for elimination of the income tax, payroll tax, and estate tax. These levies would be replaced by a 9 percent business tax imposed on gross income less purchases from U.S.-located businesses, a 9 percent personal tax on gross income less charitable deductions with no tax on capital gains, and a 9 percent national retail sales tax to be collected by the states. The plan was immediately attacked for its lack of specifics and its optimistic revenue estimates. Congresswoman Michele Bachmann's plan also calls for fewer tax brackets and total repeal of taxes included in the 2010 Health Care Act. She would also eliminate the estate tax and devise a "simpler and fairer" corporate tax system. Governor Rick Perry's plan includes allowing individuals the option of paying the regular tax or a new 20 percent flat tax with a standard exemption of $12,500 and deductions for mortgage interest, charitable contributions, and state and local taxes for families earning less than $500,000. The estate tax would be repealed. The top corporate rate would be lowered to 20 percent and the tax system would change to a territorial, not a worldwide system. Mitt Romney's plan would keep the Bush tax cuts and move toward a flatter tax rate schedule and fewer deductions. All of the candidates' tax reform plans remained broad outlines rather than detailed plans.

3

Special U.S. Issues

This chapter includes a discussion of a few special tax issues. The chapter looks at tax reform proposals involving "green" or "eco taxes," including a discussion of "carbon taxes," which have been imposed in some other countries. The chapter next examines a number of problems with state and local taxation, with emphasis on multistate taxation issues. Finally, the chapter examines the legal and practical problems of taxing Internet sales.

State Tax Systems

Complexity and Multiple Taxation

A good deal of the complexity inherent in the U.S. tax system stems from the fact there is not one government but literally thousands of different governments that levy taxes. In our federal system, which divides political power among the federal government, states, and localities, each level of government retains the power to tax. With 50 states and thousands of local cities, towns, counties, and other taxing districts, the complexity is systemic. Although some uninformed individuals have argued that taxation from multiple levels of government is illegal double taxation, in fact it is legally permissible. Different levels of government have the right to tax the same item of income or property despite the fact that another level of government has also chosen to tax it.

Different levels of government can choose to exempt all or a portion of income or property from this multiple taxation. For example, in computing the federal income tax, the federal government allows individuals and businesses to deduct state income tax paid on the same income. Individuals can claim this deduction only if they are claiming itemized deductions instead of the flat standard deduction. Allowing the deduction of state taxes is not a constitutional requirement. In fact, for one purpose—calculation of the alternative minimum tax—the federal government provides no deduction for state tax. Likewise, the federal income tax does not allow individuals to deduct state sales taxes in computing their federal taxable income if they also deduct state income tax. This rule exempts a portion of the income from being taxed by both the state and the federal government. Consider the following simplified example.

Assume State A assesses a 10 percent tax on income and Taxpayer X earns $100 of income. Further assume that X is obligated to pay a 20 percent federal tax but the state allows X to deduct this in computing her state tax.

Federal income tax on the income would be $18, computed as follows:

$100 income
−$10 state tax deduction =
$90 income subject to federal tax
× 0.20 federal tax rate (20%) =
$18 federal tax

Taxpayer X would also have to pay $10 of state income tax on the $100 of income ($100 × 10% = $10), bringing the combined federal and state tax to $28. The state can also choose to allow X to deduct the federal tax, which reduces the income subject to state tax and the state tax payable:

$100 income
−$18 federal tax deduction =
$82 income subject to state tax
× 0.10 state tax rate (10%) =
$8.20 state tax

If both the federal and state taxes are deductible, the combined federal and state tax due is $26.20. If neither the federal government nor the state allowed X to deduct the other's taxes, the combined tax would be $30 ($100 × 20% = $20 federal tax plus $100 × 10% = $10 state tax). Therefore the deductions do lower X's combined tax. However, there is still multiple taxation of the income. If there were no multiple taxation, only one govern-ment—let's use the federal government for our example—would be allowed to tax the income, and the tax would be only $20. Accordingly, when the government allows a taxpayer to deduct taxes imposed by another government, it provides some tax relief but does not really eliminate multiple taxation.

Alert readers may have noticed a computational quandary in the earlier simplified example. If both the federal government and the state government allow a taxpayer to deduct one another's tax and then to compute each tax, the taxpayer must know the amount of the other tax. The taxpayer will have to know the amount of the state tax in order to calculate the federal tax. However, the tax-payer will also have to know the amount of the federal tax before he can calculate the state tax. Theoretically, the circularity prob-lem could be solved by requiring taxpayers to use a simultaneous equation, with the federal and state tax unknowns. In practice, taxpayers do not have to brush up on their algebra because the federal government allows taxpayers to deduct the amount of state tax *paid* rather than the actual amount of state tax due. Tax-payers can merely add the number of dollars deducted from their paychecks together with any amounts they sent to the state (typi-cally as estimated tax payments). This amount paid to the state is deducible as state tax, an itemized deduction, on the taxpayer's federal tax return. Notice that the actual tax due the state may be a higher or lower amount. Accordingly, if the taxpayer receives a refund from the state because the total amount paid in withhold-ings and estimated tax payments exceeds the actual state tax due, the refund is reportable to the federal government as income. This refund is seen as income by the federal government because the taxpayer was allowed to deduct entire amount of the payments made to the state.

Historical Overview

Historically, there has been a good deal of state-by-state variation in tax. Originally, state governments were far more important than the federal government, but this balance has increasingly shifted during the 20th century. At the time of the revolution in the 1770s, the northern colonies generally relied on property taxes and to a lesser extent on poll taxes (a tax assessed on the privi-lege of voting). They also assessed miscellaneous taxes, such as taxes on certain professions, like law and medicine. Interestingly, the amount of these early property taxes did not depend on the market value of the property, as is the case today. In the 1770s, landowners were assessed a flat amount depending on the size of the land they held. Today, the government attempts to determine the market value of the property, and it assesses tax on that basis. The southern states, politically dominated by large landowners, resisted using property taxes, relying on the poll tax and many miscellaneous levies.

When the states established compulsory public school systems in the early 1800s, they uniformly passed the funding burden to the localities—a pattern that persists in many but not all states. Initially, property taxes were assessed on both "real property" (real estate) and "personal property" (non–real estate, including jewelry, vehicles, livestock, and intangible personal property like stocks and bonds). Over the years, most of the states limited their property taxes primarily to real estate. During the early 1900s the states started levying sales taxes and taxes on both autos and gasoline. Many of the states decided to let localities be the sole recipients of property tax revenue. In 1900 the states still derived half their revenues from property taxes. This figure had dropped to about 25 percent by 1940 and to less than 2 percent in 1999. A number of states continue to assess a property tax on inventory held by a business for resale to its customers, although other states have dropped their inventory taxes in an effort to attract new industry. Real estate tax incentives are discussed in more detail in the following section "Local Taxation."

One state property tax that has proven especially unpopular is the car tax. This tax is actually an ad valorem personal property tax levied on one item—the motor vehicle. The tax is relatively easy to assess because cars have a "blue book" value (a generally accepted average value), and the state can condition receipt of license plates on payment of the tax. These taxes—which can amount to several thousand dollars per year on a luxury car— have proven especially unpopular when residents in adjacent states pay no such tax. In states that have them, car taxes entice car owners to cheat by registering their cars with friends or relatives in adjoining states in order to dodge the tax. Voters in Virginia elected a new governor who had pledged to repeal this unpopular tax, and in 1999 Washington State voters used their "initiative" power to enact ballot measures as law to repeal their state's car tax. A more recent type of property tax is the real estate transfer tax, which is really a form of excise tax on larger real estate sales.

A number of states and localities have enacted these taxes and more are considering doing so. The proceeds of these taxes are used to offset the cost to the government of providing municipal services such as roads, mass transit, water, and sewers to new real estate developments.

Modern State Tax Systems

Today, state tax systems usually rely on three main types of taxes: individual income taxes, corporate income taxes, and sales taxes. A few states have only two of these three legs. Some states rely on other taxes, such as severance taxes, which are based on the extraction of natural resources. Alaska, for example, relies heavily on severance taxes imposed on oil production. We now focus on six different types of state taxes.

Individual and Corporate State Income Taxes

The majority of U.S. states assess an income tax on the earnings of both individuals and corporations. The individual income tax in most states is similar to the income tax imposed by the federal government, although the forms required to be filed by taxpayers are usually shorter. Normally, a state income tax is due at the same time as the federal return, which for individuals is April 15 of the year following the year in which the income was earned. Although details differ, these state tax systems are quite similar to the federal income tax system but are administered by departments of revenue in each of the individual states.

Most states also impose an income tax on profits earned by corporations operating within the state. Because many corporations are engaged in multistate activities, this presents certain problems. The taxation of multistate transactions in multistate corporations is considered further on.

Excise and Sales Taxes

Most states impose excise taxes in the form of a sales tax on retail sales. For example, if a retailer sells a product for $10, a state may impose a 4 percent sales tax on the proceeds. The tax would be 40 cents ($10 × 0.04 = $0.40). The retailer acts as tax collector for the state and remits the tax collected at the point of sale to the state. Although sales taxes are assessed on most sales of goods, a number of exemptions normally apply. However, these exemptions are not uniform. For example, many states exempt the sale of food from the sales tax. However, even states that exempt the sale of food often impose the tax on the sale of food that will be consumed on the premises. In other words, sales of restaurant food are usually subject to a state sales tax even in states in which food is normally exempt from taxation. Some states exclude taxation on the sale of certain necessities, such as clothing, whereas others do not. Most states exclude the taxation of services. For example, if you were to buy $100 of grass seed from a garden store, a state with a 7 percent sales tax would impose $7.00 tax on the transaction ($100 × 0.07 = $7.00). If, however, you paid a lawyer $100 to prepare a will, in most states no sales tax would be collected.

Most states also have a use tax imposed on property that is brought into the state and has not been taxed. This tax is meant to protect the state from consumers who buy goods elsewhere and bring them into the state without paying a sales tax. For example, a consumer is a resident of State A, which imposes a sales tax of 5 percent on the sale of goods within the state. Assume that this consumer buys an automobile in State A. The state will impose a 5 percent sales tax on the purchase, and if the auto costs $10,000, then $500 in sales tax would be due on the transaction and collected by the car dealer ($10,000 × 5% = $500). It is interesting to note that the tax is due and payable even if the consumer buys the car on credit rather than paying cash. If the State A consumer purchases the car outside of State A, no sales tax may be due to State A, but a "use tax" may be due. State A has no power to impose a sales tax on a transaction that happens outside its borders. In addition, states normally impose sales tax only on their own citizens, not citizens of other states and nations. Therefore the consumer should not have to pay the adjacent state's sales tax. However, a citizen of State A would have to pay State A's state use tax on an automobile purchased in an adjacent state. The use tax is normally calculated at the same rate as the sales tax, which in our example was 5 percent. Accordingly, if the State A consumer bought a car in a State B, the consumer would not have to pay sales tax to State A but would have to pay a $500 use tax to State A before registering the car in State A. No tax would be due to State B because states normally exempt sales of property that will be removed from the state.

Although states may have an easy time collecting use tax on the purchase of automobiles, because all automobiles must be registered in the state before they can be driven, the states have a harder time collecting use tax on smaller items, such as refrigerators, washing machines, or small items like books, pens, or pencils. Although a use tax may be due when consumers bring purchases back from out of state, this tax is difficult to enforce, and many consumers are simply unaware of the tax.

Mail Order Sales
A special problem concerns mail order sales. Many consumers make mail order purchases because no sales tax is typically collected. However, in the future, states will be banding together to require mail order businesses to collect use tax in addition to the purchase price and freight and handling charges on their mail order sales.

Internet Sales
The problems associated with mail order sales also generally apply to sales on the Internet. Sales tax is not collected from buyer unless the seller has "nexus" in the seller's state (nexus being some contact with the state that justifies taxation). Few buyers pay use tax. The problems surrounding the taxation of Internet sales are discussed in a later section of this chapter.

State Property Taxes
Many states impose a property tax on various kinds of property, as previously mentioned in the historical overview. However, some states impose property tax on both real property and personal property, such as autos and water craft. Many western states have taxes on specific types of property, such as timber or minerals.

Inheritance Taxes
Some states impose inheritance taxes on the privilege of inheriting property from a deceased person. Unlike an estate tax, which is assessed on the estate of the deceased individual, an inheritance tax is a tax placed on the heir and taxes the privilege of receiving the property. Typically inheritance tax rates vary depending on the closeness of the relationship of the heir and the deceased. Close family members typically pay a lower percentage of inheritance tax than strangers to the decedent.

Severance Taxes
Some states that are rich in natural resources but with little other commercial activity rely heavily on severance taxes. For example,

Montana, with rich deposits of coal and other natural resources, depends more heavily on severance taxes than eastern states having more industrial activity. Severance taxes are typically assessed on a per unit basis. For example, a severance tax might be assessed on a per barrel basis on oil pumped from the ground or on the tons of ore actually extracted from a mine. Producers can typically pass along such costs to the ultimate consumers of the natural resources.

Multistate Taxation

Each individual state has the power to collect taxes on business activities within the state. Because many commercial transactions cross state lines, there is the potential for any transaction to be taxed by at least two states. When a transaction crosses a state line, it is considered "interstate commerce."

For many years, transactions in interstate commerce were thought to be completely exempt from state taxation. However, today interstate commerce must also pay its own way as long as state tax laws do not discriminate against interstate commerce and interstate transactions. In other words, intrastate and interstate transactions are both subject to state tax. However, business taxpayers often fear that interstate transactions may be taxed by two different states. To assure that an interstate transaction will not be taxed twice, two tools have been developed: a system of credits and a system of apportionment.

When there is potential for a transaction to be taxed once by the federal government and once by a foreign country, a foreign tax credit is available. The foreign credit gives a dollar-for-dollar credit against U.S. tax for tax payable to a foreign country. For example, if a taxpayer executes a transaction from United States with a firm in Canada and Canadian law provides that a taxpayer must pay a Canadian tax on the transaction, the taxpayer will normally be given a U.S. foreign tax credit, which will allow a credit for taxes already paid to Canada. In this way, the transaction is not taxed twice but only once.

Apportionment

When a transaction starts in one state and proceeds to a second state, the method of assessing tax must rely on either allocation or apportionment. When taxes are allocated, they are allocated to one of the two states. In other words, all of the tax will be collected by one of the states. When taxes are apportioned, they are divided between the two states or among three or more states. In other words, each state will get to collect part of the tax. For example, assume that a railroad runs through the state of Kansas. Also assume that the railroad does not start in Kansas but the trains merely proceed from one end of the state to the other without stopping within the state at all. Although Kansas has the right to assess property taxes on the railroad's property within the state, it is initially hard to see how the state of Kansas could assess tax on income earned by the railroad within Kansas. If a passenger buys a ticket in Missouri and takes the train through Kansas all the way to Denver, Colorado, where he departs, the states of Missouri and Colorado seemingly have a stronger case for taxing the income earned from the trip than the state of Kansas. However, Kansas can argue that if it were not for the tracks through Kansas, the trip would not be possible and the income would never be earned. Recognition of this problem has led to apportionment.

With apportionment, each state may tax part of the income that relates to the amount of income earned within that state. In our example, Kansas will be able to tax part of the income earned by the train passing through Kansas despite the fact that the train never stops within the state but merely proceeds through. The same is true of airplane flights over Kansas. Kansas has the right to tax the part of the income generated by that flight, and in the future the states will be able to tax communication satellites operating over their land.

Nexus

Before a state can assess a tax against a corporation, the U.S. Constitution requires that there be due process of law, and due process requires "nexus." As stated previously, nexus is some contact with the states that justifies taxation. For example, conducting a business within the state normally establishes nexus, but merely sending an order for goods into a state does not. A physical presence is usually required before a taxpayer has nexus with the state justifying taxation of the corporation.

The Massachusetts Formula

When income is earned in a number of states, the states normally apportion the income between them. For example, assume that a train runs from Seattle, Washington, south through the state of

Oregon and finally into the state of California, where the train stops in San Francisco. The states typically use a three-factor formula that apportions the income among the states. This factor is known as the Massachusetts Factor, after the first state that employed it. The formula looks at the percentage of the taxpayer corporation's payroll, sales, and property within the state. The formula appears in Figure 3.1.

In our example, if the state of California were taxing the railroad, the state of California would derive the percentage of the railroad's property in California, the percentage of the railroad sales taking place in California, and the percentage of the railroad payroll that occurs in California. These three fractions would

---

Most states assess a state income tax on income that corporations earn within the state. Because corporate income is often earned in more than one state, state tax systems must "source" corporate income to particular states. Most states use the following formula to apportion a corporation's business income among the states in which the corporation operates. The overall formula employs three factors—sales, property, and payroll—to find the fraction of the corporation's income that is earned in state.

Step 1

$$\frac{\text{In-state sales}}{\text{Everywhere sales}} = \text{In-state sales \%}$$

$$\frac{\text{In-state property}}{\text{Everywhere property}} = \text{In-state property \%}$$

$$\frac{\text{In-state payroll}}{\text{Everywhere payroll}} = \text{In-state payroll \%}$$

Step 2

$$\frac{\text{In-state sales \% + In-state property \% + In-state payroll \%}}{3} = \text{In-state \%}$$

Step 3

Everywhere corporation income × in-state % = in-state income

FIGURE 3.1 State formulary apportionment of corporate income.

then be added together and divided by three to get an aggregate fraction, which would be multiplied by the railroad's income everywhere. The result would be the portion of California income earned by the railroad, which is the amount that California may constitutionally tax.

Unitary Taxation

Some states have applied apportionment to foreign income. For example, if a Japanese company headquartered in Tokyo has a California subsidiary, the state of California may apportion a part of the Japanese parent corporation's income in determining the business's overall California income. The use of the formulary apportionment with either a domestic or overseas parent corporation is normally referred to as "unitary taxation." Unitary taxation has become a controversial issue, and Japanese companies and companies in other nations have strongly objected to such state taxation. However, the U.S. Supreme Court has uniformly upheld the use of unitary formulary apportionment.

Most states assess a state income tax on income that corporations earn within the state. Because corporate income is often "earned" in more than one state, state tax systems must "source" corporate income to particular states. Most states use the following formula to apportion a corporation's business income among the states in which the corporation operates. The overall formula employs three factors—sales, property, and payroll—to find the fraction of the corporation's income that is earned in state.

Local Taxation

Localities—cities, towns, and counties—rely primarily on real estate property taxes and miscellaneous levies. Many local governments also impose a retail sales tax, which is added onto the sales tax imposed by the state. In some states the city sales tax is uniform, but in others the sales tax varies from locality to locality. Businesses that operate in more than one location rightly complain that this variation in sales tax rates greatly contributes to the complexity of complying with the tax laws. A few larger cities and metropolitan areas like New York City also have local income taxes that apply not only to residents but also to nonresidents who work within the taxing jurisdiction.

Local Property Tax

Taxes on land and buildings have been a part of the U.S. tax system since colonial days. Before the rise of income taxes and retail sales taxes, real estate taxes were the mainstays of state tax systems. Although property taxes are assessed by both state and local governments, today these taxes are relatively more important as a revenue source to local governments because states rely more and more on income and sales taxes. In those states without a sales tax or income tax, property taxes are typically far more important to state treasuries.

Property taxes go to pay for local government services, including schools, parks, police and fire protection, streets, snow plowing, street lighting, and other local government services as well as the salaries of government workers. Roughly half of all property taxes go to support schools in most areas. Traditionally, local property taxes have gone to support local schools, but in an increasing number of states, school tax revenues are being split so students in all school districts get roughly equal amounts of tax support. Those who favor the old system complain that their tax dollars are being used to finance expenses elsewhere, whereas those who favor the reformed system argue that all children in public schools should get a decent education no matter where they live. Disparity in the quality and funding of public schools promises to remain an issue for some time. Property taxes are paid by the owners of the property. The tax is calculated by the tax rate times the tax base. The tax base is typically based on a valuation of the property. That basic scheme fails to reveal the complexity that has crept into property taxation. Not all property is included in the tax base to be taxed, and not all property pays the same tax rate. Real estate—land and buildings—is typically taxed, but in most states intangible property, like stocks and bonds, is not. Government property at all levels, including public schools, is off the tax rolls, as well as property owned by recognized nonprofit groups, such as charitable, religious, and private educational organizations. Towns and cities with large numbers of government buildings, military bases, hospitals, colleges, museums, and churches find themselves forced to shift the financial burden to homeowners and businesses. In some cities more than half the real property is exempt from property taxation. Some cities have experimented with negotiating user fees from the owners of these exempt properties on the theory that the owners should still bear their fair share of the cost of police and fire protection in the city.

Although property owners are required to pay taxes, renters are not. Landlords, who must cover all their costs to make a profit, try to pass on the cost of property taxes to their tenants. A landlord's ability to pass along property taxes depends on local rental conditions. If there is a surplus of rental housing with plenty of empty rental units, a landlord might not be able to raise rents sufficiently to cover a tax increase. Accordingly, renters normally pay property taxes indirectly.

Interestingly, citizens in an area can vote on both tax and borrowing measures whether or not they own property in the town or city. Property owners whose residences are elsewhere do not get to vote. In areas with a large number of vacation homes or with out-of-area property owners, many property owners feel disenfranchised because they do not get to vote on the level of taxes or borrowing but are required to pay property taxes nevertheless.

State and local governments are typically required to balance their budgets—spending cannot exceed their combined taxing and borrowing, and long-term borrowing must be voted on by the citizens. The amount of property tax is directly linked to government spending. Elected officials must be mindful that they need tax revenues to offset their spending. If there is a shortfall, they must borrow—and pay interest costs—to meet the shortfall. Accordingly, elected officials must coordinate their budgets and local tax collections. When spending increases, taxes normally must also increase. In most areas elected officials can increase tax rates on their own initiative to cover operating expenses. If voters find the tax rates too high, they can vote the officials out of office. In some localities any tax rate increases must be submitted to the voters.

An important feature of property taxation is assessment (valuation) of the property. The assessor creates a list of all taxable property (property not eligible for an exemption) and then assesses a value of the property. Although many jurisdictions require this assessment to be as near to fair market value as possible, in other areas the value is a percentage of the property's current value—or even a value at some date in the past. In some areas the land and buildings are assessed according to different formulas. Additionally, because local appraisers typically lack the staff to physically appraise every parcel every year, appraisers usually apply trending techniques. For example, the appraiser may decide that the assessment of all properties in a given neighborhood be raised by 5 percent based on the current real estate market. Of course, this average rise will benefit property owners whose properties actually appreciated by more and will penalize those whose property has not increased or has decreased in value. Property tax assessment is a frequent cause of taxpayer discontent. Therefore all property tax agencies allow some sort of appeal process so as to permit property owners to contest valuations.

Because of rising residential home values since 1970, many states, including California, have enacted special legislation to give property tax relief. Several areas of the country have adopted what has been nicknamed a "Hi Neighbor" system. Under this system, homes are reappraised only when sold. If a homeowner stays in his or her home, the appraised value may be frozen or presumed to rise by only a few percentage points per year. The net effect of this system is that homeowners who have owned their homes for a number of years will have underappraised homes and will be paying low property taxes. A homeowner who purchases a similar home will have a current appraised value and will have to pay substantially higher property taxes. Declining residential values may reverse this situation, with newcomers paying lower taxes than long-time homeowners. To reduce their property taxes, these long-time homeowners will have to prove that their home values have declined.

Property tax rates often differ within a locality. Some localities have special low tax rates for senior citizens or allow senior citizens to postpone payment until they sell their homes. This dispensation allows elderly homeowners to stay in their homes and not be forced to move just to pay the property taxes. When they—or their heirs—sell their homes, they will be able to pay the postponed taxes from the cash proceeds of the sale. Some areas have preferential property tax rates to encourage certain activities, like farming or keeping land in open space for esthetic reasons. A controversial measure is property tax incentives granted to encourage new industries to locate in a town or city. A city might waive all property taxes for five or more years to encourage a business to build a new facility that brings a number of jobs to an area. These incentives have been criticized on a number of fronts. Existing businesses feel that the government should not be subsidizing competitors. Others have noted that there are no hard data to show that these tax breaks really influence where businesses locate their facilities. They argue that factors like the price of land, transportation facilities, and the quality of the local workforce are the real deciding factors in plant location decisions. Despite these observations, governments continue to compete with one another in waiving property taxes for firms willing to relocate. Some governments, however, have pledged not to lure away businesses from their neighboring states.

School Funding Reform

Since the early 1800s the states have mandated public school for all children but have left localities to come up with their own funding. Local school districts either levied their own property taxes or received funds from the local government's property tax to operate the schools. Because local property taxes are based on value, wealthier areas raised more money and had better-funded schools. Schools in areas with a small tax base—poverty-stricken areas or areas with little industry—typically had poor school systems. Poor funding led to dilapidated facilities, low teachers' salaries and rapid staff turnover, poor performance, and high dropout rates. This situation contributed to an enduring cycle of poverty, with adults ill equipped to advance economically because of their limited education. Limited local wealth kept schools poor.

In the 1970s, reformers, alarmed at the wide disparity of quality in the public schools, brought lawsuits against state education departments. Many state constitutions and state laws require the states to provide a uniform system of education for all children. Until recently it was assumed that the uniformity requirement applied to the programs. For example, a state education department might require that every 10th grader take a course in U.S. history. The course requirements would be uniform in all the high schools throughout the state. However, the reformers urged the courts to interpret the word *uniform* as requiring a uniform—or nearly uniform—*quality* of education. Many courts, starting with the New Jersey Supreme Court, held that the state was required to ensure that every public school student receive an adequate education.

These court cases caused a major tax policy shift. For almost 200 years, localities had provided funding for local schools. Wealthy areas had strong schools while poorer areas generally had poorer schools. At the same time, wealthier areas normally not only had more property to tax but also higher property tax rates to support their schools. Wealthier people are better able to afford to pay higher property taxes to support the public schools and are normally willing to do so. Even property owners without children in the public schools are often willing to pay higher taxes to support the schools. Families are often willing to pay a premium for a home in an area with strong schools despite the high taxes. Childless property owners realize that the high taxes contribute to better schools, which translates into higher and more stable real estate values. Businesses, too, are not always averse to high school taxes. In today's competitive employment market, strong school systems are an important factor in attracting and retaining employees. Keeping school systems strong in cities where a business operates is simply good business. Responsible corporations are often at the forefront of efforts to improve local schools and local school funding.

When reformers brought lawsuits to require states to provide uniform education for all children attending public schools, the states normally responded by trying to equalize school funding. To equalize funding on a per student basis, states were required to make much larger payments to poorer districts to bring their per-student support up to state averages. In some states, state aid to wealthier suburban districts was cut. Some states have replaced their traditional local funding of education with a state-funded system aimed at achieving greater uniformity.

This state funding of education is a type of income redistribution, but it is hardly the only type. Whenever a government funds an activity or builds a facility, there is normally a tax subsidy and income redistribution. The redistribution is not always, or even normally, to the benefit of the less fortunate. When a local government subsidizes arts or culture by building a performing arts center or museum, the taxpayers are subsidizing the activity. Normally the wealthier citizens are the recipients of the benefits. At the state level, public colleges and universities are another example of income redistribution. Some think that public funding of higher education results in a redistribution of wealth to the needy. However, because low-income students are far less likely to attend college than their middle- and upper-middle-class counterparts, funding of public higher education provides no significant redistribution of wealth from the rich to the poor.

The reform of school funding and school property taxes has been criticized. Many individuals have bought homes in high tax areas only because of the quality of the schools. When funding for these schools is cut, these individuals feel betrayed. In fact, many public schools in wealthier areas have been able to make up for the shortfall in government funding through private fundraising. For example, some local PTAs have formed foundations to solicit voluntary contributions for computers and teachers' aides. These efforts have had mixed results and have also generated controversy. More than one district has banned the practice on the grounds that such fund-raising will perpetuate the disparity between schools in rich and poor neighborhoods. Controversy around school funding reform is expected to continue during the first decade of the 21st century.

Taxing Internet Sales

Current tax systems were designed before the invention of the Internet. Tax systems were generally devised when economic activity was more localized and transactions did not cross state or national boundaries. Internet transactions are much more likely to cross such boundaries. Internet sales have posed a number of challenges for taxing authorities. Both the U.S. federal government and state and local governments have cast an envious eye on taxing commercial activities on the Internet, but with little success.

At the outset one must keep in mind that general principles of taxation apply. If an individual or a business sells an item on the Internet and makes a profit, that profit is subject to federal and state income taxes. For example, if an individual buys an antique fishing reel at a garage sale for $10 and sells it on EBay for $100, the $90 profit is subject to income tax. The seller at the garage sale may have taxable income if he or she paid $5 for the fishing reel and sold it for $10. Most casual sales by individuals are not taxable because the items are typically sold for less than their original purchase price, so there is no profit involved.

Another basic principle to keep in mind is that a state does not have authority to impose a tax on a transactions that occurs outside the state. Accordingly, the state of New York can impose its sales tax on sales within the state but cannot impose its sales tax on a sale that occurs outside New York. Recall, however, that all states—including New York—have reciprocal "use taxes," which impose a tax on the buyer of an item who "uses" the purchased item within the state. For example, assume a resident of New York State buys a laptop computer in New Jersey then drive home and uses the laptop in his home in New York. New York State has no authority to impose its retail sales tax on either the buyer or the seller because the transaction took place in New Jersey, not in New York. However, New York could impose its use tax on the purchaser, who is using the laptop within the state of New York. State use taxes are invariably imposed at the same rate as the state sale's tax. Few individuals pay the use tax voluntarily.

One advantage of buying items on the Internet is the avoidance of local sales tax. If a buyer has the option of buying a $100 item in a local "brick and mortar" store in a state with a 7 percent sales tax or over the Internet, the buyer can avoid paying an extra $7 in tax ($100 × 7%) by buying online. Local stores believe that exempting Internet sellers from collecting use tax gives the Internet sellers an unfair advantage.

A 1992 U.S. Supreme Court case held that states could not force mail order businesses to collect use taxes from purchasers unless the seller had a physical presence in the purchaser's state. For example, if the seller had a retail store or warehouse in the purchaser's state, the purchaser's state could require the seller to collect use tax from the purchaser. If the seller had no physical presence in the state, then the state could not legally compel the mail order seller to collect a use tax from the purchaser. Although some states argued that economic nexus should be enough to allow a state to compel sellers to collect use tax from all purchasers, the Supreme Court has never extended state taxing power that far.

By analogy, Internet sellers are treated like mail order sellers. Thus, until recently, sellers like Amazon.com and Overstock. com have not had to collect a use tax from a retail purchaser unless they has a physical location in the state. State revenue departments, however, made novel arguments in support of requiring Internet sellers to collect use taxes. Until recently, Internet sellers could avoid nexus by operating within a state through a subsidiary corporation. State revenue departments again started to adopt the view that they could "look through" such legal formalities, claiming that doing business in a state through a subsidiary was no different than the parent corporation doing business in the state. Because Amazon.com and other seller use affiliates who send them business, state revenue departments have started to argue that these affiliates are sufficient to give them nexus over Amazon and other national retailers. During the severe recession that began in 2009, several states passed an "Amazon tax," requiring online sellers to collect their use tax if they utilized in-state affiliates. Significantly, Amazon mounted a $5 million public relations campaign to convince California voters to pass a law banning sales tax on the Internet. California and Amazon eventually compromised and Amazon agreed to collect a California use tax in exchange for a 1-year postponement.

Many have called for a federal solution to the state sales tax problem. The proposed Main Street Fairness Act would overrule the 1992 Supreme Court ruling and permit the 21 states that have voluntarily adopted the Streamlined Sales and Use Tax Agreement to tax Internet sales.

The Internet has created a number of potential sources of government tax revenue. The government could tax the physical connection to each computer or tax the amount of bandwidth a user uses. Federal legislation passed in 1998, the Internet Tax Freedom Act, prohibits federal, state, and local governments from imposing access taxes or other "Internet only" taxes on Internet connections. The law does not prohibit the imposition of normal sales and use taxes. In contrast, phone connections are subject to many taxes, and cell phones are subject to extremely high taxes in some areas. As more people access web sites using phones and other handheld devices rather than by personal computers, government stands to collect more in taxes. Several members of Congress have proposed bills to limit but not eliminate such access taxes.

Business Taxes and International Competitiveness

Although most political candidates tend to talk about individual tax reform, business tax reform is also an important topic. During the last few decades many businesses have worked hard to reduce their overhead expenses. This development has made tax expense relatively more important and businesses are increasingly concentrating their efforts on tax reduction. The U.S. tax system contains many tax breaks that allow businesses to legally reduce their taxes. For example, when a corporation pays for employee medical insurance or puts away money for employee pensions, the company gets a tax deduction. In effect, if a big company in the 35 percent tax bracket puts away $10 million for its employees' medical insurance and pension plans, the U.S. Treasury foregoes $3.5 million in corporate income taxes. Although the foregone tax revenue is costly, Congress wants to encourage companies to offer medical insurance to workers and their families and also to encourage private pension plans. Without private medical insurance and private pension plans, the government would evidently have to pick up much of the cost of caring for the sick and the elderly. Another way to view that example is that the government is providing a $3.5 million subsidy to the company to offer medical insurance and pensions to it workers. In the United States, tax breaks like this are more acceptable than writing checks to companies for their good deeds.

Other tax breaks are "targeted" to specific industries or even specific companies. For example, at the time of this writing, plug-in electric cars are quite rare. To encourage companies to develop and produce such cars and to encourage consumers to buy them, the federal government has employed a combination of tax breaks and subsidies. Taxpayers who buy plug-in electric cars reduce their federal taxes by $7,500, which makes such a vehicle far more affordable. Additionally, the federal government had loaned billions of dollars to three electric car producers and made grants of over $2 billion to help industry develop the cars, batteries, and charging stations. Without these direct and indirect subsidies, electric cars would be too expensive to compete with conventional cars.

Although such tax breaks are well intended, the result is a disparity in how much similar-sized businesses pay in tax. Most people agree that to be fair, taxpayers who earn the same amount of income should pay roughly the same amount of tax. For example, assume that two companies, Company A and Company B, each earned exactly $10 million in profits in a given year. Most people would conclude that it would be unfair if Company A paid $3 million in tax while Company B legally paid only $1 million. This is exactly what happens because of the tax code's numerous and uncoordinated tax breaks. In fact, each year several large, profitable corporations legally pay no income tax at all. This is nothing new. One of the major reforms of the 1986 Tax Reform Act was to try to equalize the tax load on businesses. Congressional hearings had revealed that businesses in certain industries were paying a 40 percent tax while others were paying next to nothing.

Tax breaks are generally deductions or tax credits that try to reward companies for making certain transactions, like contributing to pension plans or buying equipment. Senators and congressmen like to help companies that employ their constituents. Congress sometimes gives the tax breaks to help distressed industries or to encourage investments in new technologies like plug-in electric cars. Although such measures may be well-intentioned, the net result is to increase the disparity in tax.

The route to eliminating this disparity is to broaden the tax base, which would allow the stated tax rate to be dropped. Currently the tax rates are progressive—the more the business earns, the higher its tax rate. Corporations that can claim lots of deductions not only lower their amount of profits subject to tax but also the rate at which those profits will be taxed. Although the maximum stated corporate rate is 35 percent, many corporations pay far less.

International Business Operations

The U.S. tax system operates differently from the systems of most other countries. Most western countries other than the United States have adopted a value added tax (VAT), which imposes a tax that operate like a sale tax but at each level of production. Canada's Goods and Services Tax (GST) is an example. Manufacturers, wholesalers, and retailers all pay the tax as products move through the supply chain, but the consumers ultimately pay these taxes in the form of higher prices. VATs do not apply to exports. This gives foreign manufacturers an advantage over U.S. manufacturers because foreign firms can price their exports more cheaply. So far, proposals for a U.S. VAT have found little support.

The U.S. income tax system is increasingly unique because it taxes U.S. firms' profits earned in all countries. Under U.S. tax law, U.S. corporations pay U.S. taxes only if the profits are repatriated (brought back) to the United States. This rule has been roundly criticized by politicians from both major political parties. To avoid paying U.S. taxes on those foreign profits, U.S. corporations typically invest their foreign profits overseas, thus creating jobs overseas rather than in the United States. If the United States ever adopts a territorial tax regime, it would not even try to tax profits earned overseas.

The ability of businesses to shift income to lower-tax nations allows many companies to legally reduce their taxes. Over the past 3 years, General Electric, which has many operations overseas, reportedly paid an effective tax rate of 3.6 percent, while retailer Wal-Mart Stores, with primarily domestic operations, paid 33.6 percent.

Another tax reduction strategy that is currently legal is to transfer income overseas. Businesses with operations in low-tax countries can arrange to have income earned taxed in those countries rather than in the United States. A common technique is to transfer "intangible assets" like franchise rights or patents to subsidiaries in low-tax countries. Newspapers have reported that Google legally reduced its tax bill by about $1 billion a year by moving profits through subsidiaries in Ireland, the Netherlands, and Bermuda. Google reported an effective tax rate of 18.8 percent (which also included state taxes) in the second quarter of 2011, far lower than the stated 35 percent top corporate rate.

Carbon Taxes and Cap-and-Trade Programs

The content of this section of the chapter is broader than the heading "Carbon Taxes" suggests. In the 21st century, tax reform efforts will undoubtedly include efforts to adopt taxes that promote environmental sustainability. These efforts have been dubbed "environmental taxes," "ecotaxes," or "green taxes." To date, the most important of these taxes in the carbon tax.

For the last 2,000 years, taxation has been imposed on wealth and income. Governments seeking wealth and income from citizens focused on collections that directly transferred either wealth or income from the private sector to the government. Real estate and other properties were taxed because they were difficult to hide and governments correctly reasoned that by targeting property owners they would be more likely collect the taxes. Although "head taxes" were also employed—with each person paying the same tax—they were difficult to enforce because of the vast number of taxpayers involved. Initially the levies were devised to produce the largest transfers while causing the least problems, without any thought to social engineering.

During the 20th century, governments realized that taxes could be used to achieve economic and social goals, such as the elimination of poverty, the discouragement of vices, and the provision of incentives to engage in activities the government thought worthwhile, such as encouraging homeownership. Even in the 19th century, economists and governments realized that taxes could be used not only to fund expenses like those associated with fighting wars but also to tamper down inflation by preventing money from chasing scarce goods. Economists and governments soon learned that taxes could achieve other ends in addition to raising revenue.

Progressive income tax rates—systems with higher tax rates imposed on the rich—are a form of income redistribution. "Sin taxes" on cigarettes and alcoholic beverages are designed to discourage smoking and drinking as well as to raise revenue. Income tax breaks for homeowners make owning a home more financially attractive. Tax breaks for businesses that invest in new business assets are a government tool to stimulate the economy. The experience of using conventional taxes for social and economic engineering led thinkers to suggest that taxes might be used to tackle perhaps the major challenge of the 21st century—human destruction of the natural environment.

Although not everyone will agree on a list, there are several human-made problems that have contributed to the degradation of the natural environment. These include the burning of fossil fuels, like oil and coal, which produce air pollution as well as carbon dioxide, which, when retained by the atmosphere, contribute to global warming. Other problems include improper disposal of chemicals and other toxic materials into the air, land, and water. Many view overpopulation as a root cause of many of these problems.

Even conventional property and income tax systems can be used to promote environmentally friendly activities. For example, for a number of years the U.S. income tax code has included measures to support clean air and water. Similarly, the income tax code has given tax breaks to taxpayers who insulate their homes or buy energy-saving windows. Similarly, the tax code has provided subsidies for buyers of fuel-efficient and low-pollution hybrid and electric cars. Although these kinds of measures help encourage environmentally sensitive activities and discourage wasteful actions, many believe that the tax system can go much further to change citizens' behaviors.

The basic idea behind an environmental tax is to provide tax breaks for those who engage in environmentally sensitive activities and to impose taxes on polluters. Although there are a variety of taxes to achieve these ends, the carbon tax has gained the most traction in industrialized countries. Although the United States has not enacted such a tax, proponents of the tax come from across the political spectrum, from Al Gore on the liberal side to the conservative probusiness American Enterprise Institute. Carbon taxes have been used internationally, and this experience is detailed below.

How Carbon Taxes Work

A carbon tax is a tax on the carbon content of fossil fuels like coal, oil, and natural gas. A tax on carbon content would make fossil fuels more expensive compared with other fuels or energy-saving measures. The logic is fairly simple. When electricity is cheap, people turn up the heat or air-conditioning using more electricity and causing more air pollution. If the cost of staying warm or cool is greater, demand and emissions will fall. Without other reforms, carbon taxes can be regressive, because they would simply make basic needs like heating and transportation more expensive for the poor. The better off and those who could charge more for their service would not feel the same impact. Accordingly, in enacting a carbon tax, there must be some way to refund tax money to the needy. Another criticism is that in the short term, a carbon tax may cost domestic jobs, as businesses accelerate the trend to produce manufactured goods overseas, where costs are lower and environmental regulations lax. Critics of carbon taxes argue that cap-and-trade programs relying on individual market-based decisions will be more effective in reducing emissions than a centralized tax system run by the government.

Cap and Trade

A cap-and-trade system is an alternative to a stand-alone carbon tax. A cap-and-trade program attempts to minimize pollution by monetizing emissions. Because industry will have to buy the right to pollute, they will try to modify their operations or install cleaner equipment to avoid the costs. In a cap-and-trade system, government sets an upper limit to carbon emissions and then allocates shares of the total to manufacturers and other producers, thus distributing emission allowances. The allowances—or permits—can be transferred or sold if a producer emits less pollution than expected. Environmental organizations could buy and "retire" allowances, which would increase the cost of the remaining allowances. Critics of cap-and-trade systems argue that they will not be able to reduce emissions as effectively as a carbon tax.

At the time of this writing, there is no federal cap-and-trade program, although a bill is making its way through Congress. However, California has adopted a statewide program for utilities, and 10 northern states have signed onto the Regional Greenhouse Initiative and the Western Climate Initiative, joined by 7 other states and 4 Canadian provinces.

4

Chronology

1607	Jamestown, Virginia, is founded as the first permanent British settlement in North America.
1620	Pilgrims arrive at Plymouth, establishing a permanent settlement.
1630	Puritans found the Massachusetts Bay Colony.
1643	Pilgrims enact a modest income tax on a person's "faculties."
1646	Massachusetts Bay Colony copies the Pilgrims' lead, enacting a tax on returns and gains of tradesmen.
1760	George III is crowned King of England. George is king during the American Revolution and the tax revolt preceding it.
1763	The Treaty of Paris ends the French and Indian War (also known as the Seven Years' War) between France and England. France cedes all North American territory east of the Mississippi River, including Canada, to England. France retains vast stretches of land west of the Mississippi. The English government had borrowed heavily to pay for the war and started a program of increasing taxes in both England and the American colonies to pay down the government's debt.
1764	The English Parliament passes the Sugar Act, which actually decreases import duties on sugar. The act also

95

cracks down on smuggled and untaxed French molasses used by American distillers. The act harms John Hancock and others who profited from smuggling. To enforce the act in the colonies, the British set up several vice admiralty courts, which hear smuggling cases in place of the local courts. In a break with established practice, the courts have no juries. Violators are tried by judges sent over from England.

1765   English Parliament passes the Stamp Act. To raise revenue for the government, this act requires colonists to purchase stamps to affix to many legal documents, and also to newspapers and playing cards. American colonists feel that this taxation is unconstitutional. Although the British have no written constitution, their unwritten constitution is based on custom and the decisions of previous court cases. The colonists argue that the Stamp Act and similar revenue-raising "direct taxes" are unconstitutional under the unwritten British constitution. The colonists also argue that imposition of the Stamp Act is taxation without representation because the American colonists have no representatives in the British Parliament. The British answer this objection by arguing that the colonists enjoy "virtual representation." They reason that every member of parliament represents British citizens whether they live in England or the colonies. In that view, the colonists are in fact represented. The colonists reject this argument and demand their own representatives— but to no avail.

There is widespread nonpayment of the tax. Organized groups like the Sons of Liberty harass British officials and interfere with the distribution of the stamps. In December, representatives from the various colonies meet at the Stamp Act Congress, denounce the tax, and plan additional resistance to the tax. The Congress passes the Stamp Act Resolves, which declare the imposition of the tax illegal and the use of courts without juries to be contrary to the people's rights and liberties. The congress concludes by petitioning Parliament for the repeal of the Stamp Act and its stamp tax.

1766   American colonists join in a boycott of British manu-
          factured goods to pressure Parliament to repeal the
          Stamp Act. English merchants who rely on sales to the
          American colonies and who are hurt by the boycott
          lobby Parliament to repeal the law. A new prime min-
          ister in England who is less concerned with taxing the
          colonies pushes for repeal. To placate those in Parlia-
          ment who want to punish the colonies, Lord Rocking-
          ham, the prime minister, devises a compromise: the
          Declaratory Act.

          The British Parliament passes the Declaratory Act.
          This act repeals the hated Stamp Act but also declares
          that Parliament has full power and authority to makes
          laws for the colonies in all cases. Although the act is a
          small victory for the colonists because the Stamp Act is
          repealed, the Declaratory Act also rejects the colonists'
          arguments about representation by establishing that
          Parliament has the right to impose further taxes on the
          colonists as it sees fit.

1767   When Charles Townshend becomes prime minister,
          he reverses course and increases taxes in the colo-
          nies. The Townshend Act imposes a duty on many
          items used by colonists, including tea, paper, paint,
          and lead. Although the taxes are low, they are a
          source of irritation. Many political tracts protest this
          new round of taxation, including John Dickerson's
          "Letters from a Farmer in Pennsylvania." The Sons
          of Liberty and other groups continue to agitate for
          noncompliance and resistance to the taxes. A second
          boycott of British manufactured goods is begun and
          proves effective during the next 2 years. In a serious
          escalation of the dispute, England stations several
          thousand troops in Boston to back up its tax adminis-
          trators.

1770   Lord North becomes prime minister, bringing another
          change in direction for the British government. He
          engineers the repeal of the Townshend Acts, primar-
          ily to help British merchants. The tea duty remains as
          an irritant to the colonists. Lord North remains prime
          minister through the American Revolution.

1773 Parliament passes the Tea Act. Ironically, the act does not raise taxes but lowers them. The British East India Company imports tea from Asia to England and the American colonies. During the boycott on British goods, American colonists had deserted British tea in favor of untaxed Dutch tea. In an attempt to help the ailing East India Company, Parliament grants the company a near monopoly over tea. Although the tea is subject to a 3 percent duty, the company's tea is actually the least expensive available. Despite this, the American colonists view the scheme as a duplicitous way of collecting the unconstitutional tea tax.

    On December 16, colonists dress as Indians to carry out the protest now known as the Boston Tea Party. They storm aboard a ship called the *Dartmouth* tied to a pier and throw the entire cargo of tea overboard into Boston Harbor. The reaction by Parliament is both swift and harsh.

1774 Parliament passes the Coercive Acts (also called the Intolerable Acts), which repeal the Massachusetts colonial charter. The acts limit the power of the colony's House of Representatives and ban most town meetings. Boston Harbor is closed to shipping until the colonists pay for the jettisoned tea. The Boston Tea Party and the resulting Intolerable Acts galvanize colonial opposition to the tax in particular and to British administration in general.

    Representatives from all the colonies meet in Philadelphia at the first Continental Congress to air grievances against the British government. The Congress passes the Declaration of Rights and Grievances. The declaration objects to the Intolerable Acts as well as the Declaratory Act of 1766.

1775 First shots of the Revolution fired at Lexington and Concord, Massachusetts.

1776 The second Continental Congress encourages all the colonists to break their ties with the English Parliament. At the time, most colonists still have an allegiance to the crown. What started as a movement for modest tax reform quickly escalates into an armed conflict.

On July 4, the Declaration of Independence, penned by Thomas Jefferson with the concurrence of the Continental Congress, proclaims that the colonies are independent of England.

1777   The Continental Congress passes the Articles of Confederation, the first written constitution of the United States. It does not give the central government the right to tax. The power to tax is reserved to the states.

1781   Calls for a national tariff are rejected by the Continental Congress.

With the assistance of French reinforcements and the French fleet, General George Washington forces General Cornwallis to surrender his entire army at Yorktown, Virginia. The British lose interest in continuing the war against the colonists.

1783   England signs the Treaty of Paris, recognizing the American colonies' independence.

1785   Although the fledgling U.S. government has an enormous war debt, it refuses to levy taxes or adopt a national tariff. Manufacturing states like New York are opposed to any tariff and, under the Articles of Confederation, each state has veto power over pending legislation.

1786   When the Confederation government repudiates millions of dollars in Continental currency (the currency used during the Revolution), there is a shortage of cash in many colonies. Mobs of distressed farmers call for debt relief, lower land taxes, and paper money. In Massachusetts, Daniel Shays leads a brief armed rebellion. Although Shays and his followers are sentenced to death, they are later released and some of the requested debt and tax relief are granted.

1788   The U.S. Constitution is ratified. The new Constitution gives power to the national (federal) government to tax citizens directly as well as to collect tariffs. The

Framers adopt the taxation of imports but reject the taxation of exports.

The Constitution establishes a legislature called the Congress, with two bodies: the House of Representatives, whose members are to serve two-year terms and be directly elected by the people, and the Senate, whose members are to serve six-year terms and be chosen by the state legislatures.

The Constitution gives the House of Representatives power over money and tax bills. However, the Senate has to approve any tax measures. To prevent Congress from oppressing a particular state through taxation, the Constitution requires that any "direct tax" be apportioned among the states on the basis of population. If a state's population is 10 percent of the nation's total, the tax levied in that state must also be 10 percent of the total tax levied in all states. The constitution limits the states' taxing power by vesting in the national government the sole authority to coin money, issue bills of credit, and impose import duties.

1789   The Tariff of 1789 is the first tax levied by the new national government, a modest 5 percent duty on all imports. Prior to 1789 the national government had no taxing authority of its own and had to rely on contributions from the states. This marks the beginning of a 100-year period in which the tariffs provide the major revenue needs of the national government.

1790   The federal government—at the behest of Secretary of the Treasury Alexander Hamilton—assumes the unpaid revolutionary war debts of the states. The measure is controversial because some states, like Virginia, have already paid their debts in full. Accordingly, citizens of Virginia think they are unfairly being asked to help pay the debts owed by citizens of other states. The measure is also controversial because much of the debt has been bought up by northern speculators, who are to receive a windfall under the plan. Rural farmers and veterans who sold their debt to the speculators are outraged. When southern states, including Virginia, object to payment of the war debt, Congress agrees to locate the national capital on the Potomac River at what is to become Washington, D.C.

1791   Congress rejects Alexander Hamilton's proposed protective tariff designed to encourage domestic industry.

1792   In place of the tariff, Congress enacts a whiskey excise tax to be paid by distillers. The tax is immediately unpopular, especially at the western edges of the colonies, where whiskey has become a staple of barter trade. Westerners protest and refuse to pay the tax.

1793   Bowing to pressure, Congress cuts the whiskey excise tax rates in half. Despite the cuts, westerners still refuse to pay the tax.

1794   President George Washington orders the governors of four states—Pennsylvania, New Jersey, Maryland, and Virginia—to call out their militias to put down rioting over the whiskey tax. Leaders of the rebellion are promptly arrested and the unrest subsides. Ultimately no one serves jail time, but the government's authority to collect the tax is established.

The court case of *Hylton v. United States* upholds the federal government's right to impose a tax on luxury carriages and generally upholds the federal government's right to tax its citizens.

The Jay Treaty with England, negotiated by statesman John Jay who later served as the first Chief Justice of the Supreme Court, prohibits an anti-British tariff for 10 years in exchange for a promise that Britain will remove troops from land claimed by the fledgling United States.

1798   To pay for the expenses of the undeclared naval war with France, Congress enacts a number of taxes on land, slaves, and homes.

1800   Thomas Jefferson becomes president, pledging to reduce costs and taxes. He immediately removes the taxes imposed in 1798 as well as the unpopular whiskey excise tax. With increased trade, the federal government is able to reduce its war debt while still relying solely on revenue from the tariff.

1808   England fights Napoleonic France. Although the United States attempts to be neutral, the British harass U.S. ships. In response, Jefferson declares an embargo on the export of raw materials or finished goods to Europe. Although some shippers ignore the embargo, tonnage slips and government collections from the tariff plummet.

1812   The War of 1812 with England requires new revenue. Congress opts for doubling the tariff on imports rather than imposing "internal" taxes.

1813   The war interrupts trade across the Atlantic, and collections from the tariff continue to drop. Faced with deficits, Congress imposes taxes on whiskey, carriages, and sugar refining to help fund the war effort.

1815   Congress considers but fails to enact an income tax to help pay for the war. Secretary of the Treasury Alexander Dallas argues that the tax would be an "indirect tax" not required to be "apportioned" under the Constitution.

1816   Wartime taxes expire and are replaced by a protective tariff with rates of up to 25 percent. Although the high tariff rates are designed to raise revenue, they are also intended to encourage development of indigenous industry.

1819   In the landmark constitutional case of *McCulloch v. Maryland*, Justice John Marshall, writing the opinion for the U.S. Supreme Court, holds that a Maryland tax on state bank notes issued by the Second National Bank of the United States is illegal. Maryland enacted the tax to help its own state-chartered banks. Marshall writes the famous phrase, "The power to tax is the power to destroy." The case stands for the proposition that the states are not allowed to tax federal instrumentalities and also establishes the supremacy of federal power over state governments.

1828   Population growth in the Northeast and the West gives those regions more power when Congress is reapportioned. These areas, which favor protectionist tariffs, gain power at the expense of the South, which is generally in favor of a low tariff. Congress passes the Tariff of 1828, with high protective rates.

Tariffs help New England textile makers and manufacturers by pricing cheap imports out of the market. Some tariff rates range as high as 50 percent of the value of the imported products. Although the tariff benefits American native industry, it also means higher prices for consumers who have no access to the cheaper imports.

The Tariff of 1828 is especially unpopular in the South and leads to a political crisis that presages the Civil War. In reaction to the tariff, John C. Calhoun of South Carolina pens his famous "South Carolina Exposition and Protest," in which he argues that states have the power and right to nullify federal laws that are unconstitutional. Calhoun reasons that if three-quarters of the other states ratify the federal law, the protesting state should have the option of seceding from the union.

1832   Congress lowers a few tariff rates below their 1828 levels. South Carolina calls a Nullification Convention, which votes to declare the Tariffs of 1828 and 1832 unconstitutional.

The South Carolina legislature orders that customs duties not be collected within the state. President Andrew Jackson responds by issuing his Nullification Proclamation, repudiating Calhoun's nullification arguments and rejecting the idea that states have the right to secede if they object to specific federal laws passed by Congress.

1833   The Compromise Tariff of 1833 defuses the crisis over the Tariff of 1828. Negotiated by Senator Henry Clay of Kentucky, usually a strong supporter of high tariffs, the Compromise Tariff includes automatic reductions in tariff levels over a 10-year period. However, Congress also passes a law called the Force Bill, authorizing the president to use state militias to enforce customs duties. Clay works with Calhoun to forge the compromise.

1840   President William Henry Harrison, a Whig, wins election with a promise to raise tariffs. High tariffs are part of the "American System" championed by Henry Clay, which favors high tariffs to keep out foreign goods to protect fledgling American manufacturers. The revenue from the tariffs would be used to improve infrastructure, like roads and canals.

1842   John Tyler, the vice-president, becomes president after President Harrison dies in office. Tyler is less enthusiastic about the American System. Although some members of his party—the Whigs—urge him to cancel the tariff reductions scheduled to take place under the Compromise Tariff of 1833, Tyler generally lets the reductions take place on schedule. Tyler does abandon sharing tariff revenues with the states for local improvements.

1846   Democrat James Polk is elected president. Although his party is split between protariff and antitariff factions, Polk cuts tariff rates. The Walker Tariff (named after Secretary of the Treasury Robert Walker, a southerner from Mississippi) makes deep cuts in tariff duties, putting an end to the American System initiated by the Whigs. Because England also reduces trade restrictions, foreign trade booms and tariff revenues increase despite lower tariff rates on imported goods.

1848   Zachary Taylor, a war hero from the Mexican War and a Whig, becomes president. Taylor, who has strong political support in the South, abandons the Whigs' traditional support for high tariffs and continues the low-tariff policy started by the Democrats.

1857   Democrats regain power and again lower tariffs. Shortly thereafter, a business depression causes trade to plummet and tariff revenues also plunge. The debate over slavery takes the political center stage.

1861   President Abraham Lincoln, a member of the then-new Republican Party, serves as president throughout the Civil War. The war requires the government to find vast sums of money to finance the military effort. Ultimately, the "Union" side uses a combination of borrowing, higher tariffs, and a new income tax. The southern states are less equipped to raise revenue from taxes; they rely primarily on loans and issue Confederate paper money that the rebel government promises to repay after the war.

Because shipping is disrupted by the war, revenues from tariffs prove unreliable and the North needs additional funds. The North is able to finance much of the war effort through the sale of war bonds purchased by individuals. The North's Morrill Tariff of 1862 raises rates, as does a subsequent tariff in 1866. Although the North also resorts to printing more paper currency, issuing the legal tender called greenbacks, inflation in the North is not excessive.

Congress enacts the first American income tax. The British experimented with an income tax to finance the Napoleonic Wars earlier in the century and used it again to finance their Crimean War with Russia. The Constitution requires all "direct taxes" to be apportioned so that the tax revenues would be exactly proportional to each state's population. In 1861, Congress assumes that an income tax is not a direct tax because it does not tax property, so apportionment is not required. The original income tax, a flat tax, is replaced the following year and is never actually put into effect.

1862   In 1862, Congress passes the Internal Revenue Act, placing excise taxes on a number of items, including whiskey and tobacco products, as well as placing a number of taxes on business. The act also creates a new agency, the Bureau of Internal Revenue, to collect the taxes.

Congress enacts the first inheritance tax, replacing the older federal tax on land. The original 1861 income tax is replaced by a revised version with progressive tax rates. The tax rates are modest: they are graduated from 3 to 5 percent, and the tax falls most heavily on the wealthy. Only about 10 percent of households are required to pay the tax. Patriotic Americans pay the tax willingly.

1864   Congress increases both the excise tax and income tax rates. The top income tax rate is doubled to 10 percent, and an "emergency supplement" increases the maximum effective rate to 15 percent.

1867   Congress reduces income tax rates, instituting a tax rate of 5 percent on incomes above $1,000 and 2.5 percent on income above $2,000. It maintains the tax to help pay for Reconstruction of the South and expansion into former Native American territory in the West. Despite the name, Reconstruction is really a military occupation of the former Confederacy. With the return of peace, trade increases, as do tariff revenues. Congress is able to use these funds to run its operations and also to pay off war bonds. Confederate bonds and currency are not redeemed by the Union and become worthless. Republicans, safely in power for the decade, continue their enthusiasm for high protective tariffs.

1872   The Civil War Income Tax expires and is not renewed. Congress also makes a small reduction in tariff rates.

1873   The Panic of 1873 signals the start of the worst business depression in U.S. history up to that time. Collections from tariffs decline with the reduced foreign trade.

1875   1872 reductions in tariff rates are repealed to help make up revenue shortfalls from decreased business activity.

1883   The Tariff Act of 1883 makes few changes in tariff rates, retaining the protectionist theme initiated during the Civil War.

1884   Democrat Grover Cleveland wins the presidency. A supporter of lower tariffs, Cleveland is supported by the "Mugwumps," a faction of the Republican Party that advocates lower tariffs and government reform. Tariffs became a major campaign issue in the 1888 presidential election, with Cleveland advocating low tariffs and his Republican opponent Benjamin Harrison advocating high tariffs and protectionism. Cleveland runs poorly in the industrialized North, and

Harrison recaptures the presidency for the Republicans.

1888   The popular Joe Forcker ("Fire Engine Joe") loses his bid for a third term as senator from Ohio, after proposing a tax on saloon keepers.

1890   Republicans in Congress pass the McKinley Tariff, which raises tariffs but allows the president to negotiate lower rates with other nations. This tariff act is the first to contain such "reciprocity" provisions.

1891   Ohio Democrats call for the passage of a state income tax, several years before the passage of the federal income tax.

1892   Democrat Grover Cleveland wins the presidential election, besting the incumbent Republican Benjamin Harrison by a wide margin. Perhaps stung by the electorate's rejection of his low-tariff stance in 1888 and influenced by protectionists in his own party, Cleveland abstains from lobbying for major rate reductions. He does not veto Congress's Wilson-Gorman Tariff, which lowers rates only slightly.

1894   Cleveland's supporters in the South and West are generally also proponents of a federal income tax. Republicans and Democrats from the wealthier and more industrialized East oppose the income tax, which they were more likely to be paying. Scores of income tax bills are proposed in Congress between the Civil War and 1894.

Congress enacts the first income tax since the Civil War. The tax is in an amendment to the Wilson Tariff Bill of 1894 and provides for an income tax for 5 years. During the Civil War the income tax had provided about one fifth of the nation's tax revenues. After its expiration in 1872, the federal government relied almost solely on customs duties imposed by the tariff and excise taxes on whiskey and tobacco. The excise taxes represented about 90 percent of all taxes on domestic economic activity. Supported mainly by southern Democrats and reformers known as the Populists, the income tax is attacked as socialistic by its opponents, who argued that the tax is a "soak-the-rich" provision.

1895 The U.S. Supreme Court rules in the case *Pollock v. Farm Loan and Trust Company* that the 1894 income tax is unconstitutional. Although legal precedents favor the tax—the Supreme Court itself had upheld the constitutionality of the civil war income tax measure just 20 years before—the Court finds the income tax legally suspect. The Court reasons that the tax is a "direct tax" and under the Constitution has to be apportioned: the amount of tax collected in each state has to precisely correspond to the number of citizens in that state. In earlier court cases, judges had routinely decided that an income tax was an indirect tax rather than a direct tax on property. Accordingly, those courts had concluded that, like a tariff, an income tax would not have to be apportioned. The Supreme Court in the Pollock case, however, reasons that because taxes on real estate are direct taxes, a tax on income from real estate must also be a direct tax. Interestingly, the court holds that income from real estate or state and local municipal bonds is direct but income from wages might not be. Because that issue is not before the Supreme Court, that issue is not decided.

Tax revolt in Spanish Cuba—the Marti revolt—leads to a Spanish crackdown, precipitating the Spanish-American War.

1896 William McKinley, a Republican, wins the presidential election over William Jennings Bryan, a Democrat and a supporter of an income tax. McKinley favors protectionist tariffs.

1897 Congress passes the Dingley Tariff, bringing U.S. tariff rates to an all-time high. Congress also enacts an inheritance tax, in part to pay for the costs of the Spanish-American War. The maximum rate of the tax is 5 percent.

1902 Congress repeals the inheritance tax passed in 1897.

1908 President Theodore ("Teddy") Roosevelt, a Republican from New York, endorses an income tax. Although

Roosevelt is a wealthy New Yorker, much of his political support is drawn from the West, which is strongly in favor of an income tax.

1909   Republican senators from western states join with Democrats in calling for an income tax. A compromise is achieved and is supported by President Taft: Congress enacts a corporate income tax, the Corporation Excise Tax and proposes the ratification of the 16th Amendment to the Constitution, which would lift the Pollock case's ban on the individual income tax.

1911   The U.S. Supreme Court holds the Corporation Excise Tax of 1909 constitutional. The tax is actually an excise tax on the "privilege of doing business" but is measured by net income. The court distinguishes this tax from the 1895 version, which it had declared unconstitutional.

1913   The 16th Amendment, authorizing an individual income tax, is formally certified. It nullifies the Supreme Court's Pollock decision of 18 years earlier that an individual income tax is unconstitutional.

The 1913 Income Tax Act is passed by Congress with President Woodrow Wilson's support. The tax applies to both individuals and corporations. The act imposes a "normal tax" of 1 percent on income above $3,000. Married individuals can exempt an additional $1,000 of income. An additional graduated rate schedule imposes additional tax from 1 to 6 percent on income above $20,000. The 6 percent rate is imposed on income above $500,000—a vast amount in 1913. Although the tax is attacked in the courts on a variety of legal grounds, it is routinely upheld.

1917   The income tax deduction for federal income tax itself is eliminated. A deduction for children is introduced and expanded the following year. Charitable contributions become deductible to encourage private charity.

1918   A number of business tax innovations are introduced that will become extremely important later in the century. Corporations are allowed to merge tax-free and to carry forward net operating losses. Taxpayers are allowed a credit against their U.S. income tax for foreign income taxes paid. Oil and gas depletion are put into the law, allowing tax-free cost recovery for oil and gas producers.

1919   Congress relies on the newly enacted income tax to help pay for World War I. The exemption (amount of income not subject to tax) is lowered from $3,000 to $1,000, and tax rates are raised. The normal tax is raised to 6 percent and the graduated surtax is applied at rates ranging from 1 to 65 percent on income above $1 million. A 12 percent corporate tax rate is also enacted, along with an "extra profits" tax. Although the income tax exemption is lowered, thereby exposing more individuals to the tax, only about 5 percent of Americans must pay the tax. The income tax is still a tax on the wealthy. However, the volume of tax collected increases geometrically. In the year 1913 the federal government collected just $350 million from the income tax. The amount increases to $5.5 billion by 1920 under the lowered exemptions and increased rate structure.

1921   Congress repeals the excess profits tax on corporations that was imposed during World War I.

The capital gains concept is added to the tax code. A capital gain is a profit from the sale of an investment. The income tax rules now divide income into "ordinary income" and "capital gains." Capital gains are afforded preferential treatment—in the form of a lower effective tax rate to encourage and reward those who have invested in the economy.

As a reform measure, the law is changed so that the "basis" of property acquired by gift is no longer fair market value. *Basis* is the amount that can be recovered tax-free when property is sold. After 1921, a donee generally takes the donor's original basis but uses the lower of the donor's basis or the fair market value at the date of the gift if the property has decreased in value. When the wealthy give their relatives "appreciated" stock or real estate, the relatives will now have to pay income tax if the property is sold at a profit. Prior to 1921, no tax would have been paid.

The tax law is changed to allow taxpayers to form corporations tax-free.

1924   A federal gift tax is enacted. Taxpayers had been able to avoid paying the federal estate tax merely by making gifts of property to family members. The gift tax is enacted to allow the Treasury to tax any transfers of wealth, whether made during life or after death. The estate and gift taxes are in addition to any income tax imposed.

President Harding proposes a national sales tax but support proves slim.

1926   The federal gift tax is repealed.

1928   Congress continues its trend of increasing the exemptions started after the end of World War I. In 1928 the exemption is increased to $1,500 for an unmarried individual, $3,500 for a married individual, and $400 for each dependent. The normal tax and surtax rates are also reduced.

1929   California becomes the second U.S. state to enact a new type of tax—the retail sales tax. Many states follow the Golden State's lead and enact retail sales taxes of their own.

1932   The Great Depression, the most severe business depression since the Panic of 1873, causes tax collections to plummet. Congress lowers exemption amounts and increases tax rates to bolster revenues.

Proposals for a federal sales tax are considered but rejected. Instead, Congress enacts a comprehensive system of excise taxes on consumer goods. Excise taxes will bring in roughly the same amount of income as income taxes for the federal government until the start of World War II. Congress also reestablishes the gift tax.

1933   To enhance revenue, the federal government reduces corporate depreciation deductions (cost recovery deductions). The "temporary measure" persists until 1953.

1935   The Social Security Act is passed and signed into law by President Franklin D. Roosevelt. This is a radical and highly controversial provision that requires both employees and employers to pay a tax to fund workers' retirement pensions. The measure is intended to reduce poverty among the elderly—a serious social problem. Later in the century the basic program would be augmented by Medicare—a joint federal-state system to provide basic medical care and hospitalization insurance for retired workers. Although employee and employer payments to Social Security are labeled "contributions," they are really payroll taxes because they are mandatory. Overall, workers are anticipated to receive more than they pay into the system. The system is expected to remain sound because of the increasing population of workers whose contributions will support the retirees. The system is also designed to produce a modest income redistribution. Benefits received by lower-income workers will represent a higher percentage of their actual wages than benefits paid to higher-paid workers.

1936   The corporate tax rate becomes graduated.

1937   The Revenue Act of 1937 contains a number of rules to close loopholes. Previously, the wealthy were able to use foreign personal holding companies and incorporated yachts and other devices to reduce their tax. These loopholes are eliminated.

1938   The Revenue Act of 1938 continues a pattern of reducing the exemption amount and increasing tax rates. Payroll taxes are adopted to pay for the newly introduced federal Social Security system designed to pay retirement benefits to retired workers.

1939   The first Internal Revenue "code" continues a process begun in 1928. All federal tax laws are organized in one section of the U.S. Code, to be known as the Internal Revenue Code. The 1939 tax code will remain in force until it is replaced in 1954 by the 1954 code.

Congress passes the Public Salary Tax, which specifically requires state employees to pay federal income tax. Before passage of the act, it was argued that under the legal doctrine of Intergovernmental Tax Immunity, employees of state governments were immune from federal taxation and federal employees were immune from state taxation. Federal judges are also required to pay tax under the new law. States are still allowed to keep their own employees out of the Social Security program.

1941   Congress reenacts the Excess Profits Tax on corporations used in World War I. Small tax increases are also enacted for both individuals and corporations.

The U.S. Supreme Court in *Higgins v. Commissioner* rules that taxpayers may not deduct the expenses of a home office used to manage investments. Congress responds by adding the home office deduction to the tax code, opening the door to 60 years of enforcement problems.

1942   After the United States joins the Allies in World War II, the government requires massive new revenues to fund the war effort. Congress makes major changes in the tax code. The Revenue Act of 1942 radically changes the scope of the income tax. Prior to 1942, fewer than 4 million Americans, less than 4 percent of the U.S. population, were subject to income tax. After passage of the act, 50 million individuals, about half the population, are required to pay tax and file annual tax returns. This act is arguably the greatest change made to the U.S. tax system since the inception of the income tax in 1913.

The act lowers the exemption amount to $500, exposing most working people to the tax. The initial tax rate is 23 percent, and those earning over $14,000 face a tax rate of 50 percent. Corporate rates are 40 percent, and an excess-profits tax is imposed at an 89.5 percent rate. The high rates are enacted partly to raise revenue for the war effort but also partly to control inflation. The huge government expenditures for the war effort give people a lot of purchasing power. However, consumer goods are scarce because factories have converted to build military supplies and armaments. Without the high tax rates, the excess money in the economy would result in runaway inflation.

As a reform measure, efforts are made to simplify the filing of tax returns. A standard deduction is introduced so that millions of new taxpayers can avoid itemizing deductions. Medical expense deductions are allowed for those who do not use the standard deduction.

1943   Congress passes the Current Tax Payment Act of 1943. This law established the pay-as-you-go tax system in which employers withhold income tax from employee's wages and submit it to the government. Self-employed individuals are required to pay their tax on a quarterly basis, making estimated tax payments. This wartime measure will remain an important feature of the U.S. income tax system after the war's end in 1945. Prior to withholding, individuals were required to make the four quarterly tax payments. The income tax deduction for federal excise taxes is repealed.

Although bills for a federal sales tax are proposed, revenue from the income tax and the sale of war bonds proves sufficient.

1945   With World War II over, Congress repeals the Excess Profits Tax on corporations. Individual income tax and corporate income tax rates are slightly reduced.

1947   President Truman vetoes an income tax reduction passed by Congress.

1948   Congress overrides Truman's veto and reduces income taxes.

Congress passes the Revenue Act of 1948, which introduces the "joint return," allowing married couples to report their combined income on one tax form. The combined tax is low because the rates allow the couple to pay twice the tax on half their combined income. The averaging effect is beneficial because in 1948 few wives had incomes as high as those of their husbands. Because of the progressive tax rates, the averaging provides a major tax break to married couples. Later in the century, when spouses' incomes become more similar, the joint return often works in reverse and creates a "marriage penalty": some married spouses will have to pay higher taxes merely because they are married.

1950   Although Congress intended to cut excise taxes, entry into the Korean conflict requires new revenues. The Revenue Act of 1950 increases income tax rates for both individuals and corporations. The excess profits tax on corporations is also reenacted.

Congress enacts a "marital deduction" for estate tax purposes, which reduces the impact of the estate tax when the first spouse dies.

1951   The Revenue Act of 1951 again raises income tax rates; individual income tax rates now range up to 88 percent.

Congress considers extending the benefits of the low joint-return rates (available only for married couples) to all family units. Congress compromises and enacts head-of-household rates. To be eligible, an individual generally must provide more than half the financial support for themselves and a dependent living in the household. The new Schedule Z gives these taxpayers 50 percent of the tax reduction available to married couples from income splitting.

Life insurance proceeds are made nontaxable. Despite repeated attempts to repeal this provision, it will be successfully defended by the insurance industry and will remain a part of the tax code. If a product is classed as insurance, the buildup—or appreciation of the fund—remains tax-free. Insurance products enjoy a unique tax advantage under the code.

1952   A congressional inquiry finds the Internal Revenue Bureau is rife with incompetent and untrustworthy employees who accept bribes to overlook nonpayment of income taxes. The bureau undergoes a major reorganization to root out corruption.

1954   With the end of the Korean conflict, the Revenue Act of 1954 follows the lead of the revenue act of the previous year by lowering of both individual and corporate taxes.

The 1939 tax code is recodified into the Internal Revenue Code of 1954, which will continue in use until 1986. The 1954 code includes many technical changes in the tax law and is the basis for the tax law until 1986.

Between 1954 and 1969, few changes are made in the tax laws. The top individual tax bracket is set at 91 percent. Numerous federal excise taxes augment income taxes, providing about one quarter of the federal government's revenue needs.

Accelerated depreciation is added to the tax code, which allows corporations to "write off" their property faster, resulting in lower taxes.

1958   Congress adds the category "Sub S Corporations" to the tax code. This provision allows owners of small corporations to get "partnership" tax treatment—one level of taxation rather than two. Conventional corporations are taxed on their earnings, and earnings distributed to shareholders as dividends are taxed a second time. In an S corporation the corporation pays no tax on earnings.

1960   President John F. Kennedy, a Democrat, is elected, replacing President Dwight D. Eisenhower, a Republican and former Army general. During the Eisenhower years ("We Like Ike") the highest tax rates averaged around 90 percent on every type of income. During this period (1954–1960), productivity increases (the increase per worker) averaged slightly over 3 percent. In later decades when tax rates are cut to a top rate of 50 percent on earned income and 70 percent on unearned income (generally investment income), productivity increases actually drop to slightly over 1 percent. A similar rise in productivity occurs after tax rates are raised in 1993. Although there is no evidence the tax rate cuts cause the declines in productivity increases, it does call into question the argument that low tax rates increase productivity.

1961   The deduction for many state and local taxes (auto licenses, driver's licenses, and alcohol) are repealed.

1962   The Investment Tax Credit (ITC) is added to the tax code. This provision grants generous tax breaks to businesses and individuals engaged in business who invest in new equipment and machinery. The goal is not tax reduction but economic stimulus. By providing a tax break, Congress hopes that private sector investment will stimulate the economy. Congress learns that the tax code can be used to control the growth of the economy. The ITC will be expanded in 1964, suspended in 1967, and repealed in 1969. It will be reinstated in 1971 during a recession and extended again in both 1975 and 1978 until it is again repealed in 1986. President Clinton considers suggesting reinstatement in 1990, but the economy responds before a proposal is made.

Congress establishes H.R. 10 Plans (also known as Keogh Plans), which allow self-employed taxpayers to set up their own retirement plans. Contributions up to a limit are tax deductible. Keogh plans will be greatly expanded in 1982.

1964   In 1963, President Kennedy calls for a major reduction in income tax rates. When asked about the fairness of cutting taxes for the wealthy, he responds that the expected productivity gains will benefit all taxpayers. In a message that presages Ronald Reagan's message 20 years later, he argues that "a rising tide raises all ships." The Revenue Act of 1964 decreases individual tax rates from 20 to 91 percent to 14 to 70 percent. The standard deduction is also raised so that lower-income individuals would not be subject to any income tax. Corporate tax rates are reduced, with a maximum of 48 percent.

Income averaging is added to the tax code as a reform measure. Because of the progressive tax rates, an individual whose income can be "bunched" in 1 year, such as a salesman, pays higher taxes than an individual who earns the same amount of money but earns it over several years. Income averaging allows the taxpayer with bunched income to use a lower tax rate. This provision will remain in the code until 1986.

1965   Individual income tax rates are reduced from 91 to 70 percent for individuals. Most federal excise taxes imposed during the Korean War are repealed. Excise taxes on alcohol, tobacco, cars, and telephone calls are allowed to continue in force.

1966   The Tax Adjustment Act of 1966 repeals the ITC. The credit is reinstituted by Congress 6 months later.

1968   At the urging of President Lyndon Johnson, Democrat of Texas, Congress enacts a 10 percent income tax surtax, which requires all taxpayers to pay 110 percent of their computed tax, to help pay for the Vietnam War.

1969   Tax Reform Act of 1969 is the most important tax reform measure in the tax law since 1913. Although a number of deductions are eliminated or reduced, others are liberalized. The 1969 act also adds the alternative minimum tax (AMT) to the tax code—a political measure to ensure that all wealthy taxpayers pay some tax despite legal tax planning that may reduce their tax burden to zero. The ITC is again repealed. The use of multiple corporations to reduce taxes is curtailed. The act also reduces the attractiveness of capital gains by making the taxation of capital gains and ordinary income more equal.

The 1969 Tax Reform Act marks a turning point in tax reform. During the prior 15 years there were very few changes in the tax code except for the Kennedy rate reductions of 1962. Starting in 1969, the tax code would undergo nearly constant revision for nearly 30 years. Although some of these so-called reforms are enacted merely for revenue raising or to address specific abuses, other acts—especially the 1981 and 1986 acts—will be driven by Congress's desire to reform the tax system. Whether the trend toward change will continue in the new millennium is a matter of conjecture.

1970   A new tax schedule is introduced for taxpayers filing as individuals. The new Schedule X uses the tax rate enacted the prior year to apply to single individuals. The rate is lower than the Schedule Y, which is still to be used by married filing separate tax returns, but higher than either the Schedule Y (married filing jointly) or Schedule Z (head of household) tax rates.

1971   The Revenue Act of 1971, proposed by the Nixon administration, reverses many of the tax reforms enacted in 1969. The act is generally probusiness in tone. The ITC is revived.

1974   The 1974 Pension Reform Act, also known as the Employment Retirement Income Security Act (ERISA), creates a new system for pensions. This act is both major social engineering and a major tax reform provision. Enforced by both the IRS and the Department of Labor, ERISA sets up a complex series of rules governing private pensions. Responding to the pension scandals of the 1960s and the 1970s merger mania, the law provides a tax deduction for companies that invest cash or securities with a pension plan trustee. The law requires minimum vesting rules (when pension rights are considered permanent) and nondiscrimination rules to ensure that most employees are pension plan participants. The rules also require companies to account and report to both the IRS and the Department of Labor.

1975   The Tax Reduction Act of 1975 adds the Earned Income Credit to the tax code. Alarmed at the growth of welfare for the needy, Congress seeks to reduce the complexity of the welfare system by passing a tax provision that operates as a "negative income tax." Qualified needy individuals get a cash refund from the Treasury that, depending on their income and family status, can exceed their tax payments. Hence the payments would be a negative income tax. Originally proposed as a replacement to welfare payments, the Earned Income Credit never provides sufficient income for this purpose, but it remains a part of the tax code. It is expanded in 1993. In the early 1990s the credit becomes controversial as unscrupulous tax return preparers file electronic returns claiming cash refunds for taxpayers who did not qualify as well as for fictitious taxpayers.

1976   Congress enacts and President Nixon signs the Tax Reform Act of 1976, which includes an attack on "tax shelters," which are investments designed to produce enormous legal tax breaks. Tax shelters are increasingly perceived to be a growing abuse. In its first major challenge to tax shelters, Congress passes the "at risk" rules, which limit the deduction from investments in which the investors are not personally at risk on the financing. The at-risk rules are strengthened in 1978 and 1986.

The act limits charitable deductions for businesses and repeals "qualified stock options," which were used extensively by corporations to benefit executives. The move is made to ensure that all employee compensation is subject to tax. The act also makes substantial changes in the federal estate and gift taxes, which had been promised for many years. The changes free many upper-middle-income taxpayers from being subject to these "transfer taxes." The act also includes the highly controversial elimination of the step-up-of-basis-at-death rule. Under this rule, untaxed appreciation in the value of property is not subject to income tax when a person dies and leaves property to heirs. Later, under intense pressure from constituents, Congress reverses the elimination of the step-up-at-death rule.

The Tax Reform Act of 1976 includes the Credit for the Elderly and Disabled, meant to give tax reductions to both needy elderly and needy disabled taxpayers. Although this reform is initially useful, Congress then refuses to index the amounts for the following 25 years.

1977   President Jimmy Carter proposes a massive tax simplification. Although his Democratic Party enjoys comfortable majorities in Congress, Congressional leaders and the public are lukewarm to the proposal, which Carter withdraws in favor of the more modest Tax Reduction and Simplification Act of 1977.

1978   Alarmed at declining tax revenues, Congress passes the Revenue Act of 1978, which repeals many of the reforms in the 1969 and 1976 tax acts. Capital gains preferences repealed in 1969 are reinstated. The controversial carryover basis rules are postponed just before their effective date. The act makes the 10 percent ITC permanent.

The Foreign Earned Income Act repeals the foreign earned income exclusion, which allowed Americans to earn a limited income overseas tax-free. By closing this loophole, Congress seeks to equalize the tax of taxpayers no matter where they earn their income. The repeal is short-lived, and the exclusion will be reenacted in 1982 but limited in the 1986 Tax Act.

1979   The Windfall Profits Tax passes. The act includes the final and permanent repeal of the carryover basis rules included in the 1976 tax act. These rules would have taxed capital gains when a deceased's property passes to heirs at death. The carryover basis rules will be reintroduced in 1999 as a replacement for the estate and gift tax.

1981   Following Ronald Reagan's landslide election victory over incumbent president Jimmy Carter, Congress enacts the Economic Recovery Tax Act of 1981 (ERTA). The electorate had given a strong endorsement to Reagan's promise of smaller government and lower taxes. Top individual tax rates are scheduled to fall 23 percent over 3 years. During the late 1970s the country grew alarmed at the success of manufacturing in both Japan and some European countries. Low-cost high-quality autos from Japan and Europe captured nearly a third of the U.S. auto market. The popular press published many reports about the Midwest rust belt and the decline of American business, especially in the manufacturing sector. Many blamed government policies—especially high taxes—for the decline. Probusiness proponents championed various cures, including "10-5-3" depreciation—a radical idea that would let businesses take rapid tax write-offs over 3, 5, or 10 years for new business equipment and buildings.

Governor Ronald Reagan of California embraces these ideas, which, after his election to the presidency, find their way into the 1981 tax act, which also includes substantial tax rate reductions for both individuals and businesses.

Congress reenacts qualified stock options that were repealed in 1976. Stock options, granted to employees by their employers, allow recipients to buy employer stock at bargain prices. Now called "incentive stock options," the provision allows upper-income executives a major tax break because the options are lightly taxed.

Indexing is introduced, which increases the standard deduction and personal exemptions as inflation rises. This provision is a true reform and lightens the tax load on millions of lower-income taxpayers who had experienced "bracket creep." During the inflationary period of the 1970s, wages and salaries rose but the standard deduction and exemptions failed to keep pace. The government was able to raise more revenue without officially raising taxes merely because taxpayers "crept" into ever-higher tax brackets.

The accelerated depreciation rules in the tax act cause a massive investment in new buildings. Many of these investments are set up as tax shelters to give investors the benefits of extremely generous tax deductions. These tax shelters contribute to overcapacity of office space and storefronts in many areas and to the failure of the Savings and Loan Associations who financed many of the speculative real estate ventures. Taxpayers eventually pick up the multibillion dollar cost of bailing out the savings and loans.

Eligibility for Individual Retirement Accounts (IRAs) is expanded to include nearly all taxpayers rather than just those uncovered by an employer retirement plan. In 1986, IRA eligibility is almost restored to its original pre-1981 limits.

1982   Alarmed at plummeting revenues that resulted from the previous year's tax cuts accompanied by no spending reductions, Congress reverses course and passes the Tax Equality and Fiscal Responsibility Act of 1982 (TEFRA), which contains a number of business tax increases to help stem the mounting budget deficit. Although the 1981 tax act was the largest tax cut ever, the 1982 is probably the greatest tax increase to date.

1983   Social Security benefits become taxable for higher-income retirees. However, Congress also enacts the Credit for the Elderly and allows taxpayers over age 55 to exclude the first $125,000 of gain on the sale of a personal residence. In a strange balancing of "reform" measures, Congress increases some taxes on the elderly while it also enacts rules that would significantly reduce their taxes.

The Social Security Amendments of 1983 raise payroll taxes for millions of working Americans. Although income tax rates are declining, the Social Security tax is increasing, resulting in a net increase in taxes for those in the middle and working classes but a net reduction in tax rates for those at the top.

1984   The Deficit Reduction Act of 1984 drops the capital gain holding period from 1 year to 6 months, allowing many more investors to benefit from the lower tax rate imposed on long-term gains.

1985   Alarmed at the ever-increasing deficit, Congress passes the Balanced Budget and Emergency Deficit Control Act of 1985 (better known as the Gramm-Rudman Act), which requires the president to make across-the-board budget cuts if Congress fails to meet specific deficit targets.

1986   Congress passes the 1986 Tax Reform Act, a truly significant change in the income tax code, although not as much a reform measure as the 1969 act. Based on a bill originally proposed in 1982 as the Bradley-Gephardt bill, named after Bill Bradley and Richard Gephardt, its Democratic sponsors, the act cuts individual income tax rates from the high of 50 percent to 28 percent. Corporate rates fall from 46 to 34 percent. For individuals the rate structure replaces the traditional progressive rates with a much flatter tax rate schedule. Although rates at the bottom are progressive, a flat tax–type 28 percent individual income rate applies once a married couple's taxable income exceeds $29,750 ($17,850 for single taxpayers).

In a major change, the tax code abandons the preferential treatment of capital gains, a fixture of the code since 1922. All income is to be taxed alike. This change is made with equity in mind. Wealthy investors who had been paying a maximum of 20 percent tax on stock market profits now face a 28 percent tax. Ironically, this measure causes a surge of revenue in the Treasury the year before it is applied, as investors sell stock in record numbers at year's end to avoid the higher tax. This provision stays in the code only until 1990, when the capital gains tax preference is brought back.

Deductions for business meals and entertainment are limited to 80 percent. The act also places strict limits on miscellaneous deductions like tax preparation expenses, investment expenses, and employee expenses—areas of taxpayer "creativity." Income tax deduction for state sales taxes is repealed for individual taxpayers, but the deduction for state income tax continues as part of the tax code. The act also creates a new form—Form 1040-EZ—meant to simplify filing for millions of lower-income taxpayers.

The act contains a major assault on tax shelters, which remain a problem despite the changes made in the 1976 act. The new rules about passive-activity losses are aimed at making tax shelters far less attractive to investors. Drafters of the bill include two major reforms for businesses: corporate taxpayers will be paying a higher proportion of taxes overall, and corporations in various industry categories will be taxed more equitably. Before the passage of this act, manufacturing firms were taxed much more lightly than service sector firms.

The Low Income Housing Credit is added to the tax code. The federal government resolves to cease building and subsidizing low-income housing, and

Congress enacts the tax credit to encourage private entrepreneurs to build low-cost housing.

1987   The "Kiddie Tax," enacted the year before, creates a special tax rate rule for children under fourteen years of age who have net unearned income (investment income). Prior to this time, wealthy parents frequently transferred income-producing assets to children because the income would be taxed to the child. The result was either that the income was sheltered from tax by the standard deduction or the income would be exposed to much lower taxation because of the child's lower tax rate. Although this technique was legal under the tax rules, Congress decided this area was in need of reform. Beginning in 1987 only small amounts of a child's income could be taxed at the child's rate while the remainder was taxed at the parent's highest tax rate. The law is made retroactive to the extent that the new Kiddie Tax also applies to income from property given as a gift to children before 1987.

1988   The Technical and Miscellaneous Revenue Act of 1988 (TAMRA) includes the first Taxpayer's Bill of Rights, which gives taxpayers a number of important procedural protections when dealing with the IRS.

1989   The Revenue Reconciliation Act of 1989 increases tax collections by accelerating withholding and the payment of payroll taxes.

1990   The Budget Enforcement Act of 1990 adds additional requirements to the Gramm-Rudman balanced budget requirements. Congress adopts a resolution that requires all tax legislation to be revenue-neutral (it must bring in as much revenue as it loses). The economy is in the midst of a minor recession. The Revenue Reconciliation Act of 1990 raises individual tax rates, which become 15, 28, and 31 percent. The maximum capital gains rate stays at 28 percent, restoring the capital gains preference dropped in the 1986 tax act. The deduction for an individual's investment interest is limited.

1991   The presidential campaign pits the Republican incumbent George Herbert Walker Bush against former

Arkansas governor Bill Clinton. Clinton prevails. Bush's support from his own party is shaky because he was forced to retreat from his famous pledge: "Read my lips . . . no new taxes."

1993   President Clinton signs the Revenue Reconciliation Act of 1993, which raises income taxes significantly for individuals. The top rate rises from 31 to 39.6 percent. Republicans in Congress split, and some support the tax increases proposed by the president. Corporate rates are hiked by 1 percent. Despite the tax increases, the economy booms and tax collections increase with the rise in overall national income. The boom continues for the next 7 years, during which time the government collects increasing revenues without the need to raise taxes.

1995   The presidential campaign is notable because tax reform becomes a central issue. Steve Forbes, a candidate who unsuccessfully seeks the Republican nomination, forces the issue to center stage by championing a flat tax proposal. All the candidates stake out a position.

1996   The incumbent Bill Clinton wins a surprisingly easy victory in the presidential election. Although he had raised taxes in 1993, the economy boomed despite predictions to the contrary.

The Small Business Job Protection Act contains a number of business provisions. The Taxpayer Bill of Rights 2 includes additional protections not included in the original 1988 Bill of Rights. Two other small tax acts include relatively minor reform measures.

A National Commission on Restructuring the IRS is formed to review the structure of the agency and its tax collection function. The commission is charged with exploring new options, including the outright abolition of the IRS. The commission's findings were the basis of the 1998 IRS Restructuring and Reform Act.

1997   The Tax Reform Act of 1997 includes a number of technical changes, including new tax incentives for higher education and retirement savings. The movement for tax simplification has been forgotten, and the act is notable for the complexity of the new provisions. Capital gains rates for individuals are sharply reduced. With the stock market at a record high, taxpayers welcome the move.

The U.S. Supreme Court declares the Line Item Veto Act, passed the prior year, unconstitutional. The law gave the president the power to delete revenue-losing tax benefits.

1998   After well-publicized Congressional hearings in which taxpayers testified about alleged IRS collection abuses, Congress passes the IRS Restructuring and Reform Act of 1998. Although the agency is not abolished, Congress attempts to refocus the agency from enforcement to taxpayer education and encourages the agency to speed computerized tax reporting and collections.

The 1998 act also provides that the estate and gift tax will only apply to the truly wealthy. The amount exempt from these taxes is scheduled to rise gradually from $600,000 to $1 million in 2006.

The Republican-controlled Congress passes a tax bill containing a major tax cut. The act is vetoed by President Clinton, a Democrat, and the Republicans fail to gain enough votes to override the veto. The public remains apathetic, perhaps signaling that the promise of tax cuts have lost their luster. The robust economy is no doubt partly responsible.

1999   Government tax collections grow faster than even the most optimistic predictions as the economy continues its unprecedented growth. The federal government posts a surplus after decades of deficits. The states are also beneficiaries of the strong economy, and many are able to modestly reduce taxes.

The presidential election campaign for 2000 starts in earnest, with all candidates favoring some sort of tax reform that includes tax cuts for individuals. Steve Forbes still champions his flat tax proposal, but it is no longer the centerpiece of his campaign. He drops out of the race. The country ends the millennium with fundamental tax reform still unaccomplished.

2000   In this presidential election year, the healthy U.S. economy continues to generate small budget surpluses. The Republican-controlled Congress votes to completely phase out the federal estate tax. In its place the Congress would enact a system of taxing certain capital gains at the time of a taxpayer's death. President Clinton, in his last year of office, vetoed the measure, arguing that any surplus should be used to stabilize the Social Security system and to reduce the national debt. The Congress also passes a marriage penalty relief act, which the president also threatens to veto.

Republican presidential candidate George W. Bush calls for across the board income tax rate reductions plus repeal of the federal estate tax.

Congress extends the ban on state taxation of the Internet until a "final" solution is forged. The ban is supported by online retailers but opposed by traditional retailers and shopping center operators who argue that the ban is unfair and perhaps unconstitutional.

2001   President George W. Bush (son of George Herbert Walker Bush), Republican, takes office. Bush's campaign had promised tax cuts and elimination of the "death tax" (the federal estate tax) because it penalized success. Bush's plan includes the repeal of the federal estate tax and its replacement with the taxation of capital gains at death—a proposal that will reduce taxes for the truly wealthy but actually increase taxes for some middle-class Americans who were not subject to the old estate tax but would be subject to a new type of death tax under the Bush plan. The major part of the Bush plan is significant tax cuts—especially for upper-income taxpayers who saw their income taxes increase significantly under the previous Democratic administration. Taxes on most stock dividends and long-term capital gains—the tax on investment income—are slashed to 15 percent.

In effect, the income tax is reengineered to operate like a "consumption tax" (similar to a sale tax) with income only being taxed if it is consumed (spent on goods and services). Under the revisions, most lower-income taxpayers effectively now pay only Social Security tax and not income tax while some Wall Street and hedge fund owners and millionaires pay only 15 percent federal income tax on their huge investment gains.

Because of congressional rules limiting measures that increase the deficit, the Bush tax cuts had to be designed to be "revenue-neutral." This required Congress to engineer the cuts to expire in 2010, after which the tax rates would return to their previous higher levels. The federal estate tax was to be phased out between 2002 and 2009 and would disappear completely in 2010. In 2011 it would reappear on wealth in excess of $1million unless Congress eliminated it completely in the decade before 2010.

2003   The child tax credit is increased $400 to $1,000. This provision lets middle- and lower-income taxpayers to reduce their taxes by $1,000 for each eligible child. This measure proved popular with voters with children but did little to address poverty.

President George W. Bush's Advisory Panel on Federal Tax Reform issues its final report. The panel recommends either a "hybrid consumption tax" or a keeping a greatly simplified income tax that eliminates several popular tax deductions. The proposed simplification would have four tax rates between 15 and 33 percent and eliminate the alternative minimum tax. Several individual deductions would be limited or eliminated altogether. Health insurance tax-free benefits would be capped at $11,500 for families and $5,000 for single filers. A 15 percent credit would replace the current home mortgage interest deduction. The credit would be limited, with caps on the size of the loan varying among State and local income tax and real estate tax deductions would be eliminated. The top corporate income tax rate would be reduced (from 35% to 32%) and most employee fringe benefits like health insurance would be taxed. Of course the proposals proved highly controversial. Both President Bush and Congress ignore the report and no tax reform is undertaken.

Because of delays in passing a tax law at the end of 2004, the IRS has to delay printing forms and tax filing season begins a month later than normal. Congress tightens record-keeping requirements for charitable giving. The tax code adopts a uniform definition of *a child* for various tax breaks in the tax code. The tax code starts to incorporate "green" provisions. The 2005 tax act includes tax breaks for taxpayers who buy hybrid and electric cars and for those who improve the energy efficiency of their homes and buildings.

2006   Alarmed at the energy crisis with rising oil prices, Congress adds several "energy credits" designed to help individuals and businesses "go green." Among them are added breaks for buys of hybrid and electric cars and tax incentives for those who weatherize their home and buildings. Former Vice President Al Gore's movie and book *An Inconvenient Truth* bring attention to climate change and environmental issues. Gore's earlier 1999 book, *Earth in the Balance*, called for a carbon tax that would tax fuels with carbon content such as gasoline, natural gas, and coal while exempting "clean" energy generated by solar or wind power.

2007   Congress grants relief to homeowners who face foreclosure because of the housing crisis following the bust of the real estate bubble. Under the tax code, forgiven debt is considered income to the debtor. Taxpayers must pay a tax when a home mortgage debt is reduced or forgiven. Under 2007 changes, taxpayers can exclude up to $2 million of debt forgiven on their home mortgages. This provision applies to debt forgiven in 2007, 2008, or 2009, but was later extended to other years.

The Fair Tax, a proposed national sales tax designed to replace the income tax, receives national exposure when Republican presidential candidate Mike Huckabee endorses it. Bills to adopt the Fair Tax have been introduced since 1999. Generally the Fair Tax would be a national sales tax designed to replace both the federal income tax and the federal estate tax. The more an individual spends, the higher the tax. Taxpayers at all income levels would receive a monthly rebate check based on the number of individuals in their household. The tax would also eliminate Social Security taxes and the corporate income tax. The tax would be imposed on services as well as the sale of goods and would start at 23 percent. Critics of the tax argue that it will be "regressive" (the poor will bear a larger burden of the tax) and also suggest that the rate will have to be far higher than the 23 percent estimated by the tax's supporters.

2008   The Alternative Minimum Tax (AMT) originally enacted in 1969, was designed to ensure that all taxpayers paid at least some tax. Each year a relatively small number of wealthy taxpayers are able to avoid paying any income tax because they employ legal "loopholes" to minimize their tax. The AMT—which uses a different set of tax rules—is designed to compel all taxpayers to pay at least some tax. During the 1990s the AMT unexpectedly started applying to more and more upper-middle-class taxpayers. Outright repeal of the AMT proved difficult because the measure brings in millions of dollars in tax revenues. Starting in 2001, Congress tried to limit the number of taxpayers subject to the AMT with a series of AMT "patches" rather than a real solution. In 2008 Representative Charles Rangel proposed to replace the AMT with an income tax surcharge on the rich. Because of partisan bickering, the proposal was never adopted and Congress resorted to another "patch" for 2009.

2009   After the real estate bubble burst, the United States faced the prospect that the U.S. banking system might collapse. The federal government undertook emergency measures including bailouts of banks, insurance companies, and other firms. The federal government spent hundreds of billions of dollars under the Troubled Assets Relief Program (TARP) created by the Emergency Economic Stabilization Act of 2008. Faced with enormous budget deficits due to the financial bailout and the costs of the Iraq and Afghanistan wars, President Barak Obama creates a special task force to review the U.S. tax system. The group, known as the Volker task force, headed by former Federal Reserve Chairman Paul Volker, is charged with finding ways to reform the tax system while reducing the "tax gap," simplifying the system, and closing loopholes that let some corporations escape taxation.

The "Tea Party" protest movement originally sprang up in early 2009 to protest the federal government's TARP program. Tea Party activists later protested on tax day (April 15), and staged later demonstrations as the Obama health care plan made its way through Congress. In September 2009 tens of thousands joined a Tea party taxpayer march on Washington. At least at its start, the movement was not a political party but a series of rallies and antigovernment demonstrations. Antitax sentiment played a major role in several of the protests.

2010 The 2001 Bush tax cuts were designed to expire in 2010, after which the income tax rates would return to their previous higher levels. The federal estate tax was to be phased out between 2002 and 2009 and would disappear completely in 2010 but would reappear in 2011 unless Congress eliminated it completely in the decade before 2010. After Barak Obama's election, many assumed Congress would act before 2010 to extend or repeal the Bush tax cuts and certainly to prevent the estate tax from expiring before 2010. However, burdened with other matters, Congress let the federal estate tax expire for the year 2010 and did not take action on the Bush income tax cuts. By taking no action, the 2010 Congress paved the way for the 2001 income tax cuts to automatically end and tax rates to rise across the board. Without action, the estate tax will have expired for 2010 but after 2011 would be imposed on estates of more than $1 million—a significantly lower threshold than during the period 2002–2010.

Congress considers a 3 cent tax on sodas and other sugary drinks to fund the new federal health care proposal. The measure also aims at reducing chronic obesity.

U.S. Senators Ron Wyden (D-Ore.), and Judd Gregg (R-N.H.), introduce the Bipartisan Tax Fairness and Simplification Act of 2010, designed to create a simpler and fairer tax system by eliminating many of the tax breaks that benefit special interests and to promote job growth. The main feature of the proposal is a one-page individual tax form. The 2010 bill is an updated version of the senators' earlier proposals.

2011   Despite calls for bipartisan tax reform to help defray the cost of the mounting budget deficit, partisan bickering between the Republicans and Democrats prevents any progress.

Representative Paul Ryan (R-Wis.) proposes a deficit reduction plan that, in the name of tax reform, would repeal most itemized deductions. The resulting revenue would not be used to pay down the deficit, however, but to cut tax rates, mostly for the benefit of comparatively well-to-do Americans. House Republicans support the Ryan plan unanimously, as do all but four Senate Republicans, but almost no support comes from Democrats. Republicans argue that most—and in some cases all—of the added revenue should go toward cutting personal and corporate tax rates, not for deficit reduction and not for achieving the social and economic objectives largely supported by the rival Democrats.

In the early fall, President Obama proposes a $3 trillion federal budget Deficit Reduction Plan which includes $1.5 trillion in tax increases. Under this plan, the "Bush tax cuts" from 2001 would be phased out and the highest individual tax rate would increase from 35 to 39.6 percent starting in 2013. Republican critics argue that a recession was not a good time to be raising anyone's taxes. The president's plan included two new twists: first, itemized deductions would be limited to 28 percent of a taxpayer's adjusted gross income. The result would be higher taxes for the wealthy who claimed sizable tax deductions. Second, the plan included the "Buffet Rule" (named after the investor Warren Buffet), requiring taxpayers earning $1 million or more per year to pay as high a share of income taxes as middle-income taxpayers. Buffet himself pointed out the unfairness of some wealthy taxpayers paying lower tax rates than the middle class.

The president's plan also called for comprehensive tax reform for individuals and businesses. Hearkening back to the Reagan 1986 Tax Reform Act, Obama's plan called for lower tax rates, the removal of deductions and other tax breaks, and elimination of complexity from the tax code. The plan included only vague goals rather than specific proposals.

Republican presidential candidate Herman Cain gathered the most press coverage for his novel "9-9-9" tax proposal. The plan helped propel Cain from an also-ran to a leading contender for the Republican nomination. Cain's plan envisioned replacing the current income tax with a business flat-rate income tax of 9 percent, an individual flat-rate income tax of 9 percent, and a new retail income tax of 9 percent. Most tax deductions would disappear. Federal payroll taxes, presumably including Social Security taxes, and the estate tax would be eliminated. Capital gains and dividends would not be taxed. State taxes would not change.

Cain argued that the plan should draw popular support because it combined a flat tax with a national sales tax (sometimes termed the Fair Tax). Critics argued that the plan was risky and might not bring in enough revenues, which would only increase the federal deficit. Others speculated that plan would favor the wealthy, while yet others argued that given Congress's penchant for raising taxes, the tax rates would soon rise above the single digits. Although the prospects for passage were uncertain, the proposal raised people's expectations for fundamental tax reform.

5

Biographical Sketches

William Reynolds (Bill) Archer Jr. (1928–)

In 2000 Representative Bill Archer, a Republican from Houston, Texas, was the chair of the House Committee on Ways and Means, which has the primary responsibility for writing U.S. tax laws. Archer is known as a conservative who would like to downsize the federal government. He is especially critical of IRS intrusions into the lives of taxpayers. Although at one time Archer was a supporter of a flat tax, he came to support a national sales tax. In Archer's view the benefits of both the current income tax or a flat tax are outweighed by their inherent complexity and inevitable compliance problems. Eventually the IRS will have to make unreasonable inquiries into taxpayers' personal and business affairs. In Archer's view, only a national sales tax will be able to eliminate this intrusion. In fact, Archer believes that the sales tax will enable the government to eliminate not only the income and estate taxes but also the IRS itself. Prospects for a national sales tax are murky. Some economists suggest that the tax rate might have to exceed 20 percent to produce the sort of revenue needed to fund basic government programs. The effect on the economy is unknown, and sellers of big-ticket items like cars and trucks worry that a 20 percent sales tax would drive away customers. Since his retirement from Congress in 2001, Archer has been a senior policy analyst for the Tax Foundation, based in Washington D.C.

Richard K. (Dick) Armey (1940–)

Majority leader of the Republicans in the House of Representatives in 2000 and a major proponent of the flat tax, Dick Armey is the author of the book *The Flat Tax* (1996) as well as two other books. Armey, who earned a Ph.D. in economics and was formerly an economics professor, was first elected to Congress in 1984 as part of the "Reagan revolution," which promised smaller government and lower taxes. A conservative Republican, Armey has long advocated tax reform and lower taxes. When President George H. W. Bush was forced to back away from his "no new taxes" pledge during a recession in 1990, Armey submitted a resolution to the Republican Conference, a group of congressional members described on Armey's web site as opposing "new taxes and all tax-rate increases as a means of reducing the federal budget deficit." Armey broke ranks not only with President Bush but also with fellow Republicans in Congress when they agreed to a modest tax increase in 1990. Armey was also the primary author of the highly controversial "Contract with America"—a conservative agenda of 10 bills, 6 of which were eventually enacted. Armey supports a flat 17 percent income tax—which could be reported on a postcard-sized form. His proposal would exempt the first $33,800 of family income and would eliminate not only deductions and tax credits but also the preference for capital gains, Social Security taxes, and the federal estate tax. Since his retirement from Congress in 2003, Armey has been chair of the group Freedomworks, associated with the Tea Party protest movement, which is opposed to bigger government and higher taxes. Armey also penned the book *Give Us Liberty*.

William Warren (Bill) Bradley (1943–)

Although best known as a presidential candidate in the 2000 Democratic primaries, Bill Bradley was a major participant in forging the 1986 Tax Reform Act, the most comprehensive revision of the Internal Revenue Code since its inception in 1913. Bradley, a former Rhodes scholar from Princeton University and a member of the New York Knicks' championship professional basketball team, won a Senate seat from New Jersey as a Democrat. Bradley had developed an interest in taxes while he was a highly compensated NBA player (his nickname was "Dollar Bill"), and this interest continued during his Senate years. Together with Representative Dick Gephardt of Missouri, Bradley introduced a bill that would essentially reverse the Economic Recovery Tax Act(ERTA), the tax-cutting plan passed by Congress and signed into law by President Ronald Reagan in 1981. Bradley's bill was ultimately enacted, though with changes, as the Tax Reform Act of 1986. The original bill proposed low-income tax relief, elimination of many special-interest business tax breaks, and a limit on the value of itemized deductions. This last idea was eliminated when the bill was enacted. The bill's most striking idea was to radically lower the highest individual tax rate from 50 to only 33 percent and to completely eliminate the preference for capital gains—provisions that did pass. Fearful that the Democrats would use the bill to their advantage, Ronald Reagan and Republican leaders in Congress embraced the bill, which culminated in the most sweeping tax reform of the century. Few now remember that Bill Bradley was the originator of these reforms.

William Jennings Bryan (1860–1925)

During much of the 19th century, tax politics were regional—the wealthy Northeast favored a high tariff while the West favored a low tariff and eventually called for a national income tax. Bryan and other Democrats appealed to the latter group, whereas Republicans favored the tariff. Bryan was an unsuccessful Democratic presidential candidate in 1896, 1902, and 1908. A renowned orator, he gained a national reputation and the Democratic nomination in 1896, after making his "Cross of Gold" speech, aimed at eliminating the gold standard. After his three unsuccessful presidential campaigns, he became Woodrow Wilson's secretary of state. Bryan tried to keep the United States on a pacifist course in foreign policy but resigned after he broke with Wilson over U.S. involvement in World War I. Today Bryan is best remembered for his defense of the Tennessee antievolution law in the famous 1925 Scopes "monkey trial." During the hotly contested presidential campaign of 1896, Bryan was supported mostly by westerners who favored an income tax to replace the tariff and elimination of the gold standard to enlarge the money supply. Although the tariff protected eastern factories and jobs, it effectively excluded low-cost imports, raising the cost of all manufactured goods used by westerners. Additionally, because the vast majority of the wealthy lived in the Northeast, they, rather than the westerners, would be paying the tax. This had proved true with the Civil War income tax. In fact, after the demise of the federal income tax that was in place during the Civil War, scores of bills were submitted to Congress to enact an income tax. Although Bryan's campaign elicited a great deal of fervent support, it did not attract a majority of votes. William McKinley won the election on a platform supporting the gold standard and continued high tariffs.

George Herbert Walker Bush (1924–)

The 41st president of the United States and father of George Walker Bush (1946-), the 43rd president of the United States, George H. W. Bush lost his bid for reelection in part because of a famous campaign pledge that came back to haunt him: " Read my lips, no new taxes." The son of Senator Prescott Bush of Massachusetts, the first President Bush, a decorated hero of World War II, graduated from Yale and followed the family model by entering politics, serving first in the U.S. House of Representatives. He held a number of posts including Ambassador to the United Nations and headed the Central Intelligence Agency for about a year. He served two terms as vice president before winning election as president himself. He was extremely popular after the successful and brief Gulf War.

In seeking the Republican presidential nomination in 1980, Bush called Ronald Reagan's "supply-side" antitax message "voodoo economics." As Vice President, he supported Reagan's plan to cut tax rates. When Bush was nominated to run for president in 1988, his nominating speech contained the famous phrase "Read my lips, no new taxes." Although Bush generally followed traditional Republican conservative views, he signed legislation from the Democratic Congress raising taxes to fight the growing federal deficit, caused in part by lower tax revenues during a recession but also in part by the Reagan tax cuts. By breaking his "no new taxes" pledge, Bush alienated many antitax Republicans, who felt that he had abandoned their cause. In his bid for reelection, Bush was defeated by Democrat Bill Clinton in a three-way race that included third-party candidate H. Ross Perot, a businessman who received nearly 19 percent of the vote. Fairly or unfairly, Bush's abandonment of his pledge regarding taxes certainly contributed to his defeat. Other Republicans convinced themselves that the antitax pledge was essential for their party's success and their own political futures. Their inflexibility on this issue contributed to the 2011 political stalemate during the Obama administration.

George Walker Bush (1946–)

George W. Bush, the 43rd president of the United States, is the son of George H. W. Bush (1924–), the 41st president of the United States. Although best remembered for his antiterrorism effort after the destruction of New York City's "twin towers" at the World Trade Center and the invasion of Iraq, the second President Bush was extremely influential in the tax area. The 2001 "Bush tax cuts" radically changed the tax landscape and the effect of the cuts lasted far beyond his presidency. During Bill Clinton's last term in office (Clinton served as president between the two Bushes), the federal government had a small annual surplus rather than a deficit. While Clinton was in office, the individual tax rate had risen and the economy was healthy, which led to larger-than-expected tax revenues for the government. Although there were annual surpluses, they were tiny compared with the accumulated national debt. As George W. Bush came into office, government economists predicted even larger annual surpluses. Evidently Bush wanted a tax cut equal to one quarter of the projected surplus. The plan included income tax rate cuts; doubling the child care credit to please the middle class; and reduction of the "marriage penalty," which occurs because the tax rules make some married couples pay more than they would have paid if they had remained unmarried. Finally, Bush's plan included a phase-out of the federal estate tax on the well to do.

Andrew Carnegie (1835–1919)

Born in Scotland, Carnegie sailed to the United States aboard a whaling ship at the age of 13, settling with his family in Pennsylvania. As a boy, Carnegie worked 12-hour days and studied at night to help his parents maintain their modest livelihood. After a stint in the Union Army during the Civil War, Carnegie founded the Freedom Iron and Steel Company, which later became the Carnegie Steel Company. By 1900 this colossus was the largest steel producer in the world. In 1902 Carnegie sold the entire operation to the financier J. P. Morgan, who was forming the U.S. Steel Corporation, for $480 million—a colossal fortune for the day. Carnegie spent the final 17 years of his life giving away over 90 percent of his wealth. he was a believer in education and established the Carnegie Foundation for the Advancement of Education, also building 800 "Carnegie" libraries across the country on the condition that the local cities and towns buy the books. Many of these magnificent buildings are still in use. The author of many books, Carnegie was a strong supporter of death taxes—perhaps a surprising stance for a wealthy man—and was influential in raising support for a federal inheritance tax, which was enacted in 1898. In his 1890 essay "The Gospel of Wealth," Carnegie called for an inheritance tax that would confiscate most of an individual's wealth at death. He opined, "The parent who leaves his some enormous wealth generally deadens the talents and energies of the son, and leads him to lead a less useful and less worthy life than he otherwise would."

Henry Clay (1777–1852)

Henry Clay of Kentucky was largely responsible for shaping the 19th-century U.S. tax system. He was speaker of the House of Representatives, secretary of state, and finally a U.S. senator. The only major political office that eluded him was the presidency itself. However, Clay arguably was more influential than a number of presidents of his day. After he abandoned his presidential aspirations in favor of John Quincy Adams in 1828, Clay was rewarded with the post of secretary of state. Turned out of office after Adams's reelection bid failed, Clay was elected to the U.S. Senate and promptly earned the title "the great pacificator" for defusing the very serious nullification crisis: John C. Calhoun of South Carolina had theorized that in certain circumstances a state could "nullify" an act of Congress within the state and that the states retained the power to secede from the union. Clay brokered a deal whereby the tariff, so objectionable to South Carolinians, would be lowered. Clay ran unsuccessfully for president as a Whig in 1832 and again in 1844. Clay's Whig Party arose as a coalition of opponents of Andrew Jackson. Clay—known as "Harry of the West" (Kentucky was the "West" in 1824)—devised the "American System," which proposed a national bank and high tariffs to protect American manufacturing and farm products. Revenues from the tariffs would go to building roads and canals. This program appealed mostly to those in the Northeast and the Ohio Valley—areas with growing populations. Democrats, mostly from the South and West, favored low tariffs. Clay's ideas gained the widest acceptance. Although high tariffs in part precipitated the Civil War, the federal government relied mainly on them for the bulk of its revenue until World War I.

Steve Forbes (Malcolm Stevenson Forbes Jr.) (1947–)

Son of publisher Malcolm Forbes, Steve Forbes unsuccessfully sought to be the Republican Party's presidential nominee in both 1996 and 2000. Forbes is best known as a tax reformer for his advocacy of a flat income tax. Although flat tax proposals had been made before, Forbes was able to focus the country on the issue by making it the central tenet of his 1996 political campaign. A flat tax would use a single tax rate and abolish most deductions, thereby eliminating much of the complexity inherent in the current income tax code. Forbes's critics argued that the plan would shift much of the tax burden to low- and middle-income taxpayers because it would exempt capital gains and interest income from any tax and would eliminate the high federal estate tax. Although Forbes's tax plan generated a huge amount of interest in 1996, his 2000 campaign for president focused on more diverse issues. Although he was not elected president, Forbes did change the tax reform debate by popularizing the idea of a flat tax and taking the initiative to advance it.

Henry George (1839–1897)

A 19th-century political reformer, George was a champion of the "single tax"—a tax on land. A native of Philadelphia, he was largely self-educated. He worked as a ship's boy on a sailing vessel and then learned typesetting as a trade. After his marriage in 1861, he and his family moved to California, where he became a newspaper reporter and later editor of his own paper, the *San Francisco Daily Evening Post*. George was a vocal critic of entrenched interests, and he regularly criticized the railroad magnates, land speculators, and corrupt politicians of the time. He was alarmed by the growing disparity of wealth in the period following the Civil War. In 1871 George formulated his theory of a single tax on land, which would tax the wealthy. In George's view, landowners derived their wealth from the hoarding of a scarce resource. He reasoned that most of society's ills could be cured by a tax on land, which would discourage this hoarding. George expanded his initial pamphlet into a book, *Progress and Poverty*, which he finished in 1879. Undaunted by his inability to find a publisher, he published it himself. After selling out his initial printing, George found a commercial publisher to accept the book. It became an international best-seller and established George's reputation as a tax reformer. Moving to New York, he became a correspondent for the *Irish World*. He later edited the newspaper the *New York Standard* and wrote several other books on politics. A popular figure, he twice ran for mayor of New York. Support for the one-tax idea survived George's death: one-tax societies advocating George's single tax exist worldwide and seem especially influential in Australia, where George visited in 1890.

Alexander Hamilton (1757–1804)

The first secretary of the U.S. Treasury, Hamilton was influential in establishing the fiscal framework of the early republic. He was born in the British West Indies and had a distinguished military career before entering politics. An author of *The Federalist Papers*— along with John Jay, the first chief justice, and James Madison, the fourth U.S. president—Hamilton was a strong supporter of the new Constitution, a strong national government, and the national government's power to tax. At the time, the anti-Federalists— advocates of states' rights—wanted tax collecting to be vested in the states, which would then contribute to the upkeep of the national government. Hamilton and his allies argued that the national government required a stable source of revenue, and this view prevailed. The new Constitution, which replaced the Articles of Confederation, gave the national government not only the right to tax but also the sole right to issue money—a right the states had previously enjoyed. As secretary of the Treasury, Hamilton successfully persuaded the new Congress to enact a number of taxes, although customs duties from the tariff were the government's primary revenue source. Hamilton was killed in a duel by political rival Vice-President Aaron Burr. By actively advocating his support for a national taxing power, Hamilton was the most influential of the founders in setting the stage for the national tax system employed by the United States into the 21st century.

Howard Jarvis (1902–1987)

Howard Jarvis was a California tax reformer best known for supporting Proposition 13, which limited the growth of property taxes in California. During the 1970s the state of California enjoyed remarkable prosperity. One consequence was rapidly rising residential real estate prices. Homes in California became increasingly expensive for young, first-time homeowners and newcomers to the state. Modest homes that had been bought in the 1950s for $10,000 were suddenly worth $200,000. California also had the finest school systems in the country: elementary and secondary public schools, community colleges, and universities. Half the cost of the school system came from local property taxes. These taxes were calculated on the appraised value of the home. Accordingly, higher home prices led directly to higher property taxes, and homeowners on fixed incomes were in near panic at the tax increases. In 1978 a coalition headed by retiree Howard Jarvis and Paul Gann put a state initiative called Proposition 13 (or Prop 13) on the ballot. California and other western states allow citizens to propose their own state laws via the initiative process. Prop 13—approved by 65 percent of voters—effectively capped property taxes for people living in their homes. Although Jarvis's Prop 13 helped keep older Californians in their homes, it came at a price: the tax limitation forced massive cuts in spending—especially in education. The Howard Jarvis Taxpayers Association continued his work into the 21st century. Jarvis's tax revolt also spread beyond California as a number of states adopted measures similar to Prop 13. Jarvis did as much as anyone to change the tax system in the second half of the 20th century.

Jack French Kemp (1935–2009)

Kemp is a former U.S. secretary of housing and urban development and, as of 2000, a long-term member of the House of

Representatives. He has been one of the most influential Republican leaders among those who have called for reform of the U.S. tax system. After playing quarterback in the American Football League, Kemp entered politics as a Republican, representing western New York and serving nine terms in the House of Representatives. Kemp became known as a champion of entrepreneurship, calling for less government regulation and lower taxes. His lasting contribution to tax reform was the Kemp-Roth bill, introduced in 1977 and calling for a massive cut in individual tax rates. This proposal remained the center of attention during the next 10 years and helped to focus attention on the possibility of real tax reform. During the administration of President Ronald Reagan, Kemp was influential in shepherding the passage of the 1981 the Economic Recovery Tax Act, known as ERTA, which drastically cut top individual tax rates and delivered huge tax breaks to businesses, especially manufacturers. Long a potential Republican candidate for president, Kemp surprised many by accepting the post of secretary of housing and urban development and abandoning a run for president. In this post he was responsible for implementing "enterprise zones" to encourage entrepreneurship and job creation in low-income neighborhoods. Kemp's lasting contribution to tax reform came with his chairmanship of the National Commission on Economic Growth and Tax Reform, generally known as the "Kemp Commission." During the 1996 presidential election, various tax reform proposals were advocated, including a flat tax, and the Republican leadership created the commission to ensure that the subject got serious study. To Kemp's credit, the commission worked in a nonpartisan manner and created sophisticated proposals for reforming the system rather than politically attractive but ill-conceived schemes.

John Fitzgerald Kennedy (1917–1963)

The 35th president and first Roman Catholic to serve in the Oval Office, John Fitzgerald Kennedy was also a major figure in tax reform. The son of a millionaire, JFK, as he was known, graduated from Harvard and briefly attended the London School of Economics. A PT-boat commander in World War II, Kennedy received the Navy and Marine Corps medal for heroism. He entered politics and was elected to the House of Representatives and later the Senate, representing his native Massachusetts. In 1960, Kennedy defeated Richard Nixon for the presidency in a close election. Although his Democratic Party controlled Congress, Kennedy was unpopular with some of his own party for his support of civil rights. Although best known for his actions in the Cuban missile crisis and his assassination in Dallas in November 1963, Kennedy also revolutionized the way the government used the tax system to stimulate the economy. When Kennedy took office in 1961, individual tax rates on earned income ranged between 20 and 91 percent. The Revenue Act of 1964 enacted the major tax rate cuts Kennedy asked for in his 1963 tax message: rates were cut to 14 to 70 percent. Criticized for the fact that the cuts would benefit the wealthy, he answered that the cuts would help the economy and that "a rising tide raises all ships." The Kennedy tax cuts also came during a federal budget deficit. Instead of raising taxes to stem the deficit, Kennedy lowered taxes to increase private business activity, which would produce more taxes—a novel idea at the time. Additionally, Kennedy introduced the Investment Tax Credit (ITC) in 1962, which was designed to encourage investment in equipment and machinery and thus to modernize industry and stimulate job creation. Kennedy was also interested in more fundamental tax reform, and some of his ideas were finally enacted after his death in the Tax Reform Act of 1969.

Russell B. Long (1918–2003)

A Democrat from Louisiana, Senator Long was a long-time chair of the Senate Committee of Finance, the Senate committee responsible for tax matters. Although the Constitution stipulates that the House is to initiate revenue bills, in fact the House Ways and Means Committee and the Senate Finance Committee share the burden. Chairman Long enjoyed immense power because, apart from taxes, the committee also controls other important legislative areas. Long was normally receptive to giving tax breaks to business and was suspicious of tax reform. He was well known as a protector of the oil industry, which was a significant component of the economy in his home state of Louisiana. Long was also largely responsible for adding the Employee Stock Ownership Plan (ESOP) to the tax code—a method of transferring corporate stock and ownership of corporations to the corporations' employees. He was generally resistant to "tax reform," favoring changes that benefited special interests. The actual tax law is written by the committees, whose chairmen wield power over the final legislation. All major industries employ lobbyists to "educate" committee members about the advantages of giving their industries tax breaks. Long, as was the case with many chairmen, often had little sympathy for "reformers." Often humorous in person, Long may be best remembered in tax lore for his short verse "Don't tax you, Don't tax me, Tax the fellow behind the tree."

N. Gregory Mankiw (1958–)

Mankiw is a leading conservative economist who at one time advocated the carbon tax. He graduated from Princeton, earned a Ph.D. in economics from MIT, and rose to prominence as a Harvard professor and author of a leading undergraduate economics textbook. Mankiw was tapped by President George W. Bush to be chairman of the president's Council of Economic Advisers in 2003 (he had worked as a staff economist for the council for about 10 years earlier before completing his graduate work). In his role as chairman, Mankiw advocated for the Bush tax cuts even though he realized that they would not "pay for themselves," as others in the administration predicted. Mankiw pointed to the favorable impacts of tax cuts, including the stimulation of investment, growth, and jobs. After leaving his government post, Mankiw acknowledged the Bush tax cuts' effect on the growing federal deficit but pointed out that about half the growth in the deficit arose from the weakening economy and about a quarter from increased spending, including expenditures on homeland security and defense. Only about a quarter of the deficit's growth was due to reduced revenue from the tax cuts. Mankiw also served as economic adviser to Mitt Romney when he sought the Republican nomination for the presidency in 2012.

Wilbur D. Mills (1909–1992)

A Harvard-educated lawyer from Arkansas, Mills was the powerful chair of the House Ways and Means Committee from 1957 until 1974 and oversaw many of the tax reform efforts of the late 1900s, including the important Tax Reform Act of 1969. American tax laws are very much a product of politics, no less so now than in Mills's day. Mills was notorious for his iron grip on the committee. Before 1973 most of the tax writing was done in secret. Mills reputedly wielded enormous power over this process simply because he was able to hand-pick committee members and was a true tax expert who worked enormously hard at the chair's job. His career, however, came to a dramatic and memorable end. Mills, who had a problem with alcohol, had an affair with an exotic dancer who used the name Fannie Foxe (and was also known as the Argentine Firecracker). Although, in those days, the press was less inclined to publish accounts of the personal lives of politicians, Mills landed in the headlines after he and Ms. Foxe were arrested by the capitol police when, late one evening, they were found splashing in the reflecting pool of the Washington Monument.

Mills was succeeded as chair by Representative Al Ullman of Oregon, who started opening up the tax-writing process to more outside scrutiny. Ullman was receptive to tax reform proposals. Ironically, he was defeated for reelection in his rural Oregon district after proposing that the United States consider a VAT tax.

Ronald Wilson Reagan (1911–2004)

As the 40th president, Ronald Reagan was responsible for one of the largest, if not the largest, income tax cuts in U.S. history. A former movie actor and governor of California, Reagan was leader of the conservative wing of the Republican Party. At the time of his election, the United States was still suffering from the shock of the oil embargo adopted by the Organization of Petroleum Exporting Countries (OPEC). Moreover, American industry—especially manufacturing—was increasingly falling behind foreign competitors. A frequent critic of big government and high taxes, Reagan was elected on a platform that stressed tax cuts and increased business incentives. The Democrat-controlled Congress enacted Reagan's promised tax cuts in 1981. During the campaign, Reagan had promised that tax cuts would so stimulate the economy that productivity and tax revenues would soar. His own vice-president, George Bush, had labeled this plan "voodoo economics" during the primaries, in which Reagan prevailed. Bush's assessment was largely correct. Tax collections were far less than anticipated. When Congress failed to cut government spending but rather increased it, the federal budget deficit soared, forcing Congress to raise revenues largely through tax accounting changes to avoid an actual tax rate hike. But by 1986, with ever-increasing deficits, tax rates had to be increased. After serving two terms, Reagan was replaced by Vice-President George H. W. Bush, who in turn was defeated by Democrat Bill Clinton, who promptly raised taxes.

Franklin Delano Roosevelt (1882–1945)

President Franklin Delano Roosevelt (known as FDR) implemented the most radical change ever made in U.S. tax laws. Although the federal income tax had been collected since 1916, the tax fell only on the wealthiest Americans. When Roosevelt took office, only about 5 percent of Americans paid the tax. The relatively small national government was supported by customs duties from the tariff, various excise taxes, and an assortment of other taxes, including the income tax and the estate tax on the wealthy. When the United States joined the Allied side against the Axis powers in World War II, the government needed a massive amount of money to fund the war effort. Government economists also knew that higher taxes would be needed to control inflation during the war. The Roosevelt administration turned to the income tax, which had been used successfully in both the Civil War and World War I to raise large amounts of revenue. After those wars the income tax was scaled back. After World War II, however, it became a permanent fixture of the U.S. tax system. To make it work, the government instituted the pay-as-you-go system, which required employers to withhold the tax from workers' paychecks. The basic system enacted in 1942 continued into the 21st century. Initiation of this broad-based income tax system was the biggest change ever made in the U.S. tax system.

Irwin Schiff (1928–)

Irwin Schiff is a well-known author, tax protester, and self-proclaimed tax expert. Schiff is the best known of several tax protesters who believe that the income tax system is being imposed on the American people illegally. Unfortunately the president, Congress, the IRS, and the entire federal court system feel otherwise. The courts have consistently held since 1916 that the federal income tax is fully constitutional and enforceable. Schiff and other protesters argue that for tax purposes, *income* means only corporate profit and that the IRS and the government are illegally tricking Americans into paying their taxes. Schiff—who has had several run-ins with the federal government—appears to be sincere in his beliefs, which makes his arguments sound more persuasive. Schiff advocates filing "zero" tax returns—Form 1040s with zeros for entries to claim all withheld income taxes. Nearly all reasonable people reject the protesters' arguments. They point out that the protesters—few of whom are lawyers—base their arguments on twisted reasoning and court language taken out of context. Despite these criticisms, many people want to believe that the protesters' arguments are correct.

In the spirit of Schiff's argument, an unknown but large percentage of Americans are participants in an "underground economy." These people pay little or no tax because they underreport their income. Although individuals involved in illegal activities frequently fall into this category, otherwise respectable people are also members. They have a common characteristic: they have cash income that is not reported. Workers whose employers report their salaries and wages and withhold taxes from paychecks have much less opportunity to underreport. The self-employed, however, do underreport in large numbers. Flagrant nonreporting is contagious and is the surest way to undermine the integrity of the self-assessment tax system. Schiff, like several of his followers, was convicted of tax evasion and sentenced on 2006 to prison. He is scheduled to be released in 2016.

Adam Smith (1723–1790)

Improbable as it seems, an 18th-century Scot is still the most widely cited expert on tax reform. The Oxford-educated Adam Smith grew up around taxes—his father was comptroller of customs. Although Smith was a professor of philosophy at the University of Glasgow, he is now known as a political economist because of his landmark work *The Wealth of Nations*. Smith was acquainted with David Hume, Edward Gibbon, Edmund Burke, Samuel Johnson, and Sir Joshua Reynolds; he also met Voltaire, in Paris, where he started work on *An Inquiry into the Nature and Causes of the Wealth of Nations*. Economists normally cite the book for Smith's theory that self-interest drives the economy and competition controls it. The book also contains Smith's canons of taxation—Smith's view of a rational tax system. In Smith's opinion, a "good tax" should be equitable, certain, and economical. Two hundred years later, these canons are still the basic tests against which any tax reform must be judged. Interestingly, Smith is reputed to have shown Benjamin Franklin an early draft of his book and commented that he had written the book with the American colonies in mind.

6

Data and Documents

Understanding the Tax Reform Debate: Background, Criteria, and Questions

The following document is an edited version of a larger report prepared by the Government Accountability Office (GAO) that provides an overview of tax reform options. The excerpt omits a detailed discussion about specific tax reform criteria, including equity issues. Students should consult the full report, which is available at http://www.gao.gov/new.items/ d051009sp.pdf.

Source: Government Accountability Office, "Understanding the Tax Reform Debate: Background, Criteria, & Questions" (GAO #05–1009SP). September, 2005.

This report provides background information, criteria, and key questions for assessing the pros and cons of tax reform proposals, both proposals for a major overhaul of the current federal tax system and incremental changes to the system. First, we discuss how the size and role of the federal government drive the government's revenue needs. Second, we describe a set of widely accepted criteria for assessing alternative tax proposals. These criteria include the equity, or fairness, of the tax system; the economic efficiency, or neutrality, of the system; and the simplicity, transparency, and administrability of the system. The weight one places on each of these criteria is a value judgment and will vary among individuals. As we note, there are trade-offs to consider among these criteria, and we discuss how these criteria can sometimes be in conflict with each other. Finally, we turn to a consideration of the issues involved in transitioning from the current tax system to an alternative tax system.

The primary purpose of the tax system is to collect the revenue needed to fund the operations of the federal government, including its promises and commitments. Tax revenues may not fully match government spending each year, but over time, the federal government needs to be able to raise sufficient revenue to cover its current and expected financial obligations. Decisions about spending and the role of government have a direct impact on the government's ultimate revenue needs.

Whether the resources to fund government spending are provided through taxes or borrowing has consequences for the economy and the federal budget. Borrowing (which has often led to budget **deficits**) may be appropriate for federal investment such as building roads and scientific research, and during times of recession, war, and other temporary challenges. However, federal borrowing also absorbs scarce savings that would otherwise be available for growth-enhancing private investment. In addition, large amounts of borrowing may increase the share of interest payments in the federal budget overtime, placing additional pressure on future budgets.

One's view about the equity of a tax system is based on subjective judgments about the fairness of the distribution of **tax burdens**. The actual burden of a tax—the reduction in economic well-being caused by the tax—is not always borne by the people who pay the tax to the government because tax burdens can be shifted to other parties. For example, the burden of a tax on business can sometimes be shifted to consumers by increasing prices or to workers by decreasing wages. Public debates regarding the equity of the tax system reflect a range of opinions about who should pay taxes and how much of the tax burden should be shouldered by different types of taxpayers.

Taxes impose **efficiency costs** by altering taxpayers' behavior, inducing them to shift resources from higher valued uses to lower valued uses in an effort to reduce **tax liability**. This change in behavior can cause a reduction in taxpayers' well-being that, for example, may include lost production (or income) and consumption opportunities. Efficiency costs, along with the tax liability paid to the government and the costs of complying with tax laws, are part of the total cost of taxes to taxpayers. One of the goals of tax policy, but not the only goal, is to minimize compliance and efficiency costs. The extent to which efficiency costs can be reduced by reforming the tax system depends on the design features of the new tax system, such as the nature and number of any **tax preferences**.

Simplicity, transparency, and administrability are related but different characteristics of a tax system. Simplicity is a gauge of the time and other resources taxpayers spend to comply with the tax laws. This includes the time and resources spent on record keeping, learning about tax obligations, and preparing tax returns. The transparency of a tax system refers to taxpayers' ability to understand how their liabilities are calculated, the logic behind the tax laws, what their own tax burden and that of others is, and the likelihood of facing penalties for noncompliance. Administrability refers to the costs, ultimately borne by taxpayers, of collecting and processing tax payments as well as to the costs of enforcing the tax laws. While simplicity, transparency, and administrability are related concepts, they are not the same thing.

A very simple tax rule may not be transparent if the rationale for the rule is not clear. Similarly, not all simple taxes are easy to administer.

Designing tax policy requires making trade-offs among these criteria. For example, a proposal to improve the efficiency and simplicity of the tax code may involve eliminating exemptions or deductions originally introduced to improve the equity of the system. Moreover, some criteria include subjective elements. One individual's perception of the equity of a tax proposal can differ from another's. However, being subjective or objective does not make a criterion superior.

In addition to determining the type of tax system, policymakers also determine the amount of revenue to be raised, which involves balancing the costs of taxes against the benefits of government services. Despite the fact that no tax system is perfectly fair, efficient, simple, transparent, and without administrative costs, in general people are willing to pay taxes and bear the other costs of the tax system because they desire the benefits of government and understand that sufficient tax resources are necessary for a sound fiscal policy in the long term.

Finally, because moving to an alternative tax system creates winners and losers, transition rules may be included in tax reform proposals to mitigate some of the windfall gains and windfall losses that are likely to occur. However, debate exists as to whether transition rules, which are usually proposed on equity grounds, are appropriate because they may also reduce the efficiency of the tax system and temporarily make the tax system more complex.

Tax reform proposals can range from small changes to the tax code to more comprehensive changes. The issues and questions we discuss in this report are designed to apply to both incremental changes to the tax system, such as changing tax expenditures to encourage savings, and to more comprehensive tax reform proposals, such as switching from a predominantly income-based tax to a consumption tax base.

In addition to discussing the criteria used to evaluate changes to the tax system, this report provides information about economic and budgetary trends, the current tax system, and definitions of important tax concepts. For each section of the report, we provide a set of key questions designed to help identify the important features of the proposals. This is information that we believe would be useful for evaluating the proposals and identifying limitations of the data and analysis.

Revenue—Taxes Exist to Fund Government

Taxes exist to fund the services provided and the promises made by the government. Since tax revenue may not match spending in each year, the resources needed to fund government can be also be raised by borrowing (deficit financing). Both taxes and borrowing affect economic performance. Taxes can affect the economy because they alter decision making by people and businesses. Federal borrowing absorbs savings otherwise available for private investment and postpones the need to tax or reduce spending.

The Current Tax System

The federal tax system in the United States primarily consists of five types of taxes: (1) personal income taxes; (2) social insurance taxes (employee and employer contributions for Social Security, Medicare, and unemployment compensation); (3) corporate income taxes; (4) estate and gift taxes; and (5) excise taxes based on the value of goods and services sold and other taxes. The tax bases, rates, and collection points of the major federal taxes are summarized in table 6.1.

The revenue raised by the major federal taxes is determined by the size of their bases, their rates, and their levels of compli-

TABLE 6.1
Features of the Current Tax System

Type of tax	Tax base	Tax rates	Collection points
Personal income taxes (PIT)	**Regular PIT** Personal income, including income from wages, interest and dividends, capital gains, and small business income. Numerous tax expenditures exist that reduce the size of the tax base.	**Regular PIT** Graduated rate structure: Statutory marginal rates of 10%, 15%, 25%, 28%, 33%, and 35%. Deductions and other tax expenditures, such as refundable tax credits like the Earned Income Tax Credit, create a group of taxpayers who have no tax liability or a negative tax liability.	**Regular PIT** Employers withhold payments, but individuals file tax returns wherein they are also required to disclose nonwage income and remit appropriate taxes. Small business owners self-report income and remit taxes to the government.
	Personal alternative minimum tax (AMT) Taxable income exceeding certain threshold amounts based on filing status.	**Personal AMT** 26% or 28% depending on taxable income subject to the AMT. Individuals are eligible for a credit for a portion of the AMT paid in a prior year.	**Personal AMT** Individuals compare their regular PIT liability to their AMT liability and pay the greater of the two (less taxes previously withheld or paid during the year).
Corporate income taxes (CIT)	**Regular CIT** Corporate profits (total revenues less total expenses). Numerous tax expenditures exist that reduce the size of the tax base.	**Regular CIT** Statutory marginal rates range from 15% to 35%.	**Regular CIT** Corporations file tax returns and remit payment to the government.
	Corporate AMT Broader definition of the tax base (corporate income) than regular CIT; less generous accounting rules.	**Corporate AMT** 20% for all corporate income subject to the tax less the AMT credit for that tax year.	**Corporate AMT** Corporations compare regular CIT to corporate AMT liability and pay the greater of the two.
Social insurance taxes	**Social security** First $90,000 of employee wages.	**Social security** 6.2% employee contribution. 6.2% employer contribution. 12.4% for self-employed.	**Social security** Employers withhold taxes from employee paychecks. The self-employed remit taxes themselves.
	Medicare All wages.	**Medicare** 1.45% employee contribution. 1.45% employer contribution. 2.90% for self-employed.	**Medicare** Employers withhold taxes from employee paychecks. The self-employed remit taxes themselves.

(Continued)

TABLE 6.1
Features of the Current Tax System *(Continued)*

Type of tax	Tax base	Tax rates	Collection points
Unified transfer tax—estate, gift, and generation skipping tax (GST)	**Estate tax** Fair market value of the decedent's cash and securities, real estate, trusts, annuities, business interests, and other assets included in the decedent's estate at death less allowable deductions in excess of $1.5 million in 2005. There is an unlimited deduction for transfers to a surviving spouse.	**Estate tax** Rates range from 45% to 47% in 2005. As a result of recent tax legislation, estate tax rates will fluctuate before the estate tax is eliminated in 2010. However, the estate tax will be reinstated in 2011.	**Estate tax** Decedent's estate is responsible for filing returns and remitting payment to the government.
	Gift tax Tax is imposed on the value of lifetime taxable transfers of gifts of property. Applicable exclusion amount of $1 million for 2005. In addition, there is an annual exclusion of $11,000 per donee and an unlimited exclusion for tuition and medical payments.	**Gift tax** Rates range from 41% to 47% in 2005. Rates fluctuate in the same manner as for the estate tax in coming years. Gift tax will be retained following repeal of estate and GST.	**Gift tax** Gift donor is responsible for filing returns and remitting payment to the government.
	GST Total generation skipping transfers (such as from a grandparent to a grandchild) in excess of $1.5 million in 2005.	**GST** 47% (or highest statutory marginal tax rate for the estate tax) in 2005. GST rates decrease until the tax is repealed in 2010. GST is reinstated in 2011.	**GST** Depending on the form of the generation skipping transfer, gift donor, donee trustee, or decedent's estate is responsible for filing returns and remitting payment to the government.
Excise and other taxes	Selected goods, services, and other items (i.e., gasoline, alcoholic beverages, tobacco, airline tickets, etc.).	Various rates apply to different goods, services, and other items.	Generally collected by businesses, which remit payments to the government on a quarterly basis.

Source: Government Accountability Office, "Understanding the Tax Reform Debate: Background, Criteria, & Questions" (GAO #05-1009SP). September, 2005. Full report available at http://www.gao.gov/new.items/d051009sp.pdf.

ance. In addition, each tax base is affected by the size and growth rate of the economy.

Although called income taxes, the current federal individual and corporate income taxes have some features characteristic of a consumption tax. The current income tax system taxes the income of individuals and corporations, such as wages, interest, **dividend income, capital gains**, and other types of business income, including that of sole proprietorships and partnerships. (Some income is double taxed—corporate earnings are subject to the corporate income tax and are taxed again under the individual income tax when they are distributed as dividends or as realized capital gains when shareholders sell their stock.) However, some income is treated as it would be under a consumption tax where income that is saved or invested is exempted from tax until it is consumed. For example, up to certain limits, income that is contributed to individual retirement accounts and defined contribution pension plans is tax-deferred during accumulation. The result is a hybrid income consumption tax base wherein some types of savings and investment are exempt from taxation, but other types are not.

The current tax system includes tax expenditures, also called tax preferences, which reduce the size of the tax base. Tax expenditures are usually justified on the grounds that they promote certain social or economic goals. They grant special tax relief (through deductions, credits, exemptions, etc.) that encourages certain types of behavior by taxpayers or aids taxpayers in certain circumstances. Tax expenditures can promote a wide range of goals. For example, individual retirement accounts, discussed above, promote the goal of increased personal savings and investment, and the tax expenditures for owner-occupied homes encourage homeownership.

Summing one measure of tax expenditures, called outlay-equivalents, indicates that the aggregate value of tax expenditures was about $850 billion in fiscal year 2004. Outlay-equivalents are budget outlays that would be required to provide the taxpayers who receive the tax expenditures with the same after-tax income as would be received through the tax expenditures.[1] As an indication of the size and impact of tax expenditures, figure 6.1 compares them to discretionary spending. In some years the outlay-equivalents for income tax expenditures exceeded federal discretionary spending.

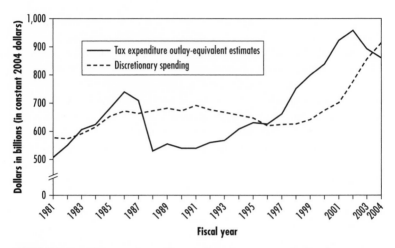

FIGURE 6.1: Sum of tax expenditure outlay-equivalent estimates compared to discretionary spending, 1981–2004.
Source: Government Accountability Office, "Understanding the Tax Reform Debate: Background, Criteria, & Questions" (GAO #05-1009SP). September, 2005. Full report available at http://www.gao.gov/new.items/d051009sp.pdf.

A few large income tax expenditures account for most of the aggregate value. The 10 tax expenditures . . . accounted for over 60 percent of the outlay equivalents in fiscal year 2004.

In the current tax system, tax rates vary across types of tax. Individual income and corporate income above certain levels are generally taxed at graduated rates. Taxes on individual income have six statutory marginal tax rates (the rate of tax paid on the next dollar of income that a taxpayer earns), ranging from 10 percent to 35 percent. Income earned by corporations has a statutory marginal rate structure that ranges from 15 percent to 35 percent. A separate rate structure exists for the individual Alternative Minimum Tax (AMT)—a tax on individual income that was originally designed to keep taxpayers with higher incomes from taking advantage of various tax provisions in order to pay little or no income tax. The current tax system also includes social insurance taxes, which are applied to wages at flat rates and remitted in equal shares by employees and employers. However, currently the first $90,000 of an individual's wages is subject to payroll taxes for Social Security, while all wages are subject to payroll taxes for Medicare.

The government's administrative burden and taxpayers' compliance burden vary depending on the type of taxpayer, the type of tax, and the collection point of the tax. For the individual income tax and social insurance taxes, the primary collection point occurs at the business level: employers bear the burden of withholding employees' taxes from their wages and remitting the tax payments to the government.

However, all individuals with income above certain thresholds based on personal allowances and a standard deduction still must file tax returns. The Internal Revenue Service (IRS) bears the administrative burden of monitoring taxpayer compliance and applying penalties to noncompliant taxpayers when necessary.

Historical Trends in Tax Revenue

Total federal tax revenues have fluctuated from roughly 16 to 21 percent of gross domestic product (GDP) over the last 43 years. In figure 6.2, total federal revenue is highest in 2000 at 20.9 percent of GDP and lowest in 2004 at 16.3 percent of GDP.

As figure 6.2 also illustrates, there have been important changes to the composition of federal revenues over the last 43 years. Corporate and excise tax receipts as a percentage of GDP have declined since 1960, while social insurance tax receipts have grown. The individual income tax and social insurance taxes have accounted for the majority of federal revenues during this period.

General Options Suggested for Fundamental Tax Reform

Recent years have seen a variety of proposals for fundamental tax reform. These proposals would significantly change the tax base, tax rates, and collection points of the tax.

Some of the proposals would replace the federal income tax with some type of consumption tax. The **retail sales tax, value-added taxes**, the personal consumption tax, and the **flat tax** are all types of consumption taxes. They vary in their collection points and structure. Similarly, collection points and rate structure will vary under an **income tax base**.

Text box 6.1 briefly summarizes the general categories of proposals.

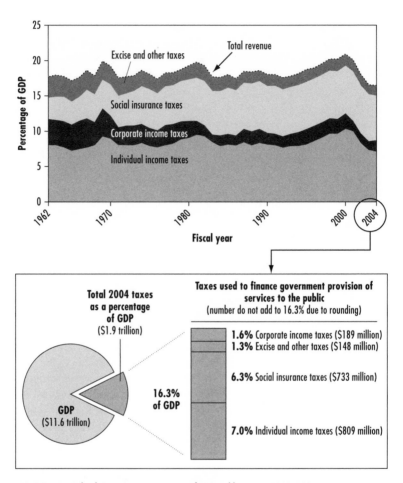

FIGURE 6.2: Federal revenue as a percentage of GDP and by source, 1962–2004.
Source: Government Accountability Office, "Understanding the Tax Reform Debate: Background, Criteria, & Questions" (GAO #05-1009SP). September, 2005. Full report available at http://www.gao.gov/new.items/ d051009sp.pdf.

Text Box 6.1: General Categories of Tax Reform Proposals

In recent years, lawmakers and analysts have suggested a variety of tax reform proposals that would change the way in which Americans pay taxes.

- *National retail sales tax (NRST)*: An NRST would be collected by businesses with, in most cases, no need for individuals to file tax returns (some taxpayers may be required to file tax returns in order to get back taxes that they paid on items for business use). The base would be retail sales of goods and services to final customers. Rates could not vary by individual.
- *Value-added taxes (VAT)*: VATs, now widely used in other countries, are collected by businesses with no need for individual tax returns. The VAT taxes all sales to both consumers and other businesses, adjusting for purchases from other businesses, which is equivalent to the base of an NRST. Rates do not vary by individual. Some experts believe a VAT would be easier to enforce than an NRST.
- *Flat tax*: A consumption flat tax would have the same base as an NRST or a VAT but would split collection between businesses and individuals by making wages deductible by businesses but taxable at the individual level. Generally, a single tax rate would apply to both individuals and businesses. Because of the individual component of the tax, wages up to some level can be exempted from tax, which would introduce some progessivity into this tax system.
- *Personal consumption taxes*: A personal consumption tax would look much like the current individual income tax. Individuals would report their income from wages, interest, dividends, and so on. It would differ in that borrowed funds would be included in the tax base, and funds that are saved or invested would be deducted. The base is equivalent to that of other consumption taxes. Rates could vary based on individual characteristics.
- *Reformed income tax system*: Over the years, the Department of the Treasury and others have discussed options for reforming the current tax system that would replace the current income tax with a more broadly based income tax. For example, proposals have been advanced to integrate the personal and corporate income tax and to eliminate preferences on certain types of income, which would broaden the tax base and could result in reduced tax rates (if the proposal were revenue neutral).

(Government Accountability Office, "Understanding the Tax Reform Debate: Background, Criteria, & Questions" (GAO #05-1009SP). September, 2005 Full report available at http://www.gao.gov/new.items/ d051009sp.pdf.)

Potential Impact of Alternative Taxes on Taxpayers and Administrators

The following document is an edited version of a larger report prepared by the General Accounting Office (GAO) that provides an accurate and unbiased appraisal of several leading tax reform proposals. The GAO is a nonpartisan federal government agency that prepares authoritative reports on a variety of subjects. Although the report is now a few years old, its content is still fresh because the report focuses on general tax reform proposals rather than specific ones. The report reviews in detail the consequences of adopting a modified income system, a national retail sales tax, a value-added tax, or a consumption tax.

This report has two stated basic objectives. The first is to describe the differences among alternative tax systems. The second is to describe how each alternative would affect taxpayers' burdens in complying with the new tax system and the government's ability to administer the system. Taxpayers' compliance includes filing of required tax returns, maintaining records to support the information on those tax returns, and accurately calculating the amount of tax to be reported—a factor that directly corresponds to the complexity of the tax system. The government's administrative responsibilities include processing the tax returns and ensuring the accuracy of those returns, collecting the tax and unpaid taxes from delinquent taxpayers, and providing taxpayer education and assistance.

Although this report is intended for policy makers, it is written in understandable language and provides many common-sense observations about the consequence of adopting a particular tax reform proposal in place of the current income tax system. This report is a good starting place for any student of tax reform. Abbreviations used in the report include:

- AMT—Alternative minimum tax
- CBIT—Comprehensive Business Income Tax
- CBO—Congressional Budget Office
- FICA—Federal Insurance Contributions Act
- IRA—Individual retirement arrangement
- IRS—Internal Revenue Service
- OECD—Organization for Economic Cooperation and Development

- RST—Retail sales tax
- TDA—Taxpayer delinquent account
- TDI—Taxpayer delinquency investigation
- VAT—Value-added tax

Source: General Accounting Office, "Tax Administration: Potential Impact of Alternative Taxes on Taxpayers and Administrators" (Letter Report, 01/14/98, GAO/GGD-98–37). Available at http://www.gao.gov/archive/1998/gg98037.pdf.

In the past few years, many proposals have been put forward to comprehensively reform the federal income tax system. Proponents of tax reform believe that replacing the current income tax system would improve the performance of the economy and make the tax system fairer. Proponents of several proposals also believe that reform would make administration of the tax law easier and less costly for the government and make compliance with the law easier for taxpayers.

To help Congress evaluate how tax reform would affect tax administration and the burdens taxpayers face in complying with the tax law, we studied, at our own initiative, the basic design features of several kinds of tax systems. The generic systems we studied are a national retail sales tax (RST), two types of value-added taxes (VAT), a flat tax, a personal consumption tax, and several versions of broad-based income taxes. Various forms of these alternative tax systems have been included in specific legislative proposals in the current and past sessions of Congress or have been prominent in tax reform discussions generally.

In this report, we describe (1) the major differences in design among the alternatives we studied and (2) how the alternatives, by incorporating different design features, may affect the taxpayers' burden of complying with the tax laws and the government's responsibilities for administering those laws. The basic design features we considered in contemplating alternative systems are the tax base (what is taxed); the types of taxpayers (whether individuals, businesses, or both are legally subject to tax); tax preferences (tax system provisions, including exemptions, deductions, credits, and multiple rates, directed at various economic and social goals); and the tax rate(s). We considered taxpayers' compliance burden to include the time, effort, and cost of filing the required returns and maintaining necessary records. We defined tax administration as including the government processing taxpayer returns, assessing compliance with tax laws, collecting taxes owed, and providing taxpayer assistance.

This report is intended to be a reference document for readers with different interests and needs. The letter summarizes (1) how the basic design features are included in the current income tax system and could be incorporated into alternative tax systems and (2) what the resulting impacts on compliance burden and administration could be. . . .

Background

Tax systems can have multiple goals. For example, in addition to the common goal of raising revenue for the government, goals can also include redistributing income, stabilizing the economy, and achieving various other social and economic objectives through the use of preferences. Generally speaking, the greater the number of goals, the more complex is the tax system.

Criteria and Trade-Offs Relating to the Design of a Tax System

Tax systems are commonly judged and compared according to four criteria: equity, economic efficiency, simplicity, and administrability. A tax system is generally considered better than alternatives that raise the same amount of revenue if it is more equitable, more economically efficient, simpler for taxpayers to comply with, and easier and less costly to administer. In this report, we focus on simplicity and administrability and do not analyze equity and efficiency. In deliberating on any changes to the current tax system, Congress would need to consider each of the four criteria.

Designing a tax system that is superior on each of the four criteria is difficult because the criteria frequently conflict with one another and trade-offs must be made. For example, a tax system that provides credits to low-income individuals may be judged by some to be more equitable than a system without this feature. However, if including credits makes it necessary for more individuals to calculate their income and file tax returns, the tax system could become more complex for both taxpayers and tax administrators.

The Current System

The federal tax system raised about $1.4 trillion in fiscal year 1995 through individual and corporate income taxes, payroll taxes, various excise taxes on certain goods and services, and estate and gift taxes. Income taxes accounted for 62 percent of total federal tax revenue.

The current income tax system includes an individual tax and a business tax. Wages, interest and dividend income, capital gains, and some types of business income, including that of sole proprietorships and partnerships, are taxed under the individual income tax. Individual income is taxed at graduated rates. Income earned by certain corporations is subject to a separate business income tax, also at different rates.

The current system provides exemptions and different tax rates on savings and investment through a variety of special provisions, such as the preferential treatment of pensions, individual retirement accounts, life insurance, annuities, state and municipal bonds, and capital gains. The result is a hybrid income-consumption system of taxation that exempts some types of saving and investment from tax but taxes others.

The current system includes numerous other tax preferences. Examples include the earned income credit; specific deductions for home mortgage interest, charitable contributions, and state and local taxes; and exclusions of employer contributions for health insurance.

Requirements for filing returns and performing other tax-related functions vary. All individuals with gross income above certain thresholds based on personal allowances and a standard deduction must file returns. Businesses have certain responsibilities beyond filing returns, including withholding and remitting employee income and payroll taxes, such as Social Security, Medicare, and unemployment taxes. Further, many businesses must send information returns to the Internal Revenue Service (IRS) and to individuals detailing income paid as wages, interest, and dividends. . . .

Kinds of Alternative Tax Systems We Studied

In the last several years, proposals for making fundamental changes to the tax system have been discussed by policymakers and tax experts in government, academia, and the private sector. An overview of tax reform design issues appears in [the section "Overview of Alternative Tax Systems and Design Issues"]. The alternative tax systems we studied are briefly described below. . . .

- A national RST would generally be collected by businesses making retail sales to final customers, with sales to other businesses generally not taxed.

- VATs, now widely used internationally, are business-level taxes levied directly on the sales of goods and services. All types of businesses, not just retail businesses, are subject to the tax, and sales to both consumers and other businesses are taxable. With the credit method VAT, used by most industrialized countries, businesses claim a credit for tax paid on their purchases from other businesses, and with the subtraction method VAT, businesses deduct the amount of their purchases of goods and services from other businesses. Thus, under a VAT, businesses pay tax on the value they add to the goods and services they purchase.
- The flat tax discussed in this report would have both business and individual components. The business tax would be similar to the subtraction VAT, except that wages, salaries, and pensions would be deducted by businesses. Individuals would pay tax on wages, salaries, and pensions received above levels of allowances for themselves and their dependents. The same, single (flat) tax rate would apply to both individuals and businesses.
- A personal consumption tax would look much like the current individual income tax in that individuals would continue to pay tax on many kinds of income, such as wages, salaries, and interest and dividend payments received. It would differ in that borrowed funds would be included in the tax base, and funds that are saved or invested would be deducted. In most proposals, the personal consumption tax has been supplemented by a business tax designed to ensure that business purchases of goods and services for consumption, such as nonpension fringe benefits, would be taxed.
- Income tax reform options that would replace the current income tax with a more broadly based income tax have been discussed by the Department of the Treasury and others over the years. Instead of being replaced by a consumption tax system, the current tax system could be changed to a broad-based income tax system by, for example, eliminating preferences on certain types of income. Some proposals for reforming the income tax would also change the collection point, or level, of tax. Options we studied include levying taxes on businesses

only, on businesses combined with a relatively simple individual tax, and primarily on individuals.

Results in Brief

The alternative tax systems we studied differ in their potential impacts on taxpayer compliance burden and tax administration. The different potential impacts of the tax systems can largely be explained by four basic design features: (1) the basis for taxation (income or consumption); (2) the type of taxpayer (individuals, businesses, or both); (3) preferential tax treatment (e.g., exemptions, special deductions, and credits) for certain individuals, businesses, or goods and services; and (4) the rate structure for individuals (single or multiple rates). Table 6.2 compares the design features of the tax systems we studied and shows:

- Many of the alternatives, namely, a national RST, VAT, flat tax, and personal consumption tax, would tax the same base—consumption.
- Two consumption tax alternatives—the national RST and the VAT—would levy tax only on businesses, while the other two—the flat tax and the personal consumption tax—could tax both individuals and businesses. Similarly, an income tax could be designed to tax individuals only, businesses only, or both individuals and businesses.
- Regardless of the base or the type of taxpayer, preferences could be included in any tax option,

TABLE 6.2.

Major Design Features of Alternative Tax Systems and the Current Tax System

Tax	# of rates	Tax base	Type of taxpayer indv/bus.	Preferences
Current system	Multiple	Income	x/x	x
Reformed income tax	Multiple	Income	x/x	x
NRST	One	Consumption	/x	x
VAT	One	Consumption	/x	x
Flat tax	Multiple	Consumption	x/x	x
Consumption tax	Multiple	Consumption	x/x	x

Source: General Accounting Office, "Tax Administration: Potential Impact of Alternative Taxes on Taxpayers and Administrators" (Letter Report, 01/14/98, GAO/GGD-98-37). Available at http://www.gao.gov/archive/1998/gg98037.pdf.

although the types of preferences provided would differ among systems.

- Finally, under income or consumption tax systems that include a tax on individuals, individuals could be taxed at different tax rates, possibly including a zero rate.

The differences in the four basic design features of the tax systems we studied explain in large part the differing potential impacts of the tax systems on taxpayer compliance burden and tax administration. For example, consumption-based taxes, such as the national RST, VAT, flat tax, and personal consumption tax, would eliminate many of the issues of defining and recognizing income that complicate income tax systems and, in this respect, reduce taxpayer compliance burden and tax administration activities. This is because under an income tax, taxpayers would be required to establish depreciation costs for different types of assets, account for income earned but not necessarily received, and keep records on the value of assets over time. Conversely, under a consumption tax, taxpayers could generally rely on records of sales, of purchases, or of funds actually received to calculate their tax liability. Simplifying the determination of tax liability for taxpayers could simplify assessing compliance and providing taxpayer assistance for tax administrators.

While different from income tax systems, the consumption-based systems could also differ from each other in their potential impact on taxpayer compliance burden and tax administration. For example, the personal consumption tax, requiring individuals to report their borrowing and saving, could be more burdensome for both taxpayers and administrators than other consumption-based systems. Another example involves a VAT and a national RST. Because all sales, not just retail sales, are included in a VAT, more recordkeeping and taxpayers could be required under a VAT than under a national RST. However, some experts believe that the additional records could make compliance assessment simpler for tax administrators.

Tax systems that would tax only businesses, rather than individuals and businesses, could reduce taxpayer compliance burden and the costs of tax administration by greatly reducing the number of taxpayers required to file returns. With a VAT, a national RST, or a business-level income tax, only businesses would be responsible for determining tax liability, filing returns, and remitting taxes. Individuals' compliance burdens could be eliminated. Tax administrators could focus on many fewer tax-paying entities, thus reducing the numbers of returns processed, actions taken to collect taxes owed, and taxpayer questions needing answers. In addition, businesses would no longer be required to withhold individual tax and file many types of information returns.

Tax systems that combine a business tax with a relatively simple individual tax, such as the flat tax or some versions of a reformed income tax, could add limited burden relative to a business-only tax. A simple individual tax, if administered largely through withholding and document matching, would have little need for the filing of individual tax returns. Tax systems requiring individuals to report more information about their personal finances, such as a personal consumption tax or a more complicated individual income tax, could add more burden than a business tax combined with a simple individual tax because more individuals could have to file tax returns and the returns would be more complicated. More tax returns and more complicated returns would make returns processing, assessing taxpayer compliance, and answering taxpayer questions more difficult for tax administrators.

The alternative tax systems in table 6.2 could all incorporate tax preferences. But, incorporating tax preferences—exemptions, special deductions, credits, or multiple rates on goods and services aimed at various economic and social goals—would generally add complexity. Tax preferences generally increase taxpayer compliance burden by complicating the determination of tax liability, adding recordkeeping requirements, and creating incentives to engage in tax planning. Similarly, tax administration would be made more complicated because tax administrators would need more information and time to verify the accuracy of tax returns and collect taxes owed. Tax administrators would also face more questions from taxpayers.

Tax systems with multiple tax rates for individuals, which could include income taxes and a personal consumption tax, do not need to add burden to taxpayers' calculation of tax liability compared to single-rate systems. Multiple rates for individuals add little to the burden of computing tax liability because the use of tax tables minimizes this burden. Rate schedules for multiple rate systems could include a zero rate or provide one implicitly through a standard deduction or personal exemptions. A zero rate or its equivalent would limit the number of taxpayers having to file returns and reduce the processing volume for tax administrators. However, tax systems with multiple rates could encourage tax planning, which would increase burden for taxpayers and make tax administration more complex.

In addition to impacts due to the four basic design features, the transition to an alternative tax system could affect taxpayer compliance burden and tax administration. The extent of the impact would depend on the type of transition allowed. For example, if a consumption tax system were adopted, a transition might allow for the gradual phaseout of depreciation. In the event of such a transition, taxpayers and tax administrators could be required to keep and check records for both the old and the new systems, complicating the determination and verification of tax liability during the transition period.

Major Design Differences among Alternative Tax Systems

Table 6.2 lists four basic design features of the tax systems we studied: (1) the basis for taxation (income or consumption); (2) whether individuals, businesses, or both would be subject to tax; (3) whether tax preferences could exist for certain individuals, businesses, or goods and services; and (4) the rate structure for individuals (single or multiple rates).

An Income or Consumption Tax Base

One major difference in the design of alternative tax systems is whether the tax base is income or consumption. An income tax system generally does not allow deductions for savings and requires that earnings on savings be measured and taxed as they are earned. Also, it generally requires that businesses depreciate their purchases of assets, that is, deduct the cost of assets over time rather than at the time they are purchased.

Consumption-based tax systems differ from income-based tax systems in that they generally exempt from tax income from savings and investment. The national RST, VAT, flat tax, and personal consumption tax would achieve this exemption in different ways. Under a national RST, businesses would generally not pay tax on goods and services they buy. Under the VAT and the flat tax, businesses could immediately deduct purchases of goods and services, including purchases of plant and equipment, that they made from other businesses. Under a personal consumption tax, funds that are saved or invested would be deducted by individuals.

Type of Taxpayer

Another major design difference among alternative tax systems is who would be subject to tax. Consumption and income taxes could be levied on individuals, businesses, or both. By levying tax directly on individuals, a tax system can make distinctions among individuals or households to account for varying individual circumstances by, for example, allowing deductions and multiple rates. Alternatively, a tax system could focus only on businesses and thus require fewer taxpayers.

The alternative consumption tax systems we considered differ from one another according to who would be taxed.

- The national RST and the VAT generally would only tax businesses. All types of businesses, including corporations, as well as partnerships and sole proprietorships, could be subject to tax. A national RST would differ from a VAT in that only businesses making retail sales would be subject to a national RST, while retail and wholesale businesses could be VAT taxpayers.
- The flat tax would collect much of the tax base from businesses but also would include a relatively simple individual tax.
- The personal consumption tax would continue to tax individuals. In conjunction with this tax, businesses could be subject to a supplemental tax.

Similar to the national RST, VAT, or flat tax, an income tax could be designed to collect taxes from businesses rather than from individuals. Such an income tax could, for example, disallow business deductions for wages and free individuals from filing returns. It would collect tax on all or part of individuals' incomes where the incomes were generated and before they were paid. Other income tax options would, like the current income tax system and the personal consumption tax system, tax most types of income at the individual level.

Preferential Treatment

Each of the various alternatives could include tax preferences, although the types of preferences provided would differ among alternatives. These preferences could include special deductions, exemptions, and/or credits, as well as various tax rates on different types of income or goods and services.

The types of taxpayers in a tax system would influence the type of preferences that could be allowed. Alternatives that tax individuals directly could include preferences designed to target specific groups of individuals. It would be more difficult for a tax system, such as a national RST or a VAT, that applied only to businesses to provide preferences for groups of individuals because businesses can apply different tax rates to goods and services but cannot distinguish among individuals. Preferences under businesslevel taxes could also include exemptions of specific types of businesses or activities.

Tax Rates

The fourth design difference is the rate structure for individual-level income or consumption tax systems. The alternatives that we considered that include an individual-level tax—the flat tax, the personal consumption tax, and several income tax options—could tax different individuals at different rates. All these options could include what is, in effect, a zero tax rate by providing a standard deduction or personal allowances. For example, under the flat tax, individuals with wage income under the personal allowance amount would not owe any individual tax; wage income above the deduction or allowance amounts would be taxed at a single rate. Individual-level taxes in general could apply a single tax rate or multiple rates.

Implications of the Alternative Tax Systems for Taxpayer Compliance Burden and Tax Administration

Because of differences in the four basic design features, the tax systems we studied would have different impacts on taxpayers' and tax administrators' responsibilities, and thus on taxpayers' compliance burden and the costs of tax administration. This section describes basic types of taxpayer and administration responsibilities and the potential effects of the alternative tax systems on each of them.

Taxpayers' and Tax Administrators' Basic Responsibilities

The taxpayer compliance burden created by any tax system will depend on how many taxpayers have tax-related responsibilities, such as filing tax returns, and on what difficulties these taxpayers face carrying them out. Similarly, tax administration is affected both by the number of taxpayers and by the difficulty of carrying out administrative responsibilities related to each taxpayer. Table 6.3 shows the basic taxpayer and tax administration responsibilities we identified.

In many respects, tax systems that are relatively easy for taxpayers to comply with will also be relatively easy to administer, and alternatives that are relatively burdensome for taxpayers will also be more difficult to administer. For instance, the more taxpayers that have to file returns, the more returns the administrators must process and accounts they must maintain. Likewise, a system's complexity resulting from exemptions, deductions, and other preferences could affect taxpayers and administrators similarly by increasing their respective burdens.

However, in some instances, burden could be shifted from government administrators to taxpayers or from taxpayers to government administrators. For example, U.S. businesses currently perform some duties to help ensure compliance, such as withholding and providing information returns, that tax administrators could do through other means.

Potential Effects of Alternative Tax Systems on Taxpayers'
and Administrators' Basic Responsibilities

The overall costs to taxpayers and tax administrators of carrying out their basic responsibilities under the tax systems we studied

TABLE 6.3
Basic Responsibilities of Taxpayers and Tax Administrators

Taxpayers' responsibilities	Tax administrators' related responsibilities
File tax returns	Process filed returns and maintain accurate taxpayer accounts
Determine correct tax amounts, maintain supporting documentation, and produce support for information on returns upon request of tax administrator	Devise programs, such as examination and document matching programs, to assess taxpayers' compliance with laws
Remit taxes owed	Collect taxes owed but not remitted
Get assistance, if necessary, from tax administrators or paid preparers to voluntarily comply	Assist taxpayers by answering specific questions, providing tax forms and publications, or helping with tax return preparation

Source: General Accounting Office, "Tax Administration: Potential Impact of Alternative Taxes on Taxpayers and Administrators" (Letter Report, 01/14/98, GAO/GGD-98-37). Available at http://www.gao.gov/archive/1998/gg98037.pdf.

are difficult to quantify. Even for the current income tax system, while IRS' administration costs are known, only very rough estimates exist for taxpayer compliance burden. This is because of the difficulty in separating accounting and recordkeeping costs for tax purposes from those that are incurred for other purposes and because taxpayers may not measure such costs. Estimates of taxpayer compliance burden for the current income tax vary widely, but all are many times larger than IRS' fiscal year 1998 budget of $7.8 billion.

In a qualitative sense, changing from the current income tax system to an alternative system would potentially affect each of the basic responsibilities that taxpayers and tax administrators have. The following discussion of possible impacts on each area of responsibility precedes a table summarizing them and relating them to different tax systems.

Return Filing and Processing

The tax systems we studied could differ significantly from each other in the number of returns filed by taxpayers and processed by administrators. Business-level tax systems generally have fewer filers than individual-level tax systems or systems that combine a business and individual tax. Business-level tax systems also generally require less information reporting.

The current income tax system is relatively complex in the sense that some income is taxed at the individual level, some at the business level, and some at both levels. In 1995, taxpayers filed and IRS processed about 116 million individual tax returns, of which about 18 million reported income from a sole proprietorship. Another 6 million returns were filed by partnerships and corporations. Employers, investment institutions, and others sent IRS about 1.1 billion information returns, including withholding documents for wages and information on investment earnings.

The alternative tax systems that would only tax businesses, such as the national RST or the VAT, would eliminate individual tax filing requirements. In addition, businesses would not be required to file information returns related to individuals. The total number of returns filed under these options would depend on how many businesses were subject to tax and on how frequently returns were required. For instance, while only businesses would be required to file tax returns under a national RST or a VAT, they could be required to file quarterly or monthly. Under a VAT, small businesses could be exempted, and under a national RST, wholesalers would not have to file tax returns.

The alternatives that include a business tax and a relatively simple individual tax would likely require return filing by businesses and by some individuals. However, the number of individual returns filed and processed under these alternatives could be significantly less than under the current income tax system. Under a flat tax or one reformed income tax option, a "return-free" filing system could be feasible because wages and salaries would be the only type of income subject to tax for many individuals. These employees would not have to file returns if employers withheld tax on wages during the year and made any necessary adjustments in withholding at the end of the year so that the amount of tax withheld equaled tax liability. If these alternatives also featured large standard deductions or personal allowances, the need for individual returns would be further reduced.

Under the personal consumption tax or certain reformed income tax options we studied, large numbers of individual tax returns and information returns could still be required. The individual tax under these systems would be relatively complex in the sense that many types of funds or income would be taxable for individuals. Withholding correct amounts of tax would be more difficult for employers and other businesses because final tax liability would depend on the total amount of income or funds individuals receive from many sources. Unless withholding was extended to other types of taxable funds, individuals would likely be required to account for all types of taxable funds on their tax returns, and employers and businesses could be required to provide information returns to both individuals and tax administrators. Under a personal consumption tax, additional information returns related to borrowing and saving could be required, resulting in increased burden for the businesses required to file the returns and for tax administrators.

Determining Correct Tax Amounts and Assessing Compliance

Because of differences in the four design features we discussed earlier, the tax systems we studied would differ in the burden experienced by taxpayers in determining their tax liability and in the costs to tax administrators of assessing compliance.

In terms of the first design feature, the basis for taxation, consumption-based taxes, such as the national RST, VAT, flat tax, and personal consumption tax, could make determining tax liabilities by taxpayers and, correspondingly, tax administrators' assessment of taxpayers' compliance simpler in some respects than income-based taxes. This is because many difficulties of defining and recognizing income would be eliminated. To measure income from saving and investment as it is earned, taxpayers have to estimate costs for depreciation, account for income earned but not necessarily received as cash, and keep records on the value of assets over time. Also, taxpayers could have to decide if expenses are deductible or must be capitalized. Similarly, tax administrators must be able to verify the income measurements required under an income tax. In contrast, consumption tax liability can generally be accurately calculated by taxpayers and verified by tax administrators by using records of sales, purchases, and funds actually received.

Whether an income or consumption tax system includes an individual tax and how complex that tax is would also affect the ease or difficulty of determining taxes and assessing compliance. Under the flat tax and one income tax option we considered, many individuals would face relatively few recordkeeping responsibilities and determining tax liability would be relatively simple, especially if taxes on wages were withheld by businesses. Tax administrators could largely administer these individual taxes by checking that proper amounts were withheld or by matching individual tax returns with information returns. Based on experience with the current income tax system, compliance would likely be high and few audits of individuals might be necessary. In contrast, under alternatives with more complex individual-level taxes, recordkeeping and tax determination burdens would likely be higher. For example, under some individual income tax options, individuals would have to keep records or receive information reports for many types of income. Under a personal consumption tax, individuals could be responsible for keeping records on borrowing and saving and including these amounts in their tax calculations. More extensive document matching and auditing would probably be needed to ensure a high level of compliance.

Even though a national RST and a VAT tax the same base—consumption—and the same type of taxpayer—businesses—they could still affect assessing tax compliance differently. For a national RST and a subtraction VAT, administrators would have to rely on businesses' own records to verify that the proper tax had been paid. However, with a credit VAT, there would be a certain amount of checking available through records of other businesses; this is thought by some tax specialists to improve compliance. Also, based on state and international experience, many experts believe that including sales of all types in the tax base and allowing businesses to deduct or receive a tax credit for purchases from other businesses, as under a VAT or flat tax, would have some compliance advantages over a national RST. While including sales of all types in the tax base would require more recordkeeping and more taxpayers, it could better ensure that business purchases would not be overtaxed, taxes of sales to households would be reported, and a paper trail would be created so that compliance could be better assessed.

Preferences—that is, exemptions, deductions, credits, and multiple rates on goods and services—could be part of any of the alternative tax systems we considered and could often complicate, but sometimes simplify, how tax liability is determined and verified. Preferences could force taxpayers to determine and tax administrators to verify whether an income or consumption item is taxable, nontaxable, deductible, or taxable at a different rate. The burdens associated with extensive use of preferences could include (1) more recordkeeping than otherwise, as was the case for the estimated 33 million individuals who reduced their tax liability by itemizing tax deductions for tax year 1993; (2) more time for determining and reporting tax liability; and (3) more tax planning by taxpayers. These burdens would require more audit time from tax administrators. On the other hand, in some instances, preferences given through exemptions could simplify taxpayers' burden. For example, if, as is commonly done with a VAT, large numbers of small businesses were exempted, they would not have to file returns or remit tax, thus easing their compliance burden. However, tax administrators would have to verify compliance by determining that only eligible taxpayers took the exemption.

The fact that some tax systems—the current income tax, versions of a reformed income tax, and the personal consumption tax—have or could have multiple rates on individuals imposes little additional burden on taxpayers or tax administrators except to the extent that multiple rates encourage tax planning. Graduated rates alone have little effect on the actual tax calculation burden of taxpayers who can determine their tax liability through a tax table. Tax administrators still must verify that proper rates have been applied. However, multiple tax rates could encourage taxpayers to devote resources to tax planning in order to avoid high marginal rates.

Tax Remittance and Collection

The issues related to this third area of taxpayer and tax administration responsibilities we discuss—tax remittances and collections—may not differ greatly among the tax systems we considered except that widely different numbers of taxpayers would be responsible for remitting the taxes. If individuals, including the 18 million individuals owning sole proprietorships, no longer had to file tax returns as individuals but only in their capacity as business owners, nonbusiness collection issues related to them would disappear. Similarly, if a simpler tax reduced the problems tax administrators found during examinations, or if changes in withholding or other information reporting reduced the number of mismatches requiring follow-up, tax administrators would be less likely to assess additional taxes they would then have to collect.

In its responsibility for collecting unpaid taxes from taxpayers who filed but did not pay the required tax or who did not file required returns, in fiscal year 1995, IRS' collection function disposed of millions of taxpayer delinquencies. Business delinquencies most commonly involved employment taxes.

An issue of concern to administrators in the current tax system involves businesses, particularly small ones, getting into financial difficulty and using collected taxes as working capital rather than remitting them to the administrators. This problem could continue under many of the alternatives we considered, including a national RST or a VAT, and it could be more pervasive if the amounts of taxes to be collected and remitted by businesses were higher than under the current income tax system or state sales tax systems. The amounts could be higher because specific businesses would be processing federal taxes on their sales in addition to their payrolls and could face a greater temptation to retain some of the money for their own use. More frequent remitting and filing could reduce noncompliance but increase the burden on businesses.

Taxpayer Questions and Assistance

Although the universe of taxpayers who must file returns could change under the various alternatives, those who would still need to file would likely have questions that still needed to be answered. Even if a "return-free" tax system were adopted, questions about individuals' involvement with the system would still arise. However, the probable reduction in the number of taxpayers, particularly individuals, under some of the alternatives and the removal of certain complex provisions, such as defining and recognizing income and providing deductions, would likely reduce the overall level of assistance needed.

On the other hand, the more complications introduced under any alternative tax system, such those introduced with many preferences, the greater would be the need for tax administrator assistance in those areas. Greater assistance would also be needed for certain alternatives' distinctive complicating features, such as the personal consumption tax's reliance on borrowing and savings information. The more radical the departure from the current income tax system, the more likely that assistance or education would be needed in the short term.

Table 6.4 provides primarily qualitative information about alternative tax systems in the four areas of taxpayer and tax administrator responsibilities we have just discussed. . . .

Transition to a New Tax System

A wide range of options exist for moving from the current income tax system to an alternative tax system, and the way that any transition is formulated could have significant effects for economic efficiency, equity, taxpayer compliance burden, and tax administration. Many transition issues involve how income and deductions related to saving done before the transition to the new system should be treated. Consumption taxes, while designed to encourage new saving, could tax existing saving when it is used for consumption; in general, existing saving would not be subject to tax again under the current income tax system. Special rules designed to exempt existing saving from tax could burden individuals with additional record-keeping, filing, and tax determination requirements and create additional tax compliance issues for tax administrators. Another transition issue involves whether tax credits and other tax benefits already earned under the current tax

TABLE 6.4

Potential Implications of Alternative Tax Systems for Taxpayers and Tax Administrators

Tax system alternative	Taxpayer and tax administrator responsibilities			
	Return filing and processing	Determining correct tax amounts and assessing compliance	Tax remittance and collection	Taxpayer questions and assistance
Current system	In 1995, some 116 million individual tax returns, including 18 million sole proprietorships; 6 million corporate and partnership tax returns filed; 1.1 billion information returns filed by businesses and other payers	Need to define and recognize income; wide range of exemptions, deductions, full and credits; complex calculations; documents matched, enhancing compliance; about 1.7 and 2.0 percent of individual and corporate returns, respectively, examined in fiscal year 1995	Collections needed from millions of nonfilers and filers without remittance; small businesses' employment taxes a particular problem	Almost 111 million calls answered by IRS in fiscal year 1995
Reformed income tax alternatives	For individual tax, number of filers contingent on amounts of standard deduction and withholding; number of tax and information returns reduced (or possibly eliminated) by options taxing more income at business level	Complexity owing to measuring capital income; continuing need to match documents and/or examine returns; possibly complex changes needed to tax all income but tax planning possibly reduced	For individual tax, most tax remitted by businesses through withholding, but delinquent accounts possibly increased by taxing more types of income; individual remittances and delinquent accounts possibly reduced under other options	Most current questions still relevant, unless individual-level tax simplified or eliminated
National RST	Businesses, including at least 10 million retailers and service providers, responsible for filing periodically during the year if they sell to final consumers; information returns generally eliminated	No need to define and recognize income; difficulties arising from exemptions for goods and services or sales to businesses and from incompatible state and federal tax systems; compliance chiefly verified by checking records on sales, not income	Nonbusiness collection issues eliminated; delinquent amounts a continuing concern given large collections by businesses and possible temptation for small businesses, especially, to use collections as working capital	Fewer questions than under the current system because of individuals not filing and fewer likely areas of inquiry
VAT	About 24 million businesses (corporations, partnerships, and sole proprietorships) responsible for filing, unless small businesses exempted; information returns eliminated	No need to define and recognize income; fraud potential related to exports; credit VAT: tax system complicated by exemptions of goods or services and multiple rates, administration simplified by invoice mechanism; subtraction VAT: unlike credit VAT situation, multiple rates and exemptions not suitable and auditing dependent on business' own records	Nonbusiness collection issues eliminated; tax payment spread over all businesses, not just those selling to final consumers; if small businesses not exempt, collection problems increased	Fewer questions than under the current system because of individuals not filing and fewer likely areas of inquiry

Flat tax	Both individuals and businesses responsible for filing, though nearly half of individuals possibly excused owing to large personal allowances; no information returns for savings or investment	Compliance aided by no need to define and recognize income, by fewer deductions, and by continued withholding; unlike credit VAT situation, auditing dependent on business' own records	Fewer delinquency problems for individuals likely if withholding continues, but small business difficulties similar to difficulties with employment taxes	Taxpayer assistance on many complex issues unneeded owing to tax's simplicity, although individual returns still possibly required
Personal consumption tax	Large number of individual filers likely; business filings or allocations to individuals needed; new information returns possible	Many issues of defining and recognizing income eliminated; information returns, audits needed to verify borrowing (e. g., on credit cards), proceeds from sales of assets, and savings	Withholding possibly not closely matching tax liability, with more returns owing taxes after matching, possibly leading to more delinquent accounts than otherwise	Questions on filing requirements, filing status, account information continued but not on calculations of capital income; new questions on borrowing, proceeds from sales of assets, savings

Source: General Accounting Office, "Tax Administration: Potential Impact of Alternative Taxes on Taxpayers and Administrators" (Letter Report, 01/14/98, GAO/GGD-98-37). Available at http://www. gao.gov/archive/1998/gg98037.pdf.

should be made available under a new system. For example, what would happen to depreciation expenses for existing investments that businesses would have been able to deduct if the current tax were retained? Depending on how these and other compliance issues are addressed, taxpayer compliance burden and tax administration responsibilities could be greater in the transition period than when a new system is fully phased in. . . .

Other Issues

Other issues, many of which are hard to handle even now, could also have significant implications for both taxpayers and tax administrators under most, if not all, of the alternative tax systems we discuss. Some of these issues are (1) the extent to which employee benefits, such as employer-provided health insurance, should be included in the tax base; (2) how to deal with the special complexity and difficulty of taxing financial services; (3) how housing would be taxed; (4) whether governments and nonprofit organizations should be taxpayers and filers; and (5) how international activities would be taxed.

Another important issue would be the relationship between federal tax filing and reporting requirements and those of states and localities, especially in those jurisdictions that currently piggyback on the federal income tax system. Changing the federal system could effectively force states to change or even abandon their own income tax systems because they depend on the federal tax infrastructure. For example, states depend on IRS' information reporting program and use income reported on federal tax returns as a starting point on state returns. . . .

Overview of Alternative Tax Systems and Design Issues

In recent years, several proposals for fundamental tax reform have been put forward. These proposals would significantly change tax rates, the tax base, and the level of tax (whether taxes are collected from individuals, businesses, or both). Some of the proposals would replace the federal income tax with some type of consumption tax levied only on businesses. Consumption taxes levied only on businesses include retail sales taxes (RST) and value-added taxes (VAT). The flat tax would also change the tax base to consumption but include both a relatively simple individual tax along with a business tax. A personal consumption tax, a consumption tax levied primarily on individuals, has also been proposed. Similar changes in the level at which taxes are collected could be made while retaining an income tax base.

If Congress were to decide to fundamentally reform the tax system, it would have to make choices on several basic issues, all of which have ramifications for tax compliance and administration. First, should the tax base be income or consumption or, as under the current system, contain elements of both? Second, should taxes be levied on businesses, individuals, or both? Third, should the preferential tax treatment now given certain goods and services and types of income be maintained or eliminated, thereby affecting not only the economic and social purposes for which they were established but also the ease of tax compliance and administration? Fourth, if consumption is chosen as the appropriate base for taxation, what issues arise in making the transition to a new tax base, and how should certain types of consumption that are difficult to tax be treated? Fifth, how should a new system be designed to balance other goals for the tax system with the goals of minimizing administration costs and taxpayers' costs of compliance?

This [section] provides some information to clarify these issues. To summarize, the fundamental difference between income and consumption taxes lies in the treatment of saving and investment. A broad-based income tax would tax all income, regardless of how it is used and regardless of its source. In particular, a broad-based income tax would tax income regardless of whether it is used for consumption or for saving and investment and would tax all income earned from saving and investment. In contrast, consumption taxes are designed to tax only income used for consumption, exempting from tax income used for saving and investment. Under certain conditions, this is equivalent to exempting income earned from saving and investment. As a result, different consumption taxes can in effect exempt saving and investment in different ways, so taxes that appear to be different may actually tax the same base—consumption.

Either income or consumption taxes could be levied on individuals, businesses, or both. The choice of level of tax (or collection point) alone does not determine the base of a tax or who will bear its economic burden. The choice does affect how equitable and how complicated a tax may be because it determines whether a tax can treat different individuals differently. A tax levied on individuals, whether income- or consumption-based, can tax different individuals at different rates or allow for adjustments such as standard deductions or exemptions for dependent children. Such provisions may make a tax system more equitable but may also make it more complicated. A tax levied solely on businesses (corporations, partnerships, and sole proprietorships) may be simpler to administer and less costly for taxpayers to comply with because the number of tax return filers may be substantially reduced and because only businesses would be burdened with tax-related recordkeeping and accounting tasks. Businesses may keep some of the same records for nontax purposes and are likely to be more efficient at recordkeeping and accounting than individuals. However, taxes levied solely on businesses are generally less able to make distinctions between individuals for reasons of equity.

The current income tax is actually a hybrid tax because it exempts or lightly taxes some types of saving and investment from tax but fully taxes other forms. The current tax also grants preferential treatment to some types of consumption, such as employer-provided health insurance. A reformed tax system could treat saving and investment more uniformly, either by taxing all saving and investment (income tax) or by exempting all saving and investment (consumption tax). A reformed tax system could also eliminate the current tax code preferences for certain items of consumption, or it could maintain them.

Any tax reform that replaces the current income tax with a consumption tax would have to address transition issues. In particular, the decision on whether to tax existing wealth could raise issues of fairness and administrability, as well as revenue. Moving to a consumption tax would also raise issues involving the taxation of some types of goods and services that could be difficult to tax from an administrative viewpoint. In particular, decisions would have to be made on whether to tax and how to tax financial services, housing, fringe benefits, and goods and services produced by governments and nonprofit organizations. Some of these items are also difficult to tax under an income tax.

While some information is readily available on administration costs, policymakers have little quantitative evidence on compliance costs available to help them design new tax systems. Compliance costs are costs that individuals and businesses incur, in terms of both time and money directly spent, because of the requirements of the tax system. Compliance and administrative costs are interrelated because some of the tasks that need to be done to collect taxes can be done by the public sector or by the private sector. As a result, costs can be shifted from one sector to another. The distribution of compliance costs among different businesses and individuals is also important for understanding the full effects of a tax system. A major difficulty in measuring compliance costs is disentangling accounting and recordkeeping costs due to taxes from the costs that would have been incurred in the absence of the tax system. As a result, the reliability of the results of most compliance cost studies that have been done to date is limited.

Differences between Income and Consumption Taxes

The fundamental difference between income and consumption taxes lies in their treatment of saving and investment. Income can be used for either consumption or saving and investment, so if income used for saving and investment can be exempted from tax, the result will be a tax only on consumption. As described below, the exemption of saving and investment can be done in different ways, so consumption taxes can be structured differently and yet still have the same overall tax base. In contrast, income taxes do impose a tax on income used for saving and investment. The current tax system is considered to be a hybrid between a pure income tax and a pure consumption tax because it effectively exempts some types of saving and investment from tax but taxes other forms of saving and investment.

Tax Treatment of Saving and Investment

Consumption taxes exempt income used for saving and investment in one of two ways. First, tax could be levied only on income used to buy consumption goods and services. This could be done by either taxing the sale of goods and services to consumers or by allowing individuals to deduct the amount that they saved from their income. Under either method, the income that an individual saved or invested would not be taxed until it was used to buy goods and services for consumption.

A second way to in effect exempt saving and investment from tax would be to exempt income earned by saving and investment. Over time, not taxing the earnings from savings can be economically equivalent to not taxing the amount saved originally. As shown below, under certain conditions, these two methods are equivalent in that what individuals earn through saving, the rate of return to saving and investing, is the same under these seemingly different taxes.

In contrast to consumption taxes, a broad-based income tax would levy tax on income from all sources and tax income regardless of whether it is used for consumption or saving. In particular, all income earned from saving and investment would be taxed, and income used for saving and investment would not be deductible.

A simple example focusing on the treatment of saving under alternative taxes is shown in table 6.5. The example compares an income tax to two forms of consumption taxes and also illustrates the equivalence between a consumption tax that exempts saving and a tax that exempts the income earned by saving. The three cases all assume that $100 of wage income is earned in the first year, all after-tax income is saved the first year and used for consumption in the second year, the interest rate is 10 percent, and the tax rate is 20 percent.

The first column shows how a person would be taxed under an income tax. In the first year, the individual pays $20 in tax and saves the balance ($80). In the second year, the individual earns $8 in income from saving, and pays $1.60 in tax on this income, leaving $86.40 available for consumption. Because the earnings from saving were subject to income tax, the after-tax rate of return on the individual's saving is 8 percent ($6.40 of $80) instead of the 10-percent rate ($8 of $80) that would be earned without the income tax.

TABLE 6.5

Tax Treatment of Saving Under Income and Consumption Taxes

	Income tax	Consumption tax — income from saving not taxed	Consumption tax — saving not taxed
First year			
Wages	$100	$100	$100
Tax	20	20	0
Amount saved or invested	80	80	100
Second year			
Additional income from saving or investment	$8	$8	$10
Tax	1.6	0	22
After-tax return on saving	8%	10%	10%
Present value of taxes	$21.45	$20	$20

Source: General Accounting Office, "Tax Administration: Potential Impact of Alternative Taxes on Taxpayers and Administrators" (Letter Report, 01/14/98, GAO/GGD-98-37). Available at http://www.gao.gov/archive/1998/gg98037.pdf.

The second column shows how the same individual would be taxed under a consumption tax that does not tax the earnings from saving. In the first year, the individual would be taxed on all income ($100), so as in the income tax case, $20 would be paid in tax and $80 would be available for saving. Once saved, the $80 would earn a 10-percent rate of return ($8), as in the income tax case, but the earnings from saving would not be taxed. Thus, in the second year, the individual has $80 in saving and $8 in earnings on saving available for consumption, for a total of $88. In comparison to the income tax, which reduced the after-tax return to saving, the rate of return on saving is not changed by the consumption tax, so incentives to consume today or save for the future are not affected by the tax.

The third column shows how the individual would be taxed if a deduction from income for saving were allowed and all income was taxable when used for consumption. In the first year, the individual owes no tax because all income is saved. The $100 saved earns a 10-percent rate of return, so in the second year $110 would be available for consumption before tax. The individual would owe $22 in tax (20 percent of $110), leaving $88 for consumption after tax, the same amount as under the first consumption tax.

While the two consumption taxes differ in the timing of the tax payment, as shown under this simple scenario, they would be equivalent in terms of the present value of the taxes owed. Under the first consumption tax, the individual owes $20 in tax the first year and none in the second; under the alternative consumption tax, the individual owes no tax in the first year and $22 in the second. In this case, having no tax liability in the first year would enable the person to save an additional $20 and therefore earn an additional $2, just enough to pay the additional tax in the second year. Therefore, under the consumption tax in column 2, the individual effectively prepays the consumption tax in the first year by paying $20; the individual has paid an amount that if saved, would earn just enough to pay the tax owed when the income was actually used for consumption.

Income and Consumption Taxes Can be Levied
on Individuals or Businesses

Both income and consumption taxes can be levied on individuals or businesses. Whether collected from individuals or businesses, ultimately, individuals will bear the economic burden of any tax.

The choice of whether to collect a tax at the business level or the individual level depends on whether it is thought to be desirable to levy different taxes on different individuals. A business-level tax, whether levied on income or consumption, can be collected "at source"—that is, where it is generated—so there can be many fewer tax filers and returns to administer. Business-level taxes cannot, however, directly tax different individuals at different tax rates. Individual-level taxes can allow for distinctions between different individuals; for example, standard deductions and/or graduated rates can be used to tax individuals with low income (or consumption) at a lower rate than individuals with greater income (consumption). Other individual characteristics can also be taken into account. For example, adjustments can be made for family size, and additional deductions could be allowed for individuals who have very large medical expenditures. However, individual-level taxes require more tax returns, impose higher costs to comply with the tax laws, and would generally require a larger tax administration system.

Table 6.6 shows alternative income and consumption taxes that are levied on businesses only, individuals only, or both. The current tax, while including a separate corporate income tax, could be considered primarily an individual tax because most types of income are taxed under the individual tax. As mentioned earlier, the current tax is somewhere in between a pure income and pure consumption tax because under the current tax some forms of income from saving are taxed, while others, particularly income from saving for retirement, are not taxed. We describe each of the alternative taxes in the next two sections.

Alternative Types of Consumption Taxes

The second column of table 6.6 shows two business-level consumption taxes (a national RST and a VAT), a mixed business/individual-level consumption tax (a flat tax), and an individual-level consumption tax (a personal consumption tax). . . .

National Retail Sales Tax

The consumption tax that Americans are most familiar with is the retail sales tax, which in many states, is levied when goods or services are purchased at the retail level. The RST is a consumption tax because only goods purchased by consumers are

TABLE 6.6
Alternative Income and Consumption Taxes by Level of Tax

Level of tax/ features	Consumption type	Income type
Business level	National RST	Income VAT
Tax collected at source	Consumption VAT	
No filing by individuals	Credit method	
No way to vary tax rates or base according to characteristics of individuals	Subtraction method	
Mixed business/individual	Flat tax	Comprehensive Business Income Tax discussed by Treasury, augmented with wage tax at individual level
Many parts of tax base collected at source		
Simplified individual tax base		
Standard deductions or exemptions can be used for progressivity, but no way to apply different rates to entire tax base		
Individual level	Personal consumption tax	Integrated individual income tax
Tax levied on individuals		
Business must allocate income or consumption to individuals; may also withhold and remit tax		
Tax rates can vary according to individual characteristics		

Source: General Accounting Office, "Tax Administration: Potential Impact of Alternative Taxes on Taxpayers and Administrators" (Letter Report, 01/14/98, GAO/GGD-98-37). Available at http://www.gao.gov/archive/1998/gg98037.pdf.

taxed, and sales to businesses, including sales of investment goods, are generally exempt from tax. In contrast to an income tax, then, income that is saved is not taxed until it is used for consumption.

Under a national RST, different tax rates could be applied to different goods, and the sale of some goods could carry a zero tax rate (exemption). However, directly taxing different individuals at different rates for the same good would be very difficult.

Value-Added Tax

. . . A VAT, . . . like the RST, is a business-level consumption tax levied directly on the purchase of goods and services. The two taxes differ in the manner in which the tax is collected and paid. In contrast to a retail sales tax, sales of goods and services to consumers and to businesses are taxable under a VAT. However, businesses can either deduct the amount of their purchases of goods and services from other businesses (under a subtraction VAT) or can claim a credit for tax paid on purchases from other businesses (under a credit VAT). Under either method, sales between businesses do not generate net tax liability under a VAT because the amount included in the tax base by businesses selling goods is equal to the amount deducted by the business purchasing goods. The only sales that generate net revenue for the government are sales between businesses and consumers, which is the same case as the RST.

Flat Tax

The flat tax was developed in the early 1980s by economists Robert Hall and Alvin Rabushka. The Hall-Rabushka flat tax proposal includes both an individual tax and a business tax. As described by Hall and Rabushka, the flat tax is a modification of a VAT; the modifications make the tax more progressive (less regressive) than a VAT. In particular, the business tax base is designed to be the same as that of a VAT, except that businesses are allowed to deduct wages and retirement income paid out as well as purchases from other businesses. Wage and retirement income is then taxed when received by individuals at the same rate as the business tax rate. By including this individual-level tax as well as the business tax, standard deductions can be made available to individuals. Individuals with less wage and retirement income than the standard deduction amounts would not owe any tax.

Personal Consumption Tax

A personal consumption tax would look much like a personal income tax. The major difference between the two is that under the consumption tax, taxpayers would include all income received, amounts borrowed, and cash flows received from the sale of assets, and then deduct the amount they saved. The remaining amount would be a measure of the taxpayer's consumption over the year. When funds are withdrawn from bank accounts, or stocks or bonds are sold, both the original amount saved and interest earned are taxable because they are available for consumption. If withdrawn funds are reinvested in another qualified account or in stock or bonds, the taxable amount of the withdrawal would be offset by the deduction for the same amount that is reinvested.

While the personal consumption tax would look like a personal income tax, the tax base would be the same as an RST. Instead of collecting tax on each sale of consumer products at the business level, a personal consumption tax would tax individuals annually on the sum of all their purchases of consumption goods. Because it is an individual-level tax, different tax rates could be applied to different individuals so that the tax could be made more progressive, and other taxpayer characteristics, such as family size, could be taken into account if desired.

Alternative Types of Income Taxes

Table 6.6 also shows three alternative integrated income taxes: a business-level tax (income VAT), a mixed business/individual-level tax (Comprehensive Business Income Tax (CBIT)), and an individual-level income tax (integrated individual income tax).

All income taxes, including the current tax, differ from consumption taxes in their treatment of investment. To produce the goods and services they sell to customers, businesses purchase a variety of goods and services themselves. While some of the goods and services that businesses buy are used up immediately in production, other goods and services, such as plant and equipment, for example, can be used for production over time. The purchase of goods and services of this type is referred to as investment, and such goods and services are also referred to as business assets.

Under consumption taxes, investment is either exempt from tax or deducted immediately (expensed). In fact, all business purchases of goods and services, regardless of how long they are used in production, are exempted or expensed because business purchases generally do not represent consumption.

Investment is treated differently under an income tax. Under an income tax, income is calculated by deducting costs from revenue; therefore, the costs that businesses incur from purchasing goods and services, including the costs from owning assets, should be deductible. For goods and services that are used up or become worthless in the same year as they were purchased, the economic cost to the business will be the entire amount they paid for the goods and services, and therefore the entire amount should be deductible immediately (in the same tax year as the goods or services were purchased). However, business assets do not lose all their value immediately; rather, they wear out or become obsolete over time (the assets depreciate). The economic cost incurred by owning an asset during a particular year is the reduction in the value of the asset during that year, so under an income tax businesses should be allowed a deduction for depreciation that reflects this reduction in value. Depending on the rate at which an asset loses economic value, a proportion of the amount originally paid for the asset can be deducted for depreciation each year until the total amount deducted over time is equal to the amount originally paid.

The current income tax differs from the other three income tax options in that the current corporate income tax is not integrated with the personal income tax. For example, under the current tax, corporations cannot deduct dividends paid to shareholders, and shareholders pay tax on the dividends they receive. Noncorporate income, however, is taxed only once, at the individual level. The three options would tax all forms of business income, corporate and noncorporate, once. . . .

The alternative income taxes differ in that they would tax income at different levels. The income VAT would tax all income at the business level. Wage income would be taxed at the business level by denying businesses a deduction for wages. The CBIT option would tax business income, including profits and the interest income earned by lenders, at the business level. Wage income would be taxed at the individual level.

Integrated Individual Income Tax

An integrated individual-level income tax would be much like the current tax. Individuals would be responsible for filing returns containing information on all taxable forms of income. The taxation of business income would change so that all business income, corporate and noncorporate, would be taxed at the individual level. The tax rate would apply to all forms of income that an individual receives, and individuals could be taxed according to graduated rates if desired. Other taxpayer characteristics, such as the number of dependent family members, could be taken into account.

CBIT

The CBIT option would move much of the taxation of business income to the business level, leaving a simplified individual tax return (primarily wages). Business deductions for interest and dividends would not be allowed, so this form of income would be taxed at the business level. The business tax would effectively withhold tax on business income at the tax rate that was applied to the business. Since individuals would file returns, standard deductions and dependency exemptions could be part of the system. A flat rate could be levied at the individual level, or multiple rates chosen, but the multiple rates would only apply to the simplified base.

Income Value-Added Tax

An income VAT would move the taxation of wage income to the business level as well. No individual returns would be necessary, so the burden of complying with the tax law would be eliminated for individuals. An income VAT would not allow businesses to deduct dividends, interest, or wages, so the income VAT remitted by businesses would include tax on these types of income. Calculations would not have to be made for different individuals, which would simplify tax administration and compliance burdens but not allow for treating different individuals differently.

Ten Largest Tax Expenditures

The current income tax system and most proposed tax systems contain "tax incentives" that are designed to encourage specific taxpayer behavior. For example, eligible taxpayers receive a tax deduction that results in a lower tax if the taxpayer makes a contribution to an Individual Retirement Account. The tax incentive is designed to encourage retirement savings—something Congress believes is a worthwhile goal. By allowing the deduction, however, the Treasury has foregone revenue in the amount of tax lost. Accordingly, the Treasury has labeled these amounts "tax expenditures." Tax expenditures include not only exclusions from income but also deductions, credits, exemptions, deferrals, and other preferential tax treatments. The current tax system contains hundreds of such tax incentives—all designed to encourage taxpayer behavior.

Because tax expenditures directly impact government revenues, the government needs to estimate the amount of tax that will be lost from these provisions. The Treasury annually prepares a Tax Expenditures Budget that lists the tax incentives and their "cost" to the Treasury in the form of lost taxes.

When incremental reform is undertaken—including the expected upcoming reforms—Congress examines individual tax incentives to determine whether the incentive really justifies its cost in lost revenue. The Tax Expenditure Budget is used in the same way when studying tax reform proposals. It allows an examination of how much will be lost in revenues if particular features of the present tax code are retained, such as the deduction for home mortgage interest.

Eliminating tax expenditures has the same practical effect as raising tax rates: more revenues for the government. Proponents of low taxes however may not view cutting tax expenditures as "raising taxes." Politically the distinction is important. Current tax reform proposals include cutting or even eliminating certain tax expenditures that are viewed as unfair or ineffective. Those who benefit from the tax breaks are of course reluctant to lose them.

The following chart, based on the Tax Expenditure Budget, illustrates that the 10 largest individual tax expenditures "cost" the federal government $651 billion—tax revenue the government foregoes by allowing the tax breaks. The largest tax expenditure—the exclusion for employer-provided medical insurance premiums and medical care—is also one of the fastest growing.

TABLE 6.7

2010's Ten Largest Individual Tax Expenditures (Figures in billions of dollars)

Tax expenditure	One-year cost
1. Exclusion for employer contributions for medical insurance and care	105.7
2. Deduction for mortgage interest on owner-occupied homes	90.8
3. Net exclusion of employer pension plan contributions and earnings	83.8
4. Reduced rates of tax on dividends and long-term capital gains	77.7
5. Making work to pay credit	59.7
6. Earned income tax credit	56.2
7. Child tax credit	55.1
8. Exclusion for medical benefits	54.6
9. Deduction for charitable contributions	36.8
10. Deduction for nonbusiness state and local taxes	30.7

Source: Congressional Research Service, *Compendium of Background Material on Individual Provisions,* prepared for United States Senate, Committee on the Budget, Government Printing Office, December 2010.

Excerpts from *Progress and Poverty*

The following document is an excerpt from Henry George's Progress and Poverty. Henry George was a 19th-century tax reformer whose writings are still influential today. George championed the "single tax" on land to replace all other taxes, a concept that continues to attract proponents worldwide. Many of George's economic and social observations about the operation of tax systems are still relevant today.

Source: Henry George, *Progress and Poverty* (New York: Appleton's, 1897).

Chapter 22: Changes Wrought in Economic and Social Life

The advantages that would be gained by substituting, for the numerous taxes by which the public revenues are now raised, a single tax levied upon the value of land, will appear more and more important the more they are considered. . . .

To abolish the taxation, which acting and reacting now hampers every wheel of exchange and presses upon every form of industry, would be like removing an immense weight from a powerful spring. Imbued with fresh energy, production would start into new life and trade would receive a stimulus that would be felt to the remotest arteries.

The present method of taxation operates upon exchange like artificial deserts and mountains.

To get goods through a customs house can cost as much as carrying them around the world. Today taxation operates upon energy, and industry, and skill, and thrift, like a fine upon those qualities. If you have worked harder and built yourself a good house while I have been contented to live in a hovel, the tax-gatherer now comes annually to make you pay a penalty for your energy and industry, by taxing you more than me. If you have saved while I have wasted, you are mulct while I am exempt.

We punish with a tax the man who covers barren fields with ripening grain; we fine him who puts up machinery and him who drains a swamp. How heavily these taxes burden production only those realize who have attempted to follow them through their ramifications, for their heaviest part is that which falls in increased prices. Manifestly these taxes are in their nature akin to the Egyptian Pasha's tax upon date trees. If they do not cause the trees to be cut down, they at least discourage the planting.

Taking Taxes off Industry

To abolish these taxes would be to lift the whole enormous weight of taxation from productive industry. The needle of the seamstress and the great manufactory, the horse and the locomotive, the fishing boat and the steamship, the farmer's plough and the merchant's stock, would be alike untaxed. All would be free to make or to save, to buy or to sell, unfined by taxes, unannoyed by the tax-gatherer. Instead of saying to the producer, as it does now, "The more you add to the general wealth the more shall you be taxed!" the Government would say, "Be as industrious, as thrifty, as enterprising as you choose, you shall have your full reward! You shall not be fined for making two blades of grass grow where one grew before; you shall not be taxed for adding to the aggregate wealth."

And will not the community gain by thus refusing to kill the goose that lays the golden eggs; by thus refraining from muzzling the ox that treadeth out the corn; by thus leaning to industry, and thrift, and skill, their natural reward, full and unimpaired? For there is to the community also a natural reward. The law of society is each for all as well as all for each. No one can keep to himself the good he may do, any more than he can keep the bad. Every productive enterprise, besides its return to those who undertake it, yields collateral advantages to others. If a man plant a fruit tree, his gain is that he gathers the fruit in its time and season. But in addition to his gain, there is a gain to the whole community. Others than the owner are benefitted by the increased supply of fruit; the birds that it shelters fly far and wide; the rain that it helps to attract falls not alone on his field; and, even to the eye which rests upon it from a distance, it brings a sense of beauty. And so with everything else. The building of a house, a factory, a ship, or a railway, benefits others besides those who get the direct gains.

Well may the community leave to the individual producer all that prompts him to exertion; well may it let the labourer have the full reward of his labour, and the capitalist the full return of his capital. For the more that labour and capital produce, the greater grows the common wealth in which all may share. And in the value or rent of land this general gain is expressed in a definite and concrete form. Here is a fund which the state may take while leaving to labour and capital their full reward.

Opening New Opportunities

To shift the burden of taxation from production and exchange to the value or rent of land would be not merely to give new stimulus to the production of wealth; it would be to open new opportunities. For under this system no one would care to hold land unless to use it, and land now withheld from use would everywhere be thrown open to improvement. And it must be remembered that this would apply not merely to agricultural land but to all land. Mineral land would be thrown open to use as would agricultural land; and in the heart of a city no one could afford to keep land from its most profitable use, or on the outskirts to demand more for it than would be warranted by the use to which it could be put at the time.

Whoever planted an orchard, or sowed a field, or built a house, or erected a manufactory, no matter how costly, would have no more to pay in taxes than if he kept so much land idle. The owner of a vacant city lot would have to pay as much for the privilege of keeping other people off it until he wanted to use it as his neighbour who has a fine house upon his lot. It would cost as much to keep a row of tumble-down shanties upon valuable land as it would were the land covered with a grand hotel or a pile of great warehouses filled with costly goods.

The selling price of land would fall; land speculation would receive its death-blow; land monopolization would no longer pay. Thus there would disappear the premium which, wherever labour is most productive, must now be paid before labour can be exerted. The farmer would not have to pay out half his means, or mortgage his labour for years, in order to obtain land to cultivate. The company that proposed to erect a manufactory would not have to expend a great part of its capital for a site. And what would be paid from year to year to the state would be in lieu of all the taxes now levied upon improvements, machinery and stock.

Effect upon the Labour Market

Consider the effect of such a change upon the labour market. Instead of labourers competing with each other for employment, and in their competition cutting down wages to the point of bare subsistence, employers would compete for labourers and wages would rise to the fair earnings of labour. For into the labour market would have entered the greatest of all competitors for the employment of labour, a competitor whose demand cannot be satisfied—the demand of labour itself. The employers of labour would have to bid not merely against other employers, all feeling the stimulus of greater trade, but against the ability of labourers to become their own employers upon the natural opportunities thrown open to them by the tax which prevented monopolization.

With natural opportunities thus set free to labour, with capital and improvements exempt from tax and exchange released from restrictions the spectacle of willing men unable to turn their labour into the things they want would become impossible; the recurring paroxysms which paralyse industry would cease; every wheel of production would be set in motion; trade would increase in every direction and wealth augment on every hand.

But great as they thus appear, the advantages of a transference of all public burdens to a tax upon the value of land cannot be fully appreciated until we consider the effect upon the distribution of wealth.

Effect upon Individuals and Classes

. . . Who can say to what infinite powers the wealth-producing capacity of labour may not be raised by social adjustments that will give to the producers of wealth their fair proportion of its advantages and enjoyments? Every new power engaged in the service of man would improve the condition of all. And from the general intelligence and mental activity springing from this general improvement of conditions would come new developments of power of which as yet we cannot dream.

When it is first proposed to put all taxes upon the value of land and thus to confiscate rent, there will not be wanting appeals to the fears of small farm and homestead owners, who will be told that this is a proposition to rob them of their hard-earned property.

But a moment's reflection will show that this proposition should commend itself to all whose interests as landholders do not largely exceed their interests as labourers or capitalists, or both.

Take the case of the mechanic, shopkeeper or professional man who has secured himself a house and plot where he lives and which he contemplates with satisfaction as a place from which his family cannot be ejected in case of his death. Although he will have taxes to pay upon his land, he will be released from taxes upon his house and improvements, upon his furniture and personal property, upon all that he and his family eat, drink and wear, while his earnings will be largely increased by the rise of wages, the constant employment, and the increased briskness of trade.

And so with the farmer. I speak not of the farmer who never touches the handles of a plough, but of the working farmer who holds a small farm which he cultivates with the aid of his sons and perhaps some hired help. He would be a great gainer by the substitution of a single tax upon the value of land for all the taxes now imposed on commodities because the taxation of land values rests only on the value of land, which is low in agricultural districts as compared with towns and cities, where it is high. Acre for acre, the improved and cultivated farm, with its buildings, fences, orchard, crops and stock, would be taxed no more than unused land of equal quality. For taxes, being levied upon the value of the land alone, would fall with equal incidence upon unimproved as upon improved land.

Government Simplified

The great wrong that takes wealth from the hands of those who produce, and concentrates it in the hands of those who do not, would be gone. Whatever disparities continued to exist would be those of nature, not the artificial disparities produced by the denial of equal rights. Wealth would not only be enormously increased; it would be distributed in accordance with the degree in which the industry, skill, knowledge or prudence of each contributed to the common stock.

It is not possible without too much elaboration to notice all the changes that would be wrought, or would become possible, by a change that would readjust the very foundation of society. Among these is the great simplicity that would become possible in government. To collect taxes, to prevent and punish evasions, to check and countercheck revenues drawn from so many distinct sources, now make up a large part of the business of government. An immense and complicated network of governmental machinery would thus be dispensed with. The rise of wages, the opening of opportunities for all to make an easy and comfortable living, would at once lessen and would soon eliminate from society the thieves, swindlers and other classes of criminals who spring from the unequal distribution of wealth. Thus the administration of the criminal law, with all its paraphernalia of policemen, detectives, prisons and penitentiaries, would cease to make such a drain upon the vital force and attention of society. The legislative, judicial and executive functions of government would be vastly simplified. Society would thus approach the ideal of Jeffersonian democracy.

Chapter 23: The Master Motive of Human Action

In thinking of the possibilities of social organization, we are apt to assume that greed is the strongest of human motives, and that systems of administration can be safely based only upon the idea that the fear of punishment is necessary to keep men honest—that selfish interests are always stronger than general interests. Nothing could be further from the truth.

Whatever is potent for evil may be made potent for good. The change I have proposed would destroy the conditions that distort impulses in themselves beneficent, and would transmute the forces that now tend to disintegrate society into forces that would tend to unite and purify it.

Give labour a free field and its full earnings; take for the benefit of the whole community that fund which the growth of the community creates, and want and the fear of want would be gone. The springs of production would be set free and the enormous increase of wealth would give the poorest ample comfort. Men would no more worry about finding employment than they worry about finding air to breathe; they need have no more care about physical necessities than do the lilies of the field. The progress of science, the march of invention, the diffusion of knowledge, would bring their benefits to all. With this abolition of want and the fear of want, the admiration of riches would decay and men would seek the respect and approbation of their fellows in other modes than by the acquisition and display of wealth. In this way there would be brought to the management of public affairs, and the administration of common funds the skill, the attention, the fidelity and the integrity that can now be secured only for private interests.

Short-sighted is the philosophy that counts on selfishness as the master motive of human action. It is blind to facts of which the world is full. It sees not the present, and reads not the past aright. If you would move men to action, to what shall you appeal? Not to their pockets, but to their patriotism; not to selfishness, but to sympathy.

Self-interest is, as it were, a mechanical force—potent, it is true; capable of large and wide results. But there is in human nature what may be likened to a chemical force that melts and fuses and overwhelms, to which nothing seems impossible. "All that a man hath will he give for his life"—that is self-interest. But in loyalty to higher impulses men will give even life.

How Men Are Inspired

It is not selfishness that enriches the annals of every people with heroes and saints. It is not selfishness that on every page of the world's history bursts out in sudden splendour of noble deeds or sheds the soft radiance of benignant lives. It was not selfishness that turned Gautama's back to his royal home or bade the Maid of Orleans lift the sword from the altar; that held the Three Hundred in the Pass of Thermopylae, or gathered into Winkelried's bosom the sheaf of spears; that chained Vincent de Paul to the bench of the galley, or brought little starving children, during the Indian famine, tottering to the relief stations with yet weaker starvelings in their arms. Call it religion, patriotism, sympathy, the enthusiasm for humanity, or the love of God—give it what name you will; there is yet a force that overcomes and drives out selfishness; a force that is the electricity of the moral universe; a force beside which all others are weak. Everywhere that men have lived it has shown its power, and today, as ever, the world is full of it. To be pitied is the man who has never seen and never felt it. Look around! Among common men and women, amid the care and the struggle of daily life, in the jar of the noisy street and amid the squalor where want hides—every here and there is the darkness lighted with the tremulous play of its lambent flares. He who has not seen it has walked with shut eyes. He who looks may see, as says Plutarch, that "the soul has a principle of kindness in itself, and is born to love, as well as to perceive, think, or remember."

What Prevents Harmonious Development

. . . And this force of forces—which now goes to waste or assumes perverted forms—we may use for the strengthening, and building up, and ennobling of society, if we but will, just as we now use physical forces that once seemed but powers of destruction.

All we have to do is to give it freedom and scope. The wrong that produces inequality; the wrong that in the midst of abundance tortures men with want or harries them with the fear of want; that stunts them physically, degrades them intellectually, and distorts them morally, is what alone prevents harmonious social development. For "all that is from the gods is full of providence. We are made for co-operation—like feet, like hands, like eyelids, like the rows of the upper and lower teeth."

There are people who are unable to conceive of any better state of society than that which now exists—to whom the idea that there could be a state of society in which greed would be banished, prisons stand empty, individual interests be subordinated to general interests, and no one would seek to rob or to oppress his neighbour, is but the dream of impracticable dreamers. Such people—though some of them write books, and some of them occupy the chairs of universities, and some of them stand in pulpits—do not think. If they were accustomed to dine in those eating-houses where the knives and forks are chained to the table, they would deem it the natural, ineradicable disposition of man to carry off the knife and fork with which he has eaten.

Take a company of well-bred men and women dining together. There is no struggling for food, no attempt on the part of anyone to get more than his neighbour; no attempt to gorge or to carry off. On the contrary, each one is anxious to help his neighbour before he partakes himself; to offer to others the best rather than pick it out for himself; and should anyone show the slightest disposition to prefer the gratification of his own appetite to that of the others, or in any way to act the pig or pilferer, the swift and heavy penalty of social contempt and ostracism would show how such conduct is reprobated by common opinion.

Differing States of Society

All this is so common as to excite no remark, as to seem the natural state of things. Yet it is no more natural that men should not be greedy of food than that they should not be greedy of wealth. They are greedy of food when they are not assured that there will be a fair and equitable distribution that will give enough to each. But when these conditions are assured, they cease to be greedy of food. And so in society, as at present constituted, men are greedy of wealth because the conditions of distribution are so unjust that instead of each being sure of enough, many are certain to be condemned to want. It is the "devil catch the hindmost" of present social adjustments that causes the race and scramble for wealth, in which all considerations of justice, mercy, religion and sentiment are trampled underfoot; in which men forget their own souls and struggle to the very verge of the grave for what they cannot take beyond. But an equitable distribution of wealth, by exempting all from the fear of want, would destroy the greed of wealth, just as in polite society the greed of food has been destroyed.

Consider this existing fact of a cultivated and refined society, in which all the coarser passions are held in check, not by force, not by law, but by common opinion and the mutual desire to please. If this is possible for a part of a community, it is possible for a whole community. There are states of society in which everyone has to go armed—in which everyone has to hold himself in readiness to defend person and property with the strong hand. If we have progressed beyond that, we may progress still further.

The Incentives to Progress

But it may be said, to banish want and the fear of want would be to destroy the stimulus to exertion; men would simply become idlers, and such a happy state of general comfort and content would be the death of progress. This is the old slaveholders' argument, that men can only be driven to labour with the lash. Nothing is more untrue.

Want might be banished, but desire would remain. Man is the unsatisfied animal. He has only begun to explore, and the universe lies before him. Each step that he takes opens new vistas and kindles new desires. He is the constructive animal; he builds, he improves, he invents and puts together, and the greater the thing he does, the greater the thing he wants to do. He is more than an animal. Whatever be the intelligence that breathes through nature, it is in that likeness that man is made. The steamship, driven by her throbbing engines through the sea, is in kind, though not in degree, as much a creation as the whale that swims beneath. The telescope and the microscope, what are they but added eyes, which man has made for himself? The soft webs and fair colours in which our women array themselves, do they not answer to the plumage that nature gives the bird? Man must be doing something, or fancy that he is doing something, for in him throbs the creative impulse; the mere basker in the sunshine is not a natural, but an abnormal man.

It is not labour in itself that is repugnant to man; it is not the natural necessity for exertion that is a curse; it is only the labour that produces nothing—exertion of which he cannot see the results. To toil day after day, and yet get but the necessaries of life, this is indeed hard; it is like the infernal punishment of compelling a man to pump lest he be drowned, or to trudge on a treadmill lest he be crushed. But released from this necessity, men would but work the harder and the better, for then they would work as their inclinations led them; then, would they seem to be really doing something for themselves or for others.

The fact is that the work which improves the condition of mankind, the work which extends knowledge and increases power, enriches literature, and elevates thought, is not done to secure a living. It is not the work of slaves, driven to their task either by the lash of a master or by animal necessities. It is the work of men who perform it for its own sake, and not that they may get more to eat or drink, or wear, or display. In a state of society where want was abolished, work of this sort would be enormously increased.

Mental Powers Liberated

I am inclined to think that the result of confiscating rent in the manner I have proposed would be to cause the organization of labour, wherever large capitals were used, to assume the cooperative form, since the more equal diffusion of wealth would unite capitalist and labourer in the same person. But whether this would be so or not is of little moment. The hard toil of routine labour would disappear. Wages would be too high and opportunities too great to compel any man to stint and starve the higher qualities of his nature, and in every avocation the brain would aid the hand. Work, even of the coarser kinds, would become a lightsome thing. The tendency of modern production to subdivision would not involve monotony or the contraction of ability in the worker, since toil would be relieved by short hours, by change, by the alternation of intellectual with manual occupations.

The greatest of all the wastes that the present constitution of society involves is that of mental power. How infinitesimal are the forces that concur to the advance of civilization, as compared with the forces that lie latent!

How few are the thinkers, the discoverers, the inventors, the organizers, as compared with the great mass of the people! Yet such men are born in plenty; it is the conditions that permit so few to develop.

How little have the best of us, in acquirements, in position, even in character, that may be credited entirely to ourselves; how much to the influences that have moulded us. Who is there, wise, learned, discreet, or strong, who might not, were he to trace the inner history of his life, turn like the Stoic Emperor to give thanks to the gods, that by this one and that one, and here and there, good examples have been set him, noble thoughts have reached him and happy opportunities opened before him. Who is there, with his eyes about him and having reached the meridian of life, who has not sometimes echoed the thought of the pious Englishman, as the criminal passed to the gallows, "But for the grace of God, there go I." How little does heredity count as compared with conditions. This one, we say, is the result of a thousand years of European progress, and that one of a thousand years of Chinese petrifaction. Yet place an infant in the heart of China and, but for the angle of the eye or the shade of the hair, the Caucasian would grow up as those around him, using the same speech, thinking the same thoughts, exhibiting the same tastes. Change Lady Vere de Vere in her cradle with an infant of the slum and will the blood of a hundred earls give you a refined and cultured woman?

To remove want and the fear of want, to give to all classes leisure, comfort and independence, the decencies and refinements of life, the opportunities of mental and moral development, would be like turning water into a desert. The sterile waste would clothe itself with verdure and the barren places where life seemed banned would ere long be dappled with the shade of trees and musical with the song of birds. Talents now hidden, virtues unsuspected, would come forth to make human life richer, fuller, happier, nobler. For in those round men who are stuck into three-cornered holes and three-cornered men who are rammed into round holes; in those men who are wasting their energies in the scramble to be rich; in those who in factories are turned into machines, or are chained by necessity to bench or plough; in those children who are growing up in squalor, vice and ignorance, are powers of the highest order, talents the most splendid. All they need is the opportunity to bring them forth.

Consider the possibilities of a state of society that gave that opportunity to all. Let imagination fill out the picture; its colours grow too bright for words to paint. Consider the moral elevation, the intellectual activity, the social life. Consider how by a thousand actions and interactions the members of every community are linked together and how, in the present condition of things, even the fortunate few who stand upon the apex of the social pyramid must suffer, though they know it not, from the want, ignorance and degradation that are underneath. The change I propose would be for the benefit of everyone, even the greatest landholder. Would he not be safer of the future of his children in leaving them penniless in such a state of society than in leaving them the largest fortune in this? Did such a state of society anywhere exist, would he not buy entrance to it cheaply by giving up all his possessions?

Treasury Deputy Assistant Secretary (Tax Analysis) Leonard Burman Testimony before the House Committee on Ways and Means Subcommittee on Oversight

Reformers across the world have suggested that nations adopt "green taxes"—taxes that promote environmental sensitivity and discourage environmental damage. The current income tax system contains a number of "green" tax incentives but could be reformed to include more. The following document contains testimony from a U.S. Treasury official before the House Committee on Ways and Means Subcommittee on Oversight regarding specific tax incentives included in President Bill Clinton's budget for 2000 that are designed to enhance the environment. These proposals illustrate how the tax system can be used to encourage taxpayers to make environmentally sensitive choices.

Source: Hearing on the Impact of Tax Law on Land Use, Conservation, and Preservation. Testimony of Treasury Deputy Assistant Secretary Leonard Burman, House Committee on Ways and Means, Oversight Subcommittee, House of Representatives, Washington, D.C., September 30, 1999. Available at http://waysandmeans.house.gov/legacy/oversite/106cong/9-30-99/9-30burm.htm.

I appreciate the opportunity to discuss with you today the Administration's proposed tax incentives for improving the environment.

Earlier this year, in the Administration's budget for FY 2000, the President proposed initiatives to help build livable communities for the 21st century. The Livable Communities initiative aims to provide communities with tools, information, and resources they can use to enhance the quality of life of their residents, enhance their economic competitiveness, and build a stronger sense of community. As part of that initiative, the Administration proposed a new financing tool—Better America Bonds—to help preserve green space and improve water quality for future generations. The proposed $700 million in tax credits over 5 years would make available $9.5 billion in bond authority over 5 years for investments by state, local, and tribal governments to preserve green space, create or restore urban parks, protect water quality, and clean up abandoned industrial sites. The Administration also proposed to make permanent the tax incentive to clean up brown-fields in targeted areas, generally low-income communities, which is scheduled to expire on December 31, 2000. The revenue cost of that proposal is estimated to be $0.6 billion over five years.

The Administration's budget also included a $3.6 billion package of tax incentives over 5 years to encourage energy efficiency, reduce greenhouse gas emissions, and develop renewable energy sources. The tax incentives are part of a larger package of complementary initiatives. In addition to the $3.6 billion of tax incentives, the Administration proposed to increase funding for R&D in energy efficient technology and renewable energy, a new Clean Air Partnership Fund to boost state and local efforts to reduce air pollution and greenhouse gases, and $1.8 billion for global climate change research.

My comments today will focus on an explanation of the Administration's tax initiatives for improving the environment.

Better America Bonds

Americans are concerned that the quality of the environment surrounding their communities is threatened by sprawl, that scenic vistas are being lost, that watersheds are eroding and contaminated, and that public access to outdoor recreation is diminishing.

To address these concerns, the Administration proposed the creation of a new financial tool—referred to as "Better America Bonds"—for use by state, local, and tribal governments, often in partnership with non-profit organizations, in securing more livable communities. Better America Bonds are modeled after the current-law provision for Qualified Zone Academy Bonds. The federal government would, in effect, pay all the interest on Better America Bonds for fifteen years, thereby significantly lowering the cost of financing below that attainable by state, local, and tribal governments issuing traditional tax-exempt bonds. Mr. Matsui and others have introduced a proposal for Better America Bonds in H.R. 2446.

Interest would effectively be paid to holders of Better America Bonds in the form of a credit that could be claimed by the bondholder against Federal income taxes otherwise due. The credit rate would be set by the Treasury Department on a daily basis based on "aa" corporate yields of comparable maturity. The credit rate set for the day on which the bonds were sold would apply for the life of the bonds. (This method of setting credit rates was established by Treasury regulations for Qualified Zone Academy Bonds sold on or after July 1, 1999.)

Issuers of Better America Bonds would pay no interest for the 15-year term of the bonds; their only obligation would be for repayment of principal after 15 years.

H.R. 2446 is designed to enhance the marketability of Better America Bonds by allowing buyers of the bonds to strip the "coupons," in the form of the tax credits, from the obligation to repay principal and sell the two pieces separately, much the same way that Treasury obligations are stripped. This would permit non-taxable entities, such as pension funds and endowments, to benefit from the gain between the current value of the stripped principal and the repayment of principal at par upon redemption, while another taxable investor claims the tax credit.

The proceeds of Better America Bonds could be used for the following purposes:

- Acquisition of land for open space, wetlands, parks, or greenways. Acquired land would be owned by a government or a tax-exempt entity whose exempt purposes include environmental protection.
- Construction of public access facilities such as campgrounds, hiking and biking trails on publicly-owned land or land owned by a tax-exempt entity whose exempt purposes include environmental protection.
- Remediation of publicly-owned parks and open space to improve water quality by planting trees or other vegetation, creating settling ponds to control runoff, or remediating conditions caused by the prior disposal of toxic or other waste.
- Acquisition of permanent easements on privately-owned open land that prevent commercial development and

any substantial change in the character or use of the land. Such easements could be held by governments or tax-exempt entities.

• Environmental assessment and remediation of brownfields owned by state or local governments under certain circumstances.

In general, property acquired with the proceeds of Better America Bonds would be available only for public use and use by tax-exempt entities, but not private use. The one exception is with respect to remediated brownfields, which could be sold to a private entity for private development, with the sale proceeds made available to repay principal.

After the expiration of the 15-year term of the bonds, tax-exempt entities whose purpose includes environmental protection would have first option to buy any land acquired with Better America Bond proceeds if the government decided to sell the land for development or otherwise convert it to a non-qualifying use. A tax-exempt entity's option to buy could be exercised at the original price of the land, rather than its current market price. The tax-exempt entity would be required to hold the property in its qualifying use in perpetuity.

The Administration proposes $1.9 billion of authority to issue Better America Bonds each year for 5 years beginning in 2000 (i.e., a total of $9.5 billion of bond authority). The Environmental Protection Agency (EPA) would administer an annual, open competition among state, local, and tribal governments for authority to issue these bonds, subject to published EPA guidelines. H.R. 2446 stipulates that, as part of the competitive application process, the EPA should try to distribute the credits among the states in proportion to their populations.

Projects qualifying for Better America Bonds, with the exception of remediated brownfields converted to private use, could be financed by tax-exempt bonds under current law. Indeed, states and localities occasionally use tax-exempt bonds for these purposes. But more needs to be done. Benefits from environmental projects are often so diffused over time and distance that taxpayers within particular local jurisdictions are reluctant to finance such projects with conventional tax-exempt bonds.

Compared to traditional tax-exempt bonds, Better America Bonds would significantly reduce the financing costs to local taxpayers of environmental projects. For example, annual payments of principal and interest on a traditional 30-year, $1 million tax-exempt bond issue would, at current interest rates, be about $71,000. In comparison, the annual payments into a sinking fund that would repay after 15 years the $1 million principal of an issue of Better America Bonds would be about $42,000. A state or local government issuing the bonds would thus save about $29,000 per year over the initial 15 years, and $71,000 per year over the remaining 15 years of a 30-year bond's term. Better American Bonds would cost state and local governments only about half of what a tax-exempt bond would (in present value terms). This is a powerful tool for financing investments to make our communities better.

Brownfields Remediation Costs

Brownfields are abandoned or underutilized properties where redevelopment is complicated by known or suspected contamination. Because lenders, investors, and developers fear the high and uncertain costs of clean up, they avoid developing contaminated sites. Blighted areas of brownfields hinder the redevelopment of affected communities and create safety and health risks for residents. The obstacles in cleaning these sites, such as regulatory barriers, lack of private investment, contamination and remediation issues, are being addressed through a wide range of Federal programs that includes the tax incentive for brownfields remediation.

To encourage the clean up of contaminated sites, the Administration proposed, and the Congress enacted in the Taxpayer Relief Act of 1997, a brownfield tax incentive that permits the current deduction of certain environmental remediation costs. Environmental remediation expenditures qualify for current deduction if the expenditures would otherwise be capitalized (generally costs incurred to clean up land and groundwater that increase the value of the property) and are paid or incurred in connection with the abatement or control of hazardous substances at a qualified contaminated site. A qualified contaminated site must be located within a targeted area, i.e., census tracts with at least 20 percent poverty rates (and certain contiguous industrial or commercial tracts), designated Empowerment Zones and Enterprise Communities, and the 76 EPA brownfields pilot projects designated before February 1997. In order to claim a current deduction, the taxpayer must obtain a statement from a designated state environmental agency that the qualified contaminated site satisfies the statutory geographic and contamination criteria of a brownfield.

The provision applies to qualified environmental remediation expenditures paid or incurred in taxable years ending after August 5, 1997, and before January 1, 2001.

The current-law tax incentive is designed to be temporary to encourage faster clean up of brownfields in targeted areas. However, many taxpayers are unable to take advantage of the incentive because environmental remediation often extends over a number of years. For that reason, the Administration's budget proposed a permanent extension of the brownfields tax incentive. That proposal was introduced by Mr. Coyne and several cosponsors as H.R. 1630.

Reclaiming brownfields would encourage the redevelopment of targeted communities by making unused or underutilized land productive again. Extending the special current-law rule on a permanent basis would eliminate uncertainty regarding the future availability of the incentive and encourage long range investment in the targeted areas. The revenue cost of the proposal is estimated to be approximately $0.6 billion for FY 2000–2004. Treasury estimates that the tax incentive would induce an additional $7 billion in private investment to return 18,000 brownfields to productive use over the next ten years.

Energy Efficiency and the Environment

Individuals and businesses do not invest enough in energy-saving technologies that produce benefits to society in excess of their private returns. If a new technology reduces pollution or emissions of greenhouse gases, those "external benefits" should be included in the decision about whether to undertake the investment. But potential investors have an incentive to consider only the private benefits in making decisions. Thus, they avoid technologies that are not profitable even though their benefits to society exceed their costs. Tax incentives can offset the failure of market prices to signal the desirable level of investment in energy-saving technologies because they increase the private return from the investment by reducing its after-tax cost. The increase in private return encourages additional investment in energy-saving technologies.

The proposed tax incentives for energy efficiency and the environment are designed to reduce energy consumption and greenhouse gas emissions by encouraging the deployment of technologies that are highly energy efficient and that use renewable energy sources. The proposed incentives are also designed to minimize windfalls for investments that would have been made even absent the incentives and to facilitate tax administration.

The design of the tax incentives incorporates the following considerations:

1. *Superior energy efficiency compared to conventional equipment.* The eligible items should meet higher standards for energy efficiency than conventional equipment or use renewable energy sources. This ensures that tax benefits promote energy efficiency and reduce greenhouse gas emissions.
2. *High threshold for eligibility.* The energy efficiency standards should be set sufficiently high so that eligible items presently account for a small share of the market. This minimizes windfalls for purchases that would have been made absent the credit.
3. *High up-front costs compared to conventional equipment.* The targeted technologies have significantly higher purchase prices than conventional equipment and, at current market prices, have limited cost effectiveness. These high up-front costs are another reason relatively few items incorporating the targeted technologies would be purchased without the credit.
4. *Commercially available.* The items should be commercially available or near commercialization. This ensures that the incentives encourage the deployment of new technologies that private markets have already developed.
5. *Ease of administration.* The items must be able to be defined precisely enough so that the IRS can administer the incentives. This helps to ensure that tax benefits are claimed only for items for which they are intended.

The tax incentives the Administration has proposed cover buildings and homes, vehicles, renewable energy, and industrial equipment. Mr. Matsui and others introduced these proposals in H.R. 2380.

Buildings and Homes

This sector currently accounts for about one-third of energy consumption and the related greenhouse gases. The proposed tax incentives would encourage investment in highly energy efficient building equipment and new homes, and solar energy systems.

Tax Credit for Energy Efficient Building Equipment. A tax credit of 10 percent or 20 percent would be provided for energy efficient equipment, depending upon the efficiency of the equipment. This credit encourages the purchase of equipment that will improve the energy efficiency of both residential and commercial buildings. The items covered are electric heat pump and natural gas water heaters, electric and natural gas heat pumps, advanced central air conditioners, and fuel cells.

The credit would be 20 percent of the cost of super energy efficient models, subject to a cap. It would be available for the period 2000 through 2003. A 10 percent credit would be available for electric heat pumps, central air conditioners and natural gas water heaters that meet high efficiency standards, but do not satisfy the standards for the 20 percent credit. The smaller credit would be available for the period 2000 through 2001.

Items eligible for the 20 percent credit are top-tier technologies that are much more energy efficient than conventional equipment. For example, compared to typical units on the market, the eligible advanced air conditioning systems and electric heat pumps are 40 percent more efficient, and eligible electric heat pump water heaters and natural gas heat pumps are about twice as efficient.

Items eligible for this credit embody new, cutting-edge technologies that have substantial purchase prices and limited in their cost effectiveness. They generally account for less than one percent of market sales. Therefore, the credits would benefit very few purchases that would have been made absent the credit. The 10 percent credit provides a more widely available incentive for purchases of highly energy efficient items, as well as state of the art technology, during the period 2000 through 2001. Some makes and models of qualifying items are currently available. Existing energy efficiency standards for the designated classes of equipment have been used to define eligible items precisely enough for IRS to administer the credit.

The revenue cost of this incentive is estimated to be $1.5 billion for FY 2000–2004. The credit is estimated to increase purchases by nearly 10 million items of highly energy efficient building equipment through 2009.

Tax Credit for Energy Efficient New Homes

Residences account for about one-sixth of U.S. greenhouse gases and offer one of the largest sources of energy saving potential. Over one million new homes and manufactured homes are built and sold each year. Some states and certain Federal programs require new houses to meet certain energy code standards for insulation and related construction standards, and for heating, cooling and hot water equipment. However, the energy efficiency of new homes could be improved significantly through the use of more energy efficient building practices and more efficient heating and cooling equipment that exceed current efficiency standards.

A tax credit equal to $1,000 to $2,000 (depending upon the home's energy efficiency) would be provided to encourage consumers to purchase energy efficient new homes. The tax credits would be: (1) $1,000 for homes that use at least 30 percent less energy than the standard under the 1998 International Energy Conservation Code (IECC); this credit would be available for homes purchased during the period 2000 through 2001; (2) $1,500 for homes that use at least 40 percent less energy than the IECC standard; this credit would be available for homes purchased during the period 2000 through 2002; and (3) $2,000 for homes that use 50 percent less energy than the IECC standard; this credit would be available for homes purchased during the period 2000 through 2004.

Homes qualifying for the credit would use 75 percent to 85 percent less energy than existing housing and as much as 50 percent less energy than typical new housing. The revenue cost is estimated to be $0.4 billion for FY 2000–2004.

The credit is estimated to result in purchases of over 250 thousand new energy efficient homes through 2009.

Tax Credit for Solar Energy Systems

Solar energy systems accounted for 0.02 percent of electricity generation in 1996. These systems produce no greenhouse gas emissions. The tax credit for the purchase of rooftop photovoltaic (PV) systems and solar water heating systems would be 15 percent of the cost up to a maximum credit of $2,000 for PV systems and $1,000 for solar water heating systems. The tax credit for PV systems would be available for the period 2000 through 2006, and the tax credit for solar water heating systems would be available for the period 2000 through 2004.

The revenue cost of this incentive is estimated to be $0.1 billion for FY 2000–2004.

This incentive will help to achieve the President's goal of one million solar energy roofs by 2010. The credit is estimated to reduce electricity production from non-solar sources by 3 billion kilowatt hours through 2009.

Vehicles

Cars and light trucks (including minivans, sport utilities, and pick-ups) currently account for 20 percent of greenhouse gas emissions. Those vehicles also account for about 20 to 40 percent of urban smog-forming emissions and 40 percent of total U.S. petroleum consumption. Almost all cars and trucks use a single gasoline-fueled engine.

Hybrid vehicles, which have more than one source of power on board, and electric vehicles have the potential to reduce greenhouse gas emissions, air pollution, and petroleum consumption. The proposed credits will encourage the purchase of vehicles that incorporate advanced automotive technologies and will help to move advanced hybrid vehicles currently under development from the laboratory to the highway. These vehicles can significantly reduce emissions of carbon dioxide, the most prevalent greenhouse gas.

The proposal would extend the present tax credit for electric vehicles and fuel cell vehicles. Under current law, a 10 percent credit is provided for the cost of qualified electric vehicles and fuel cell vehicles up to a maximum credit of $4,000. The maximum amount of the credit is scheduled to phase down in 2002 and be phased out in 2005. The President's proposal would extend the tax credit at its $4,000 maximum level through 2006.

The proposal also would provide tax credits of $500 to $3,000 for certain hybrid vehicles, depending upon requirements for the vehicle's design and performance.

A qualifying hybrid vehicle is a road vehicle that can draw propulsion energy from both of the following on-board sources of stored energy: (1) a consumable fuel, and (2) a rechargeable energy storage system. The tax credits would be available for vehicles purchased during the period 2003 through 2006. The credit amounts—available for all qualifying vehicles, including cars, minivans, sport utility vehicles, and pickup trucks— would be:

- $500 if the rechargeable energy storage system provides at least 5 percent but less than 10 percent of the maximum available power;
- $1,000 if the rechargeable energy storage system provides at least 10 percent but less than 20 percent of the maximum available power;
- $1,500 if the rechargeable energy storage system provides at least 20 percent but less than 30 percent of the maximum available power, and
- $2,000 if the rechargeable energy storage system provides 30 percent or more of the maximum available power.

If the vehicle actively employs a regenerative braking system, the amount of the credit shown above would be increased by:

- $250 if the regenerative braking system supplies to the rechargeable energy storage system at least 20 percent but less than 40 percent of the energy available from braking in a typical 60 miles per hour (mph) to 0 mph braking event;
- $500 if the regenerative braking system supplies at least 40 percent but less than 60 percent of such energy to the storage system; and
- $1,000 if the regenerative braking system supplies 60 percent or more of such energy to the storage system.

Hybrid vehicles eligible for the largest credit would be 50 percent to 100 percent more fuel efficient than a conventional vehicle of the same size and power. Doubling a car's fuel economy reduces its emissions of carbon dioxide by about 50 percent. The revenue cost of this initiative is estimated to be $0.9 billion for FY 2000–2004. These credits are estimated to result in purchases of 13 million electric and hybrid vehicles through 2009.

Renewable Energy

Wind and biomass currently account for about 2 percent of electricity generation from renewable sources. These renewable energy sources produce virtually no greenhouse gas emissions. To make electricity produced from wind and biomass price competitive with other forms of electricity generation, the proposal would extend the current-law tax credit for wind and biomass for five years, expand eligible biomass sources, and allow a credit for electricity produced from cofiring biomass with coal.

Current law provides a tax credit of 1.5 cents per kilowatt hour (adjusted for inflation after 1992) for electricity produced from wind and closed-loop biomass (organic material from a plant that is grown exclusively to fuel a qualified electricity generation facility). The current tax credit covers the first ten years of production from facilities placed in service before July 1, 1999.

The proposal would extend and expand the tax credit for electricity produced from wind and biomass. It would:

- Extend the current wind and biomass credit for 5 years to cover facilities placed in service before July 1, 2004.
- Expand the definition of eligible biomass for the 1.5 cent credit beyond closed-loop biomass to include certain forest-related resources and agricultural and certain other sources. This change would apply to facilities placed in service after June 30, 1999 and before July 1, 2004.
- Allow cofiring biomass with coal. This proposal adds a 1.0 cent per kilowatt hour tax credit for electricity produced by cofiring biomass in coal plants after the date of enactment and before July 1, 2004. Only the portion of electricity associated with biomass would be eligible for the credit.

The revenue cost of this incentive is estimated to be $0.3 billion over FY 2000–2004.

This incentive is estimated to increase electricity production from renewable energy sources by 32 billion kilowatt hours through 2009.

Industry

The proposal would promote energy efficiency in industry by encouraging investments in combined heat and power (CHP) systems. These systems use the thermal energy that is otherwise wasted in producing electricity by more conventional methods. These systems increase energy efficiency, lower the consumption of primary fossil fuels, and reduce greenhouse gas emissions compared with conventional methods.

To encourage and accelerate investment in CHP equipment, an 8 percent tax credit would be provided for eligible CHP investment. A qualified CHP system would be required to produce at least 20 percent of its total useful energy in the form of thermal energy and at least 20 percent in the form of electric or mechanical power, and would have to meet certain efficiency standards. The credit would apply to property placed in service between 2000 and 2002. Eligible CHP systems should reduce input energy requirements by about one-third compared to conventional systems. The revenue cost of this incentive is estimated to be $0.3 billion for FY 2000–2004. The credit is estimated to increase cogeneration electrical capacity by more than 1.2 gigawatts through 2009.

Environmental Benefits of the Proposal

The proposed incentives described above encourage businesses and consumers to increase their investment in energy-efficient items, new technologies, and renewable energy sources. The investments induced by the credits would be long-lived and, therefore, would produce energy savings and greenhouse gas reductions for many years after the investment is undertaken. The induced increase in the market penetration of energy-efficient technologies, new technologies, and renewable energy sources may lead to lower cost production and increased awareness of the benefits of such technologies that could have lasting effects.

The cumulative reduction in greenhouse gas emissions attributable to the tax incentives is estimated to be between 100 and 150 million metric tons of carbon equivalent (MMTCE) over the lifetime of the investments undertaken from 2000 through 2009. Over one-third of the emissions reduction is attributable to the tax credits for electric and hybrid vehicles and over one-fourth to the tax credits for building equipment.

Reductions in greenhouse gas emissions, however, are not the only benefits that will be realized from these incentives. The incentives will also reduce local air pollution. In addition, the proposals will produce private benefits, such as energy savings for consumers and businesses. The present value of energy savings for consumers and business over the lifetime of items purchased through 2009 is estimated to be between $22 billion and $33 billion.

Conclusion

The Administration strongly supports the proposed tax credits for holders of Better America Bonds, a permanent extension of the current deduction of brownfields remediation expenses, and tax credits for energy efficiency and the environment.

The proposed Better America Bonds provide a new financing tool that will enable state, local, and tribal governments to preserve green spaces, create and restore urban parks, protect water quality and clean up brownfields. Those governments would be authorized to issue a total of $9.5 billion of Better America Bonds to finance environmental and conservation projects. The proposed permanent extension of the current deduction of brownfields remediation costs will help return industrial and commercial sites in targeted areas to productive use. The proposal is estimated to induce an additional $7 billion in private investment and return an additional 18,000 brownfields to productive use over the next ten years. Together, these initiatives will help to preserve our environmental heritage and make our communities more livable in the 21st century.

The Administration's proposed package of tax incentives for energy efficiency and the environment is designed to achieve reductions in greenhouse gas emissions and improvements in energy efficiency. Purchases of items that offer superior energy efficiency or that use renewable energy sources would be eligible for a temporary tax credit. The proposed incentives are estimated to reduce greenhouse gas emissions by 100 to 150 MMTCE over the lifetime of purchases made through 2009 that were induced by the credits. The benefits of the proposal should increase significantly in the years beyond the ten-year budget window, through the transformation of markets after the credits are no longer in effect. Moreover, the proposed incentives also may generate other benefits to society, such as cleaner air.

In conclusion, Mr. Chairman, we believe that the Administration's proposed tax initiatives represent sound policy that can produce significant environmental benefits over the next ten years and for decades to come. The proposals represent investments that will generate long-term benefits for the Nation. We look forward to working with the Congress on these initiatives.

Note

1. Summing outlay equivalent estimates is controversial because doing so does not take into account possible interactions among tax expenditures. In addition, there are several ways to define and measure tax expenditures. The size of a tax preference can change over time. For example, accelerated depreciation of machinery and equipment drops out of the list of the top 10 tax expenditures in 2006. Moreover, what is considered a tax expenditure depends on the tax base. Some provisions of the tax code that are considered tax expenditures under an income tax base would not be considered tax expenditures under a consumption tax base. For further information on how tax expenditures are defined and measured, see GAO, *Government Performance and Accountability: Tax Expenditures Represent a Substantial Federal Commitment and Need to Be Reexamined*, GAO-05–690 (forthcoming).

7

Directory of Organizations and Associations

The following are selected organizations and associations relevant to the topic of tax reform.

American Bar Association (ABA)
750 N. Lake Shore Drive
Chicago, IL 60611
(312) 988-5000

The ABA is a voluntary association of dues-paying attorneys. As the largest organized group of attorneys in the United States, the ABA wields a powerful influence on the shape of legislation. It publishes influential legal journals relating to tax issues, including the *Tax Lawyer*. Policy makers are influenced by reports on tax reform published by the ABA's Tax Section and Real Property and Probate Section.

American Institute of Certified Public Accountants (AICPA)
1211 Avenue of the Americas
New York, NY 10036
(212) 596-6200
http://www.aicpa.org

The AICPA is a voluntary association of dues-paying certified public accountants. As the largest professional organization of CPAs, the AICPA is able to influence tax policymakers. The AICPA takes positions on tax reform and issues reports through its Tax Section.

American Taxation Association
c/o American Accounting Association
5717 Bessie Drive
Sarasota, FL 34233
(941) 921-7747
www.aaahq.org/ata/

This nonprofit association of university professors is engaged in teaching taxation and conducting tax research. Through its *Journal of the American Taxation Association* it publishes tax research on various tax reform issues. The research is truly nonpartisan, but readers must be familiar with economics to appreciate the content of this journal.

Americans for Fair Taxation
3900 Essex Lane, Suite #328
Houston, TX 77027
(713) 963-9023
www.fairtax.org

Americans for Fair Taxation is a nonprofit group that advocates for replacement of all current taxes with a federal retail sales tax called the Fair Tax. The Fair Tax plan would replace all federal income and payroll-based taxes with an integrated approach including a progressive national retail sales tax, a prebate to ensure that no American pays federal taxes on spending up to the poverty level, dollar-for-dollar federal revenue neutrality, and, through companion legislation, repeal of the 16th Amendment.

The group's tax plan is contained in proposed legislation, the Fair Tax Act. This would abolish all federal personal and corporate income taxes, as well as gift, estate, capital gains, alternative minimum, Social Security, Medicare, and self-employment taxes, replacing them with a federal retail sales tax administered primarily by existing state sales tax authorities. The IRS would be eliminated. Like other sales taxes, the Fair Tax would tax only what people choose to spend on new goods or services, not what they earn.

Proponents of the Fair Tax say that it is a fair, efficient, transparent, and intelligent solution to the frustration and inequity of our current tax system. They argue that because the Fair Tax does not tax work, savings, or investment but only taxes spending, it promotes economic growth, raises marginal labor productivity and real wages, creates jobs, and encourages upward mobility.

Critics argue that the claims for the tax are unproven and would likely result in higher taxes for poor and middle-class taxpayers, who spend everything they earn; they also say that the tax would not apply to much of the rich's income because they can invest or save it rather than spend it. It is also claimed that such a tax would decrease revenues and add to the federal deficit.

Americans for Tax Reform
1320 18th Street, NW
Suite 200
Washington, DC 20036
(202) 785-0266
http://www.atr.org

This conservative group with 60,000 members works to improve the tax system and minimize taxes. The group invites legislators to sign their Taxpayer Protection Pledge, promising that they will not raise income taxes under any conditions. The institute also gives awards to politicians for being an "enemy of the taxpayer" or "friend of the taxpayer." The group is also active in fighting tax increases at the state and local levels.

Brookings Institution
1775 Massachusetts Avenue, NW
Washington, DC 20036
(202) 797-6000
www.brookings.edu

An influential liberal research institute, the Brookings Institution is primarily involved in conducting and publishing research on economic, government, and social policy. Founded in 1916, the institute has published numerous studies on taxation and tax reform over the years. *The Brookings Review* enjoys a circulation of 18,000.

Cato Institute
1000 Massachusetts Avenue, NE (will relocate sometime in 2012)
Washington, DC 20001-0200
(202) 842-0200
http://www.cato.org

A public policy institute the Cato Institute is committed to "traditional American principles of individual liberty and peace." Most of its publications espouse reducing the size of the government and reducing taxes. The institute publishes several newsletters and journals, including special reports on policy issues of current interest.

Center on Budget and Policy Priorities
NE 820 First Street, NE
Suite 510
Washington, DC 20002
(202) 408-1080
http://www.cbpp.org

This is a liberal research organization and policy institute conducting research on a range of government policies and programs with an emphasis on those affecting low- and middle-income taxpayers. The center produces reports on tax reform issues, especially as related to their effect on groups who are not represented in the tax-writing process by lobbyists. Although not strictly a tax organization, the CBPP issues reports on the impact of federal and state taxes on low-income Americans.

The center was founded in 1981 to analyze federal budget priorities with particular emphasis on the impact of various budget choices on low-income Americans. Its work has broadened considerably over the years as it has responded to new developments and entered new areas of research. Most notably, the center initiated extensive work on budget priorities and low-income programs at the state level during the 1990s in response to the devolution of responsibility over many areas of low-income policy from Washington to the states.

Citizens for Tax Justice
1311 L Street, NW
Washington, DC 20005
(202) 626-3780
http://www.ctj.org

This liberal, nonprofit research and advocacy organization is dedicated to fair taxation at the federal, state, and local levels. It espouses a tax system that reflects taxpayers' ability to pay without breaks for the wealthy and businesses. The organization works to build coalitions at the state and local level to work for fairer taxes. The group was especially effective in advocating specific measures included in the Tax Reform Act of 1986. Its research on tax reforms was effective in promoting changes to make the tax code fairer for most taxpayers.

Committee on State Taxation (COST)
122 C Street, NW
Suite 330
Washington, DC 20001
(202) 484-5222

This nonprofit trade organization, representing about 480 multistate corporations engaged in interstate and international commerce, advocates tax laws beneficial to these corporations. Supports research on tax reforms to reduce multiple taxation and other problems of corporations operating in the interstate environment.

Federation of Tax Administrators
444 North Capitol Street
Suite 345
Washington, DC 20001
(202) 624-5890
http://www.taxadmin.org

An association whose members are state revenue departments, this organization investigates administrative problems facing state tax officials. It also conducts research into state tax reform issues.

Freedomworks
400 North Capitol Street, NW
Suite 765
Washington, DC 20001
Toll Free: 1 (888) 564-6273
(202) 783-3870
http://freedomworks.org

A conservative nonprofit group, Freedomworks is able to influence lawmakers through petitions and letter-writing campaigns. The organization is committed to promoting a strong free-market economic system with fewer government programs, lower taxes, and less government regulation. The group promotes the flat tax as a vehicle of fundamental tax reform. The foundation absorbed the Tax Foundation, which espoused similar antitax views. The group's agenda also includes energy and the environment, health care reform, workplace freedom, and entitlement reform. The organization is chaired by former U.S. House Majority Leader Dick Armey; its president is Matt Kibbe. David Koch is a major financial backer.

Freedomworks has strong ties to the Tea Party movement. Its hosting of a 4-day "summit" of 150 top Tea Party activists at the Freedomworks headquarters resulted in the creation of the Tea Party Debt Commission, modeled on the federal debt commission, to find ways to balance the federal budget through spending cuts rather than tax increases.

Henry George Foundation of UK
PO Box 6408
London
United Kingdom
W1A 3GY
0800 048 8537
http://www.henrygeorgefoundation.org/

Founded in 1929, the Henry George Foundation is involved in research on property tax reform and land value taxation (LVT), a modern version of Henry George's single tax on land. In practice, LTV shifts value from buildings to the land. Proponents of this approach believe that LVT will cure many of society's ills.

Heritage Foundation
214 Massachusetts Avenue, NE
Washington, DC 20002
(202) 624-4400
http://www.heritage.org/

The Heritage Foundation is a well-known conservative institute committed to the principles of advancing free enterprise, limited government, and individual liberty. The foundation supports research on tax reform, especially tax limitations, and issues policy statements and reports.

Hoover Institution
Stanford University
Stanford, CA 94305
(415) 723-0603
http://hoover.org

This well-known conservative think tank, housed at Stanford University in California, supports interdisciplinary research of a high level in social science areas of public policy. Some of this research has been in the tax reform area. The institute normally funds researchers who have a conservative viewpoint.

House Ways and Means Committee
U.S. House of Representatives
1102 Longworth House Office Building
Washington, DC 20515
http://www.house.gov/ways_means/

This is the congressional committee empowered by the U.S. Constitution to deal with all revenue bills. All tax bills must start here, and members of the committee—especially the chair—wield considerable influence over the tax laws. The committee issues reports, including the "blue books," on new and proposed tax bills. These documents, published in both hard copy and on the Internet, are invaluable in studying tax changes because they provide not just the law but a commentary on what types of transactions and economic activity are affected by specific sections of the tax code and how changes in the tax law will influence taxpayers. Accordingly, these publications are required reading for serious students of tax reform.

Institute for Professionals in Taxation
600 Northpark Town Center
1200 Abernathy Rd., Suite L-2
Atlanta, GA 30328-1040
(404) 240-2300
http://www.ipt.org/

Formerly called the Institute of Property Taxation, the institute comprises a group of tax professionals primarily working in the areas of property and state sales taxes. The institute analyzes existing and proposed legislation and regulations, keeping members informed of the findings.

Internal Revenue Service
U.S. Treasury
1500 Pennsylvania Avenue
Washington, DC 20220
(202) 622-2000
http://www.irs.gov

The mission of the IRS, part of the U.S. Treasury, is to handle the "nuts and bolts" of administering the tax laws passed by Congress. The IRS publishes regulations and other rulings and guidance to help taxpayers comply with the tax laws. Of course the IRS also prints forms, receives completed forms and tax payments, and conducts tax audits and collection activities. In 1998, Congress passed the IRS Restructuring and Reorganization Act, requiring the agency to reorganize itself to meet the needs of both the government and taxpayers in the next century. The general goals of the reorganization were to streamline operations, improve the use of technology to make tax collections more efficient, and shift the agency's emphasis from enforcement to taxpayer education.

Joint Committee on Taxation
Room 1915
Longworth House Office Building
Washington, DC 20515
(202) 225-3621
http://jct.gov

After the House Ways and Means Committee and the Senate Finance Committee approve tax legislation, the bills go respectively to the full House of Representatives and the Senate for ratification. However, the bills typically differ in detail. After the bills are passed in each chamber, the Joint Committee on Taxation must hammer out a compromise bill. Typically the final bill will be a compromise between the House and Senate versions. This committee also issues reports, including a "blue book," published as a hard-copy book and on the Internet, that reports on what specific provisions in the House and Senate bills were included in the final legislation. Like any other law passed by Congress, tax legislation must be signed or vetoed by the president. Congress has the ultimate authority to override a presidential veto by a two-thirds majority vote in each chamber.

Multistate Tax Commission
444 N. Capitol Street, NW
Suite 425
Washington, DC 20001
(202) 624-8699
http://www.mtc.gov/

The Multistate Tax Commission (MTC) was established by a compact between the states authorized by the U.S. Constitution. Its goal is to enhance compliance with state tax laws and to promote uniformity in state tax laws through the Multistate Tax Compact. The MTC is actively engaged in tax research and publishes reports on state tax issues.

National Tax Association
725 15th Street, NW
Number 600
Washington, DC 20006-3325
(202) 737-3325
http://www.ntanet.org

The National Tax Association promotes nonpartisan study of the tax system. Its membership is a unique blend of government and corporate tax officials, academics, economists, attorneys, and CPAs. The association is interested in reforming the tax system to promote the interest of governments in public finance and taxation. The association publishes the *National Tax Journal*, which includes articles on tax reform. However, readers must be familiar with economics to appreciate the content of these journals.

National Tax Limitation Foundation
151 N. Sunrise Avenue
Suite 901
Roseville, CA 95661
(916) 786-9400

This organization is committed to lowering taxes and government spending. The group promotes research in the area of reforming the tax system and a constitutional amendment to require a federal balanced budget.

National Taxpayers Union (NTU)
108 N. Alfred Street
Alexandria, VA 22314
(703) 683-5700
http://www.ntu.org

Claiming a membership of 300,000 the NTU is one of the leading
advocacy groups calling for the reduction of taxes and government spending. The group lobbies politicians to educate them
about tax issues and annually rates politicians for their tax-and-
spend habits. The NTU also works at the state and local levels for
tax reduction. It was instrumental in lobbying for the Taxpayer
Bill of Rights and for indexing of the tax code. The group's interests are broader than its name implies, and it has taken positions
on education, energy, and health care issues in addition to its tax
message.

Senate Finance Committee
104 Hart Senate Office Building
Washington, DC 20510
(202) 224-2441
http://www.senate.gov/%7Efinance/

This is the senate committee empowered to write revenue bills.
The Senate version of tax bills start here before being sent to
the full Senate. Members of the committee, especially its chair,
wield considerable influence on the shape of tax legislation. The
committee publishes a "blue book," both in hard copy and on
the Internet, explaining in detail the specific changes made in
tax acts.

Social Security Administration
Office of Public Inquiries
6401 Security Boulevard
Room 4-C-5 Annex
Baltimore, MD 21235-6401
http://www.ssa.gov

The Social Security Administration is in charge of overseeing the
Social Security system, which administers the Medicare system
and provides both retirement benefits and disability benefits.

Tax Executives Institute
1200 G Street
Number 300
Washington, DC 20005-3814
(202) 638-5601
http://www.TEI.org

This professional society comprises executives administering tax affairs for corporations. The institute is interested in tax reform as it affects its member organizations at both the federal and state levels. The group is influential because its members include top tax executives from major corporations. Also because the group is composed of working tax professionals—rather than advocates with a political agenda—the group's recommendations have substantial credibility with member of Congress.

The Tax Policy Center
Urban Institute
2100 M Street, NW
Washington, DC 20037
(202) 833-7200

The Tax Policy Center is a joint venture of the Urban Institute and the Brookings Institution (listed previously). The center is made up of nationally recognized experts ion tax, budget, and social policy who have served at the highest levels of government. Its website offers dozens of current authoritative articles on both taxes in general and tax reform in particular. It is a real trove of information for students of taxation.

The web site currently includes a page on tax reform that includes links to both Congressman Paul Ryan's Tax Plan as well as the Bipartisan Tax Fairness and Simplification Act of 2010, proposed by Senators Ron Wyden (D., Ore.) and Judd Gregg (R., N.H.).

Urban Institute
2100 M Street, NW
Washington, DC 20037
(202) 833-7200
http://www.urbaninstitute.org

The Urban Institute is a nonpartisan economic and social research organization whose goal is to sharpen thinking about society's problems; it focuses on efforts, especially by the government, to solve them. The institute, conducts extensive research and has produced many reports on reforming the tax system. The institute publishes not only journals and newsletters but also lengthy research reports and books through its UI Press.

8

Resources

Selected Print Resources

The works listed in this chapter are divided into three categories. The first lists both popular and scholarly books that deal with the subject of tax reform. The second lists scholarly journal articles. Many of these journals may only be available at university or law school libraries. Some law journals are available at courthouse libraries (but these are sometimes not open to the public). The third lists articles on tax reform in popular magazines. Much material on tax reform is now available on the Internet. These sources are detailed later in this chapter.

Most of the reference resources on tax reform were initially published in print form, although some are now available in databases. These articles can be accessed in a number of ways, but the most efficient way is to use a periodicals index. The most useful of these indexes are the *Index to Legal Periodicals* (H. W. Wilson), *Federal Tax Articles* (Commerce Clearing House), and *Index to Tax Articles* (Research Institute of America). For earlier coverage consult the *Accountant's Index*, which ceased publication in 1991.

There are a number of journals that discuss tax reform. Unfortunately, many of these are aimed at the specialist, which makes the material only moderately useful to most researchers. The *Tax Law Review* and *The Tax Lawyer* are legal journals that often contain articles discussing tax reform but they are aimed at tax lawyers. *The National Tax Journal* and the *Journal of the American Taxation Association* both publish articles on tax reform, but readers need to be familiar with economics to appreciate the content of these journals. Articles on tax reform also frequently appear in journals

233

dealing with political science, most specifically in journals dealing with public finance.

Tax Notes, a weekly publication, publishes much original research on tax reform. Although the articles are written for tax specialists, they are also addressed to policy makers in Washington, D.C., and the states, and authors frequently try to write their articles so that they are accessible to lay readers. Although *Tax Notes* is not widely available, those interested in tax reform will be rewarded if they find a library that subscribes to it. *Tax Notes* is also available on Westlaw and Lexis-Nexis.

Selected Books on Tax Reform

Aaron, Henry J., and William G. Gale, eds. *Economic Effect of Fundamental Tax Reform*. Brookings Institute, 1996.

American Institute of Certified Public Accountants. *Flat Taxes and Consumption Taxes: A Guide to the Debate*. Washington: AICPA, 1992.

This guide prepared by the Tax Section of the AICPA—the leading professional body speaking for CPAs—provides a clear and readable review of the leading tax reform proposals. Unlike any other resource, this guide does not advocate one approach over another but attempts to make a nonjudgmental evaluation of the different reform proposals. Because CPAs do have a vested stake in the system—they derive a significant portion of their fees from tax work—readers need to keep in mind that no resource is completely free of bias, even if it is unintentional.

Armey, Dick. *The Flat Tax: A Citizen's Guide to the Facts on What It Will Do for You, Your Country, and Your Pocketbook*. New York: Ballantine Books, 1996.

Representative Dick Armey, a former economics professor, explains in plain language the benefits of the flat tax. Army, a major political supporter of the tax, discusses the advantages in detail but skims over the disadvantages. The book is relatively short and is written for average taxpayers. The book appears to be out of print at this writing.

Birnbaum, Jeffery H., and Alan S. Murray. *Showdown at Gucci Gulch: Lawmakers, Lobbyists, and the Unlikely Triumph of Tax Reform*. New York: Vintage Books, 1988.

The authors detail the politics behind the Tax Reform Act of 1986. Participants have commented that this book is a remarkably accurate account of the back-room haggling that took place preceding the passage of the act, the largest revision of the tax code since 1913. The authors relate how supporters of reform overcame special-interest lobbying.

Boskin, Michael J., ed. *Frontiers of Tax Reform.* **Publication #435. Washington, DC: Hoover Institution Press, 1996.**

The essays in this collection, drawn from a 1995 conference, discuss the five major tax reform proposals: the flat tax, the VAT tax, the national retail sales tax, the USA tax, and a hybrid progressive consumption tax. Although the essays are written for the relatively sophisticated reader, they are useful for students of tax reform because they provide not only descriptions of the five proposals but also evaluations of their benefits and costs.

Brownlee, W. Elliott. *Federal Taxation in America: A Short History.* **New York: Cambridge University Press, 1996.**

This is a fairly brief historical overview of U.S. taxation from colonial times to 1990. The book contains detailed discussions of taxation at the founding of the republic, the Civil War, World War I, the Great Depression, and World War II. It focuses more on history than tax reform themes.

Diamond, John W, and Zodrow, George R, eds. *Fundamental Tax Reform: Issues, Choices, and Implications.* **Boston: MIT Press, 2008.**

This collection of scholarly papers discusses tax policy and the consequences of a wide range of issues raised by the prospect of significant tax reform. Papers discuss advantages and disadvantages of income-based taxation as opposed to any of the several alternative forms of consumption-based taxation as well as the strengths, weaknesses, and the political feasibility of these options. Other topics include the effect of tax reform on business investment behavior and possible problems in any transition to a consumption-based tax. Papers also discuss international taxation issues and behavioral economics.

Ekins Paul, and Speck, Stefan. *Environmental Tax Reform (ETR): A Policy for Green Growth (Creating Sustainable Growth in Europe).* **New York: Oxford University Press, 2011.**

This is an important scholarly book exploring proposals to shift taxation from conventional taxes to taxes on environmentally related activities that involve resource use, particularly energy, or environmental pollution. The text describes experience with environmental tax reform (ETR) in Europe and also considers how a more ambitious ETR in Europe could substantially reduce greenhouse gas emissions and material flows through the economy while stimulating innovation and investment in the key "clean and green" sectors of the economy. The book also includes case studies of renewable energy, construction, fuel-efficient vehicles, and waste management in Germany, showing how these fast-growing sectors are making an increasing contribution to employment, output, and exports in the German economy while improving the environment. The authors suggest that large-scale ETR could stimulate the world economy as well as improving the environment.

Graetz, Michael J. *100 Million Unnecessary Returns: A Simple, Fair, and Competitive Tax Plan for the United States?* **New Haven, CT: Yale University Press, 2007.**

This popular book by a Yale Law School professor advocates the value added tax (VAT) as a remedy for America's bloated income tax system. The author argues that adopting a VAT would free most Americans from filing income tax returns and from paying any income tax at all.

Graetz, Michael J, and Shapiro, Ian. *Death by a Thousand Cuts.* **New Haven, CT: Yale University Press, 2005.**

Two Yale law professors chronicle the background to Congress' repeal of the federal estate tax. Their nontechnical book focuses on the political realities rather than the operation of the tax itself.

Haig, Robert M. *The Federal Income Tax.* **New York: Columbia University Press, 1921.**

A classic text on income taxation. Although only of historical interest, Haig's definition of income played a large role in the development of modern tax concepts.

Hall, Robert E. *Fairness and Efficiency in the Flat Tax.* **Washington, DC: AEI Press, 1996.**

A short book of pro–flat tax essays, including submissions by Alan Rabushka and Dick Armey. Although the material is not original, the essays are accessible to students of tax reform who want to learn more about the economic advantages of the flat tax.

Hall, Robert E, and Rubuska, Alvin, *The Flat Tax,* **2nd ed. Stanford CA: Hoover Institution Press, 1995.**

The authors' flat tax proposal as set out in this volume is the basis of many of the tax reform proposals espoused by Republican presidential candidates Rick Perry, Newt Gingrich, and Michele Bachmann and possibly Mitt Romney. Herman Cain's 9–9-9 plan also envisioned a flat 9 percent income tax.

Head, John G, and Krever, Richard, eds. *Tax Reform in the 21st Century* **(series on international taxation). New York: Kluwer Law International, 2009.**

A collection of scholarly essays on tax reform from an international perspective.

Hicko, Scott E. *The Flat Tax: Why It Won't Work for America.* **Omaha, NE: Addicus Books, 1996.**

Hicko, a CPA, points out the primary disadvantage of moving to a flat tax: only the wealthy would benefit. Since the wealthy now pay substantially higher rates than middle- and low-income taxpayers, they would reap the largest benefit. Also, most of the flat tax proposals are designed as "consumption taxes," so dividends, interest, and royalties would not be taxed at all. According to Hicko, the major beneficiaries of the flat tax would be the wealthy, with all other taxpayers paying more or receiving less in the way of government services and benefits.

Seidman, Lawrence S. *The USA Tax: A Progressive Consumption Tax.* **Cambridge, MA: MIT Press, 1997.**

Of all the major tax reform proposals, the USA tax—the Unlimited Savings Allowance tax—has gotten the least attention from the public and the popular press. This short and readable book offers those who are not economists a detailed examination of the USA tax.

Simmons, Henry C. *Personal Income Taxation.* **Chicago: University of Chicago Press, 1921.**

This classic work on taxation is mainly of historical interest. Simmons's points are still important and prove the adage that those who are ignorant of the mistakes of the past are condemned to repeat them. Although Simmons was an economist, his insights are surprisingly practical compared with those now issued by practitioners of the "dismal science."

Slemrod, Joel, and Bakija, Jon. *Taxing Ourselves: A Citizen's Guide to the Debate over Taxes,* **4th ed. Cambridge, MA: MIT Press, 2008.**

Intended for nonexperts, this popular and accessible volume has no particular political agenda. It is well written, carefully edited, and filled with reliable information. The authors—both well-known professors with expertise in tax policy issues—review the major alternatives for reforming the U.S. tax system, including reforming the current income tax system and the leading proposals to reform or replace it, including adopting a "flat tax" or a consumption tax, such as a national retail sales tax. Take care to locate the current fourth edition, which contains a discussion of the Bush administration's tax cuts (which commenced in 2001 and applied until 2011) and the alternatives proposed by the President Obama's Advisory Panel on Federal Tax Reform. Because tax issues change so rapidly, no book—this one included—will be completely up to date by the time the purchaser reads it. Nevertheless, this is the best book for nonexperts who want to research current reform issues.

Steuerle, C. Eugene. *Contemporary U.S. Tax Policy,* **2nd ed. Washington, DC: Urban Institute Press, 2008.**

This is a well-written overview of U.S. tax policy and tax reform acts from 1980 through 2005 by perhaps the best-known writer on tax reform. The book capably integrates economic, policy and political concerns. The discussion of tax policy under both the Clinton and two Bush administrations is illuminating. The text contains a helpful appendix and glossary.

Zodrow, George R, and Mieszkowski, Peter, eds. *United States Tax Reform in the 21st Century.* **New York: Cambridge University Press; 2008.**

This slim volume contains a collection of accessible but scholarly essays on tax reform. Issues include consumption tax reform, distributional consequences, effects on administrative and compliance costs, transitional issues, and the political realities of implementing fundamental tax reform.

Selected Scholarly Articles on Tax Reform

Auerback, Alan J., Laurence Kotlikoff, and Jonathan Skinner. "The Efficiency Gains from Dynamic Tax Reform." *International Economic Review* 24, no. 1 (February 1983): 81–100.

The authors construct a model to project the efficiency gains from switching from the present U.S. tax system to a consumption-based tax, like a sales tax. Proponents of consumption tax usually argue that consumption taxes would help the economy because of lower compliance costs and fewer opportunities to evade the tax. The authors conclude that a switch to a consumption tax would produce large efficiency gains. The authors also conclude that a consumption tax could still include progressivity depending on its design.

Ballard, Charles L., John B. Shoven, and John Whalley. "General Equilibrium Computations of the Marginal Welfare Costs of Taxes in the United States." *American Economic Review* 75 (March 1985): 28–138.

Adam Smith argued that two of the prime requirements for a tax system are economy and convenience. Most would agree that the current U.S. tax system is not an economical way to raise revenue for the government and is a major inconvenience for taxpayers, who must comply with the complex rules. The authors attempted to measure the "welfare costs" of the present system. They found that the excess burden of the current system sometimes exceeds 50 percent of the revenue collected, which they suggest is strong evidence that tax reform should be a national priority. In another article in the June 1985 issue of *The National Tax Journal*, the same authors suggest that there would be large efficiency gains by switching to a consumption-based tax, such as a national sales tax.

Bankman, Joseph, and Thomas Griffith. "Social Welfare and the Rate Structure: A New Look at Progressive Taxation." *California Law Review* 75, no 6 (December 1987): 1905–1967.

The current income tax system includes progressive tax rates, which result in significant income redistribution as richer taxpayers pay a greater share of the tax burden. The authors of the article, who are in favor of income redistribution, explore the idea of moving from the current progressive tax rates to a flat tax and having the government make direct payments to low-income taxpayers. The authors conclude that a system using direct payments would be more effective at income redistribution than our current system, which relies on the tax rate differences.

Beaudry, Robert V. "The Flat Tax: Is It a Viable Solution to the Crisis Facing the Internal Revenue Code?" *Oklahoma City University Law Review* 9, no. 2 (Summer 1984): 219–270.

There are many articles arguing in favor of a flat tax. This article, written by a lawyer, argues that the flat tax will not be the panacea often predicted by its supporters. The author argues that although a flat tax will address some problems, it is likely to create others. The author concludes that relatively minor changes to the current tax code would be a better tax reform alternative than adopting a simple flat tax.

Cook, Eric W. "Revenue and Distribution Impacts of the Hall-Rabushka Flat Tax Proposal." *Cato Journal* 5, no 2 (Fall 1985): 477–480.

Flat-tax proponents frequently support the Hall-Rabushka flat tax plan (see the listing for the book by those economists in the previous section). That proposal is normally claimed to be revenue-neutral (meaning it will raise as much revenue as the current tax system). The economist-author of this article examines that proposal and concludes that the Hall-Rabuska plan has no chance of being revenue-neutral. Therefore according to Cook, just to maintain current government services, the rates would have to be raised far higher than 7 percent or the tax base would have to be broadened to include low-income Americans.

Donmoyer, Ryan J. "Flat Tax Strategy: The IRS as Poster Boy for Tax Reform." *Tax Notes* no 12(December 22, 1997): 1305.

Flat tax proposals have dominated the tax reform debate from the 1990s onward, from proposals by Dick Armey and Steve Forbes to the more recent proposals by various Republican candidates in the 2012 presidential election. Elimination or radical downsizing of the IRS is typically part of these "reform" measures. This article examines the genius of linking the flat tax to the elimination of the IRS.

Gale, William G. "The Kemp Commission and the Future of Tax Reform." *Tax Notes.* **(February 5, 1996).**

During the early 1990s, Republican Party leaders established a commission headed by former Representative Jack Kemp (who also served as secretary of the Department of Housing and ran for the presidency). The commission issued its report in 1996, calling for repeal of the internal revenue code and its replacement with a flat tax. This short article reviews the work of the commission and its recommendations.

General Accounting Office. *Economic, Administrative, and Taxpayer Compliance Aspects of a Gross Income Tax.* **GAO Report #GAO/GGD 89–36 (February 1989).**

This report was prepared by the General Accounting Office, a branch of Congress, at the request of a congressman. The report examines the consequences of adopting a gross income tax, which is a gross receipts tax. The current income tax taxes income, which is close to "profit," whereas a "gross income" tax would tax all income and sales without any deductions at all. Washington State has used this type of tax for decades. The report concludes that one major consequence of this change would be that unprofitable businesses would have to pay tax. The report also projects that businesses would tend to reorganize to avoid the tax. Companies would likely try to achieve more vertical integration—in other words, try to perform more functions themselves rather than relying on suppliers and customers to sell their products—to legally avoid the tax.

Harriss, C. Lowell. "Important Issues and Some Serious Problems in Flat-Rate Income Taxation." *American Journal of Economics and Sociology* **43, no. 2 (April 1984): 159–162.**

This short article raises a number of important issues about tax reform proposals. Although economists and other tax experts often make revenue projections, these projections are far from perfect. It can be difficult to devise mathematical formulas that will accurately predict actual human behavior. The author of this article points out that projections about flat tax revenue generation have ignored many issues that would affect revenues. The author asserts that very little thought has been given to how a change to a flat tax would affect the "underground economy" of nonfilers.

Likewise, there has been little or no research on how a flat tax would affect the work effort of Americans or on the savings and investment rate.

Henerson, Yolanda K. "Further Base Broadening: A Possible Source of Tax Revenues?" *New England Economic Review, Federal Reserve Bank of Boston* **(March/April 1988):33–45.**

Over time the federal income tax code has grown more and more complex as Congress has enacted deductions and exclusions to benefit certain industries and interest groups. The Tax Reform Act of 1986 eliminated only a fraction of these deductions and exemptions. The authors argue that the government could increase its revenues significantly by eliminating even more of these targeted tax breaks.

Knoll, Michael S. "Taxing Prometheus: How the Corporate Interest Deduction Discourages Innovation and Risk-Taking." *Villanova Law Review* **38, no. 5 (1993):1461–1516.**

The current income tax system provides a deduction for interest expense but no deduction for dividends. This results in incentives for corporations to borrow money rather than issue more stock. The interest expense is partially subsidized by the government because of the lower effective tax rate. When corporate income is used to pay dividends, the income is taxed twice: once to the corporation and once to the recipient. The author argues that this system misallocates capital because investment decisions are made for tax rather than business reasons.

Laffer, Arthur B. "The Complete Flat Tax," in *The Financial Analysis Guide to Monetary Policy,* **by Victor A. Canto, Charles W. Kadlec, and Arthur B. Laffer. Greenwich, CT: Greenwood Press, 1986, pp. 108–140.**

The author is the economist who devised the "Laffer curve," which suggested that reduced tax rates and government spending would jump-start productivity. In this essay, he argues that the United States should abolish not just the income tax but all federal taxes, replacing the entire system with just two taxes, a flat 11.5 percent tax on individuals and a value-added tax on corporations.

Martinez, Leo P. "Tax Policy, Rational Actors, and Other Myths." *Loyola University Chicago Law Journal* 40, no. 197 (2009).

This is an interesting and accessible law review article on the shortcomings of both federal and state tax systems, including lots of specific examples. The author believes that rational tax reform is not within reach. The author pessimistically concludes "Stated baldly, the democratic process is not up to the task of dealing with tax policy."

Minarik, Joseph J. "How Tax Reform Came About." *Tax Notes* 13 (December 28, 1987): 1359–1372.

This relatively brief article describes the political background of the passage of the 1986 Tax Reform Act—the largest tax reform act ever passed in the United States. The author traces the impetus for tax reform back to the 1960s and shows how the 1981 Economic Recovery Tax Act (ERTA) triggered subsequent tax acts. This article does an especially good job of covering the practical political aspects of tax reform.

Peachman, Joseph A., and Michael J. Boskin. "Flat Rate Taxes: Two Views." *Tax Notes* (August 16, 1982): 651–653.

Two prominent economists argue about the merits of the flat tax. Dr. Peachman, an economist from the liberal Brookings Institution, argues that the flat tax is not the panacea that its proponents believe. Dr. Boskin, an economics professor from Stanford University, argues that a flat tax would benefit the U.S. economy, which in the long run would benefit all residents.

Pollack, Sheldon, D. "Farewell to Tax Reform: The 1993 Tax Act in Historical Perspective." *Tax Notes* 73 (August 22, 1994): 341–351.

An interesting article that traces tax changes from 1980 to 1993. The author contends that the tax reform acts of the 1980s were essentially a hodgepodge of revenue raisers without a unifying theme that could be called reform. In contrast, the 1986 Tax Reform Act was worthy of the name because it decreased tax rates and attempted to broaden the tax base by eliminating many unjustifiable deductions and giveaways. The author concludes that the 1993 tax act—the last substantive tax act of the century—was a return to the unprincipled acts of the 1980s and was enacted as a revenue raiser rather than as a vehicle for tax reform.

Samwick, Andrew A. "Tax Reform and Target Saving. Symposium: What Do We Mean by 'Taxpayer Relief'?" *National Tax Journal,* **51, no 3 (September 1998): 621–635.**

This article discusses the effect on pensions and saving if the United States switches from the current income tax system to a consumption-based tax system The paper argues that the net effect of such tax reform on saving depends on household motives for saving. This paper documents the considerable variation in the reasons why households save and presents a buffer stock model of saving that allows for both life-cycle and target saving. The paper concludes that to the extent that specific targets are not currently tax-favored to motivate the savings of households during their preretirement years, fundamental tax reform that results in the elimination of current pension plans will reduce saving.

Sheppard, Lee A. "Tax Reform Redux: The State of the Record." *Tax Notes* **28 (September 9, 1985): 1215–1228.**

A brief and amusing look at the political process that underlies any tax reform effort. The author, a well-known but controversial tax expert from Tax Analysts, examines the high-stakes poker game that took place during negotiations over the 1986 Tax Reform Act. We learn that our elected representatives are all too human. Although the writing is accessible, the article requires a rudimentary tax background to enjoy all the comments. You'll appreciate this article more if you read it at the end of your research rather than at the start.

Smith Dan Throop. "High Progressive Tax Rates: Inequality and Immorality." *University of Florida Law Review* **20, no. 4 (Spring 1968): 451–463.**

In a highly original article, the author attacks high progressive tax rates not because of their economic inefficiencies but on the grounds that they encourage cheating. The author rightly points out that whenever tax rates become high, taxpayers make a cost-benefit decision about cheating. The higher the tax rates, the higher the incidence of cheating. The author argues that high rates encourage cheating, which undermines the integrity of the entire system.

Toder, Eric. "Comments on Proposals for Fundamental Tax Reform: Statement before Senate Budget Committee by Deputy Assistant Secretary of the Treasury." Reprinted in *Tax Notes* 66 (March 27, 1995): 2003–2017.

The assistant secretary for tax analysis at the U.S. Treasury Department presents the Treasury Department's views on fundamental tax reform. The statement reviews several of the proposals for new taxes to replace the current income tax. The paper specifically addresses the proposal to replace the income tax with a consumption tax—either a value-added tax or some sort of sales tax. The speaker concludes that a switch to this tax might not make much of an improvement in the economy and it would burden low-income taxpayers. The article is informative because it discusses many of the practical problems that would be encountered in changing the tax system and the uncertain consequences that might result.

Selected Popular Press Articles on Tax Reform

Bartlett, Bruce, "Tax Cuts and 'Starving The Beast': The Most Pernicious Fiscal Doctrine in History." *Forbes* 2010. Accessed October 15, 2011, http://www.forbes.com/2010/05/06/tax-cuts-republicans-starve-the-beast-columnists-bruce-bartlett.html.

"Starve the beast," a strategy promoted by President Ronald Regan and others, was first coined by the economist Milton Friedman: "the only effective way to restrain government spending is by limiting government's explicit tax revenue—just as a limited income is the only effective restraint on any individual's or family's spending." The author argues that the strategy does not work because when revenues fall Congress merely resorts to borrowing money. The brief article includes a number of interesting facts on federal spending.

Hitchens, Christopher. "Minority Report." *The Nation* (December 12, 1994): 716.

A short, irreverent essay supporting the flat tax written by a prominent leftist journalist best known for his iconoclastic book *The Missionary Position*. Although the flat tax is often championed by those who oppose income redistribution, the author argues that a flat tax will actually result in income redistribution because the present system coddles the rich and the corporations, who can buy their tax breaks.

Wildavsky, Rachel. "How Fair Are Our Taxes?" *Reader's Digest* **(February 1996): 57–61.**

Most resources on tax reform ignore one important aspect of the problem: how do most taxpayers feel about the present system? The author reports on a mid-1990s survey that found that most Americans thought a family earning $200,000 should not pay more than 25 percent of their income in taxes. The author concludes that tax rates are far too high because these families already pay 39 percent. The author makes the common mistake of assuming that the marginal tax rate, the rate on the last dollar of income, is the same as the average tax rate, which of course is far lower.

Selected Nonprint Resources

Videos

Economics of Taxation

Type: 1/2" videocassette

Cost: free

Source: Internal Revenue Service

Taxpayer Education

1111 Constitution Avenue, NW

Washington, DC 20224

High-production-value videos produced by the IRS for students. The first half, *Only What You Owe*, explains the operation of the income tax and tax accounting practices for nonaccountants. The second half, *Economics of Taxation*, presents an economist's view of taxation. An excellent learning tool for students.

Only What You Owe

Type: 1/2" videocassette

Length: 22 minutes

Cost: free

Source: Internal Revenue Service

Taxpayer Education

1111 Constitution Avenue, NW

Washington, DC 20224

Internet Resources

Materials on tax reform are available on the Internet in both proprietary (available by paid subscription) databases and at free web sites.

Proprietary Databases

There are a number of proprietary databases that contain huge amounts of information on both taxes in general and tax reform in particular. Westlaw, published by Thomson, and Lexis-Nexis are both legal databases that contain both professional tax information and scholarly journal articles, as well as articles in the popular press. Although there is a charge for accessing these databases, they are also available free of charge at many college and university libraries and even at some public libraries. Ask the reference librarian at the library about access to these databases.

Web Sites

There are several hundred web sites that contain tax information, and several devoted to the subject of tax reform. The sites vary considerably in focus, content and value. At one extreme are web sites that provide tax information primarily to CPAs, tax attorneys, and other tax professionals. These typically have extensive information about technical tax topics but often very little about tax reform. Large CPA firms, law firms, and universities often sponsor these sites, which provide a rich electronic resource for researching technical tax questions. These sites frequently have no articles for average readers about tax reform, so they are not always the best place to start your research.

At the other extreme are individuals' web sites that discuss taxes. Although some are very good, others are highly one-sided and inaccurate. These sites must be used with extreme care and skepticism. Sites maintained by "tax protesters" and tax protest organizations are in a similar vein. The material often contains distorted legal arguments and language from court cases, taken out of context and used to justify tax evasion. Again, users should approach this material with a good deal of skepticism.

Of course, the government provides a wealth of information on the web, and the IRS has a useful web site. The IRS site is helpful for those who need help in filing their returns, and it does contain some statistics that are useful for the researcher.

There are a number of "tax gateways" with links to tax sites. These gateways, probably the best places to begin online tax research, are listed below.

Although all of these web addresses were checked at the time of publication, readers need to keep in mind that web addresses constantly change. Researchers may have to use a search engine to locate a specific site if the address in the book does not bring you to the desired site.

Tax Gateways

"Taxworld." 2011. Accessed October 15, 2011, http://www.tax world.org.

This site includes links to property tax and international tax sites as well as links to federal income tax sites.

Tax Laws

Thomson Reuters. 2011. "Findlaw." Accessed October 15, 2011, http://www.findlaw.com/casecode/.

This is an easy-to-use site that provides access to both current and historical tax material. Users can locate court cases dealing with tax issues and also the tax code and regulations. The site has a user-friendly search engine to help with research. A major advantage of this site is that it allows users free access to law review articles, which can be searched by subject.

U.S. Government. 2011. "GPO Access." Accessed October 15, 2011, http://www.gpoaccess.gov/.

The official web site of the federal government publications office provides access to both federal laws and court cases. The site has its own search engine that can be used to look for specific topics, including court cases that can be downloaded in full or in summary form.

'Lectric Law Library. 2011. Accessed October 15, 2011, http://www.lectlaw.com.

This is a rewarding site that provides a vast amount of legal information and can be easily accessed. The site is organized as a "library" with various "reading rooms" that contain different subjects, including taxation.

Cornell University Law School. 1911. "Legal Information Institute." Accessed October 15, 2011, http://www.law.cornell.edu.

This site, maintained by Cornell Law School, is one of the premiere electronic law libraries available. It contains both current and historical court cases. The site has its own search engine that can be used to pinpoint material. The cases can be downloaded in word processing formats as well as text. The site also serves as a portal because it contains a large number of useful links.

Miscellaneous Tax Sites

American Institute of Certified Public Accountants. 2011. "AICPA Online." Accessed October 15, 2011, http://www.aicpa.org.

This is the home page of the American Institute of Certified Public Accountants. The site contains links to other tax and accounting sites and is aimed primarily at tax professionals

U.S. Department of the Treasury. 2011. "Internal Revenue Service." Accessed October 15, 2011, www.irs.gov.

This is the official IRS web site. It provides not only downloadable forms and tables but also news releases and other tax information. The page called "The Digital Daily" is updated on a daily basis. Note carefully that the address is ".gov" not ".com."

Tax Reform Web Sites

C-Span. 2010. "Future of U.S. Tax Policy." Accessed October 15, 2011, http://www.c-spanvideo.org/program/293010–5.

U.S. Department of the Treasury. 2011. "Resource Center: Tax Reform." Accessed October 15, 2011, http://www.treasury.gov/resource-center/tax-policy/Pages/tax-reform.aspx.

This web site contains some of the "greatest hits" of tax reform published by the Office of Tax Policy of the U.S. Treasury or commissioned by the president. The reports cover individual taxation, business taxation, and international issues spanning the period 1977 to 2011.

Joint Committee on Taxation. 2011. "Present Law and Historical Overview of the Federal Tax System." Accessed October 15, 2011, http://www.jct.gov/publications.html?func=startdown&id=3719.

This web site contains a PDF version of a report prepared by the Staff of the Joint Committee On Taxation in preparation for a January 20, 2011, hearing. The report provides a summary of the federal tax system, briefly describes its historical development since 1975, and provides an appendix of selected historical data on federal tax rates, federal tax receipts, components of adjusted gross income, and other features of the federal tax system.

U.S. Department of the Treasury. 2011. "IRS Videos." Accessed October 15, 2011, http://www.irsvideos.gov/.

Although not specifically focused on tax reform, this site contains a number of practical videos for taxpayers and practitioners alike explaining both basic and technical areas of the tax rules.

C-SPAN Video Library
The following videos are listed according to their usefulness to students of tax reform. C-Span videos are accessible on the Internet. The first video in the list is a good starting point for students potentially interested in researching this topic.

C-Span. 2010 "Future of U.S. Tax Policy." Accessed October 15, 2011. http://www.c-spanvideo.org/program/293010–5.

Video of a C-SPAN/*Washington Journal* broadcast on April 15, 2010 ("tax day"); Tax expert Eugene Steuerle talks about the future of U.S. tax policy and responds to telephone calls and electronic communications. Taxes are expected to be a major political issue over the next several years, and part of the debate concerns who will pay more taxes and how high taxes will rise. Length, 41 minutes.

C-Span. 2006. "Tax Policy." Accessed October 15, 2011. http://www.c-spanvideo.org/program/TaxPolicy17.

Video of August 3, 2006, Senate Finance Committee. Advisory Panel members and other experts testify about proposed reforms of the federal tax code. Topics included the Alternate Minimum Tax, simplification of the individual tax form, tax brackets, promotion of competitiveness, the Advisory Panel report, deductions, and President George W. Bush's 2001 tax cuts. Length, 2 hours, 11 minutes.

C-Span. 2007. "The Federal Estate Tax." Accessed October 15, 2011. http://www.c-spanvideo.org/program/FederalEs.

Video of November 14, 2007, Senate Finance Committee hearing. Witnesses—including Warren Buffet—testify about federal estate tax legislation. Topics included the burden on the families of small business owners, the complexity of the tax rules, the return to a 55 percent rate in 2011, and uncertainty in estate planning under current law. Mr. Buffett was in favor of keeping the estate tax law unchanged while the three other witnesses opposed the tax. Length, 2 hours, 3 minutes.

C-Span. 2007. "Federal Income Tax Policy." Accessed October 15, 2011. http://www.c-spanvideo.org/program/FederalInc.

Video of April 16, 2007, Americans for Tax Reform Program. This group favors tax reductions. Participants spoke to reporters about tax policy, federal spending levels, wasteful programs, burdens place on middle- and working-class taxpayers, and various reform proposals. They also answered questions from the audience. Length, 1 hour, 4 minutes.

C-Span. 2011. "Federal Tax Code Revision." Accessed October 15, 2011. http://www.c-spanvideo.org/program/297613–1.

Video of January 20, 2011, House Ways and Means Committee hearing. Witnesses testify about potential revisions to the federal tax code. They focused on the economic and administrative impact of current federal income tax structure, tax complexity, corporate taxes, and the impact of the tax system on the economy. They also spoke about tax policy related to income from foreign operations of U.S. businesses. Length, 1 hour, 53 minutes.

C-Span. 2011. "History of the Income Tax." Accessed October 15, 2011. http://www.c-spanvideo.org/program/302289–5.

Video of C-SPAN/*Washington Journal* broadcast on October 25, 2011. John Steele Gordon talked about the political and economic forces that led to the creation of the federal income tax. He also responded to telephone calls and electronic communications. Length, 43 minutes.

C-Span. 2011. "Tax Policy and Fiscal Responsibility." Accessed October 15, 2011. http://www.c-spanvideo.org/program/297804–1.

Video of February 2, 2011, Senate Budget Committee on Tax Reform and its relation to the growing federal budget deficit and corporate "tax shelters." Chairman Conrad notes that the federal government borrows 40 cents for each dollar it spends. Length, 2 hours, 28 minutes.

C-Span. 2010. "Tax Reform and Deficit Reduction." Accessed October 15, 2011. http://www.c-spanvideo.org/program/296950–1.

Video of December 7, 2010, broadcast of a panel from the Urban Institute. The panelists talked about plans to reduce the federal debt and reform the U.S. tax code. They also talk about the December 2010 compromise between President Obama and congressional Republican leaders reached the previous day on the extension of the George W. Bush administration's tax cuts and unemployment benefits. They also responded to questions from the audience. Length, 1 hour, 25 minutes.

C-Span. 2005. "Retail Sales Tax." Accessed October 15, 2011. http:// www.c-spanvideo.org/program/RetailSa Video of May 11, 2005 broadcast to President's Advisory Panel on Federal Tax Reform.

The President's Advisory Panel on Federal Tax Reform held a public meeting on specific options for federal tax reform. The third panel heard testimony from experts on retail sales taxes, their impact on the economy, and potential for revenue. Length, 45 minutes.

C-Span. 2011. "Herman Cain Tax Plan." Accessed January 20, 2012. http://www.c-spanvideo.org/program/302403-1.

Video of Cain Presidential Campaign that aired on October 31, 2011. Republican 2012 presidential candidate Herman Cain discusses his "9-9-9" tax proposals.

C-Span. 2011. "Rick Perry Economic Plan Announcement." Accessed October 25, 2011. http://www.c-spanvideo.org/program/ PerryEc.

Video of Perry for President announcement that aired on October 25, 2011. Texas Governor and 2012 Republican presidential candidate Rick Perry outlined his "Cut, Balance & Grow" flat tax proposal, which he says is bolder and more aggressive than the plans of his Republican colleagues or President Obama. His plan calls for a flat 20 percent income tax rate but gives taxpayers the option of sticking to their current rate. He is also calling for private retirement accounts for Social Security, a lower corporate tax rate, and reforms at keeping Medicare solvent. Length, 31 minutes.

Glossary

Accelerated cost recovery system (ACRS)   System of income tax depreciation used between 1980 and 1987. Depreciation allows taxpayers to recover their investment tax-free in equipment and buildings over the useful life of the assets. The shorter the useful life, the larger the depreciation deductions and the lower the tax. ACRS was originally modeled after the 3-5-10 proposal for fast depreciation to benefit American manufacturing. ACRS was replaced by the less generous MACRS in 1987.

Accrual basis of accounting   A type of accounting that requires companies to book income when sales are made, not when cash is received. Most larger companies employ this method, which is also used for income tax reporting.

Accumulated earnings tax   A penalty tax imposed on a corporation that has accumulated an unreasonable amount of cash with the intent to avoid tax on dividends to individual shareholders. The tax, which is paid by the corporation, is imposed at an individual's highest tax rate.

Acquiescence   The Internal Revenue Service will either acquiesce or nonacquiese in pro–taxpayer decisions of the Tax Court. An acquiescence means that the IRS will not litigate the issue decided by the court but does not necessarily agree with the result. A nonacquiescence indicates that the IRS will continue litigating the issue.

Adjusted gross income (AGI)   An individual's income as reported on the form 1040 individual income tax return after "adjustments" but before the subtraction of itemized deductions, the standard deduction, and exemptions. AGI affects the amount of deduction allowed for medical expenses, charitable contributions, and other deductions.

Ad valorem tax   A property tax imposed, normally by a state or city, on the value of property. Ad valorem taxes can be applied to both real estate and personal property. In addition to real estate, a few states impose taxes on the value of autos and boats.

Alimony   Support payments and certain property divisions made after a divorce or legal separation. If payments are considered alimony by the income tax law, the payer receives a deduction and the recipient must include the amount in taxable income.

Alternate valuation date   Although property in an estate is normally valued for federal estate tax purposes at the date of death, the executor may elect to use the alternate valuation date, which is 6 months after death if this results in a lower tax.

Alternative minimum tax (AMT)   A tax enacted to ensure that at least a minimum amount of income tax is paid by both corporate and high-income individuals who benefit from tax deductions and other tax breaks. Although this reform measure was devised to apply to high-income taxpayers, many lower-income taxpayers who claim exemptions for many children and have high medical deductions or state taxes are also subject to AMT. This anomaly has spurred Congress to find a "fix" to provide relief to lower- and middle-income taxpayers.

Amortization   Although *amortization* refers to establishing a fund of money, in income taxes the term is used to describe a system allowing cost recovery on intangible assets that operates similarly to depreciation (see ACRS). Amortization deductions reduce taxable income and tax. Intangible assets subject to amortization include patents, copyrights, trademarks, and goodwill.

Annuity   An annuity is a periodic payment. An example is receiving retirement benefits as a series of level pension payments. For income tax purposes, each annuity payment is typically partially taxable and partially tax-free.

Appeal   The legal process of challenging a decision. Decisions of agencies can be appealed, as can lower court decisions. IRS audit results can be appealed within the agency. A court decision can also be challenged.

Apportionment   The process of dividing corporate business income among several states for state corporation tax purposes.

Assignment of income   Income is taxable to the party who owns the asset producing the income even if the right to the income has been transferred to another. Accordingly, a parent cannot assign income from a bank account or rental property to his or her child to escape taxation of the income generated by the property.

Audit   Check of a taxpayer's tax returns and records by the IRS. The percentage of tax returns examined, known as the "audit rate," has declined steadily since 1975. After the 1998 IRS Reorganization and Restructuring Act, the audit rate declined further as the agency shifted its focus from compliance to taxpayer education. Over the years, audit rates varied considerably from one area to another, raising questions about the basic fairness of their auditing system. Additionally, the IRS typically "targeted" certain activities for audits, such as tax shelters and abusive trusts.

Average tax rate   Income tax liability divided by income subject to tax.

Bad debt   When an individual or business sells goods or services on credit and is not paid, the result is a bad debt. For income tax purposes, an accrual basis taxpayer may deduct a bad debt but a cash-basis taxpayer may not because the income has not yet been booked.

Basis   An income tax concept, similar to "carrying value" of an asset—the figure appearing on the balance sheet for accounting purposes. "Basis of property" is used to determine the gain or loss on the sale of the property or to compute the amount of depreciation.

Boot   An income tax term for cash and other property received in a tax-free exchange. Boot triggers tax to the recipient.

Burden of proof   A legal term relating to which party must provide evidence to make its case. In tax cases in court the government normally has the burden of proof. In court, two different burdens of proof are used. In a civil case, the burden is preponderance: it is more likely than not that the government's version of the facts is correct. In a criminal case, the government must prove its case beyond a reasonable doubt, a far higher standard. Burden of proof also applies to tax audits, and the taxpayer has the burden of substantiating proper treatment of income and deduction items on a tax return. However, the government has the burden in court if the taxpayer cooperated with the government during the audit.

Cafeteria plan   A type of employer-provided fringe benefit plan under which an employee may select among two or more benefits. It is sometimes called a section 125 plan. Employers receive a deduction for amounts contributed to the plan, and employees receive the benefits tax-free.

Calendar year   A 12-month period beginning January 1 and ending December 31. In contrast, a fiscal year is any 12-month period other than a calendar year.

Capital asset   In the tax law a capital asset is an "investment," including stocks and bonds. Depreciable equipment and buildings used in a business are normally not capital assets.

Capital gains   Gains from the sale or exchange of capital assets. Historically, for income tax purposes, the tax code has given capital gains lower rates than those imposed on "ordinary income." Corporations may deduct a capital loss only to the extent of capital gains. Individuals may offset up to $3,000 of capital losses against their ordinary income in addition to any capital gains.

Cash basis   A system of tax accounting in which taxpayers report income when cash is received and deductions when cash is paid. Nearly all individuals use the cash basis on their tax returns, as do many smaller corporations, partnerships, and trusts.

Casualty loss   For income tax purposes, a loss arising from fire, storm, shipwreck, or other casualty. To be deductible for tax purposes, the loss must be sudden, unexpected, and unusual.

Certiorari, writ of   The Supreme Court is required to hear very few cases and accepts most of its docketed cases by accepting a "writ of certiorari" from a claimant. The court hears very few federal tax cases but tends to hear many state cases involving federalism issues. When the court declines to hear a case, the decision is noted as "cert. den.," for certiorari denied. In this case the decision of the lower court stands.

Charitable contribution   Contribution of cash or property to a recognized nonprofit entity. For income tax purposes, taxpayers are allowed to deduct such contributions subject to dollar limitations.

Check-the-box regulations   A major reform for small businesses, the check-the-box regulations greatly simplified reporting for smaller businesses. The IRS frequently challenged the validity of smaller corporations and limited liability companies. These regulations allow such taxpayers to elect whether they want their businesses taxed as partnerships or corporations.

Child and dependent care credit   Income tax credit allowed for employment-related expenses for employed individuals who maintain a household for a child under age 13 or a disabled spouse or dependent.

Child tax credit   Income tax credit based on the number of the taxpayer's dependent children. Many countries, including Canada, use their tax systems to indirectly subsidize child rearing. Although advocates of this approach argue that the government has an interest in subsidizing children, others argue that this encourages large families and runaway population growth.

Community property   A type of ownership applied to property owned by a husband and wife in the states Arizona, California, Idaho, Louisiana, Nevada, New Mexico, Texas, Washington, and Wisconsin. Neither spouse may sell or encumber the property without the other's consent. Because each spouse has a 50 percent interest in the other spouse's income, they can each report one half of each spouse's income on a tax return.

Constructive receipt doctrine   Although individual taxpayers report income when they receive cash or property, income is subject to tax when it is "constructively received" and available to the taxpayer. An uncashed check or accrual of interest on a bank account is reportable income under this doctrine.

Consumption tax   A tax designed to tax consumption of income rather than the income itself. A flat tax that does not apply to capital gains, interest, or dividends is an example of a consumption tax. A retail sales tax is also a consumption tax.

Contribution to capital   Investment in a business by a shareholder. The amount an initial shareholder pays for stock. Return of this contribution to the shareholder (or a subsequent buyer of the stock) is not subject to income tax.

Corporation   Business entity established under a state statute with shareholders as owners and officers and managers. Such an entity is subject to a separate corporate income tax. State law controls the formation and operation of the corporation, whereas federal tax law determines the tax consequences of its activities.

Cost depletion   Depletion is an allowance for cost recovery. The tax law allows two systems of depletion, cost depletion and percentage (statutory) depletion. Cost depletion operates like depletion for financial accounting purposes.

Cost recovery   In income taxation, only "income" (profit) is taxed. Hence, recovery of your initial cost is nontaxable. A taxpayer who buys stock for $40 and sells it for $100 is only taxable on the $60 of income. The $40 is tax-free cost recovery. When an asset is depreciated, the cost recovery is spread over the asset's life in the form of yearly deductions rather than being realized in the year of sale.

Court of Federal Claims (Claims Court)   A specialized federal court, originally created after the American Revolution to create a fair forum for British creditor claims, the court hears lawsuits against the federal government including tax cases.

Credit (tax credit)   Amount subtracted from income tax liability. Credits are generally available to encourage positive behavior. A tax credit is more generous than a tax deduction because the credit is subtracted from the tax owed, resulting in a dollar-for-dollar reduction of tax. A tax deduction is subtracted from income and results in reduction in the amount of income subject to tax. Accordingly if a taxpayer in the 28 percent marginal tax bracket has a $1 tax credit, this will reduce the tax owed by $1. If the taxpayer had received $1of deduction, taxable income would be reduced by $1but the tax would be reduced by only 28 cents.

Death taxes   A term that refers to the federal estate tax and state inheritance taxes.

Deduction   For income tax purposes, an expense (cost) that the tax law allows to reduce income subject to tax. Deductions are a matter of "legislative grace." This means that Congress can both create and abolish deductions. Deductions are often used to subsidize activities or to motivate good behavior. Accordingly the tax code allows individuals to deduct large medical costs as a subsidy and provides a charitable deduction to encourage charitable gifts. Subject to limitations, most business expenses are deductible because the income tax is imposed on profits. However, most personal family living expenses are not deductible unless specifically allowed by statute.

Deficiency Amount by which the actual tax exceeds the tax reported on the tax return.

Depletion Cost recovery for natural resources. Depletion applies to natural resources such as oil and gas, minerals, coal, and timber. Depletion is similar but not identical to amortization and depreciation and is available in both financial and income tax accounting. Percentage depletion, a tax concept, is also called a statutory depletion and is more generous than cost depletion. Both cost depletion and percentage depletion are allowed by the income tax code.

Depreciation A system of cost allocation in accounting. It has nothing to do with physical wear and tear or valuation. For income tax purposes, the cost of an asset can be recovered tax-free over the usable life of the asset through depreciation deductions. The shorter the useful life selected, the larger the deductions and the lower the tax in the initial years of use. Accelerated depreciation allows owners larger depreciation deductions and lower taxes in the initial years of use.

Dividend A distribution of corporate profits to shareholders. For income tax purposes, dividends are not deductible by the corporation and are taxed as ordinary income to recipients, hence the "double taxation" of corporate profits under the current U.S. tax system. This rule discourages the payment of dividends.

Dividend received deduction Income tax deduction available only to corporations who receive a 70, 80, or 100 percent deduction for dividends received from certain domestic corporations. The deduction is designed to offset double or even triple taxation when corporations receive dividends from corporations in which they hold stock.

Double taxation Income earned by a corporation and distributed to shareholders as a dividend is taxed to both the corporation and the shareholder, hence "double taxation."

Earned income For income tax purposes, income from employment, wages, and commissions. Unearned income includes "passive" income, such as dividends, interest, and royalties. In the past, earned income was taxed at lower rates than unearned income.

Employee A worker who is not an independent contractor. Employers must withhold income taxes for their employees and must also pay employment tax on their behalf. The test to distinguish an employee from an independent contractor centers on "control" of the worker's activities but is hard to apply in practice.

Employee stock option Stock option granted as compensation that potentially allows an employee to purchase employer stock at a bargain price.

Employee stock ownership plan (ESOP) A type of retirement plan that invests in the stock of an employer for the benefit of the employees. This gives the employees an ownership interest in their employer.

Estate An artificial legal entity that holds a property after an individual's death. On death, property that is not co-owned or subject to a beneficiary designation falls into the probate estate, supervised by the executor ("personal representative"). For federal estate tax purposes, the taxable estate may be broader than the state probate estate.

Estimated tax Self-employed taxpayers and other taxpayers with income not subject to withholding must make estimated tax payments on a quarterly basis.

Excise tax A tax imposed on a specific transaction or product. The gasoline tax is a type of excise tax.

Executor An individual appointed in a will to carry out the directions in the will. Also known as a personal representative. The executor is responsible for paying any federal estate tax.

Exemption For income tax purposes, income that is not subject to tax. The term normally is applied to a "dependency exemption," which shelters from tax a fixed amount if income (annually indexed for inflation) for each person residing in the taxpayer's home whom the taxpayer financially supports.

Expense A cost. In income tax, an expense that reduces income subject to tax is called a deduction.

Fair market value The price at which a willing seller would sell to a willing buyer in arm's-length transaction (what two unrelated taxpayers would agree to).

Federal Insurance Contributions Act (FICA) Legislation that imposes Social Security taxes on both employers and employees.

Federal Unemployment Tax Act (FUTA) Legislation that imposes federal employment tax on employers.

Fiduciary A person or entity in a position of trust, such as an executor of an estate or the trustee of a trust. A fiduciary tax return is a return filed by a fiduciary.

Filing status For income tax purposes, tax rates depend on a taxpayer's filing status, which in turn depends on the taxpayer's living arrangements. Taxpayers file as single taxpayers, married filing jointly, married filing separately, and head of household.

Fiscal year Any 12-month period other than a calendar year.

Flat tax   A tax that includes one tax rate rather than several. Progressive tax rates utilize several rates that depend on income.

Foreign tax credit   An income tax credit that reduces U.S. tax to the extent that the taxpayer must also pay tax on the income to a foreign government. The credit is designed to prevent double taxation.

Fringe benefit   For income tax purposes, a working condition benefit. Most fringe benefits are tax-free to employees, and their cost is deductible to their employers.

401(k) plan   Type of voluntary retirement plan in which an employee makes contributions that the employer is free to match. The amount in the plan is invested—typically in stock—and is subject to market risk until the employee retires. Employees typically withdraw the balance as an annuity, receiving level payments over their retirement years. Contributions and growth are not subject to income tax, which allows the fund to grow far faster than it otherwise would. Retirement distributions are taxable.

Gift   Transfer of property from one to another for less than full value. A transfer can also be part gift–part sale (also termed a "bargain sale").

Gift tax   A federal tax on gratuitous transfers. Coordinated with the federal estate tax, the two taxes are referred to as "transfer" taxes because they tax the transfer rather than the ownership of wealth. The tax is imposed on the donor, not the donee (recipient). The gift tax is designed to apply only to the wealthy. By 2011, individuals could transfer up to $5 million during their lifetimes without paying a gift tax.

Graduated tax rate   Tax rate structure that is progressive, meaning that tax rates increase as income increases.

Gross income   Gross income includes all income subject to tax before deductions. Some income items, such as inheritances, are not subject to tax and accordingly are not included in gross income for tax purposes.

Head of household   A relief tax rate that applies to unmarried taxpayers who maintain a household for a qualifying dependent. It is a special tax rate between the joint and the single rates.

Head tax   A flat amount assessed on each citizen as a tax.

Holding period   The amount of time the property has been held by the taxpayer. For preferential capital gains rates to apply, capital assets must be a held for at least 12 months and 1 day after 1987.

Horizontal equity   For income tax purposes, the goal that taxpayers with similar incomes will pay similar amounts of tax.

Indexing   Adjusting an amount for inflation. The standard deduction, the personal exemption, and other amounts are indexed for inflation.

Individual Retirement Account (IRA)   Formally known as an Individual Retirement Arrangement, an IRA is a retirement account designed for individuals without employer retirement plans. Although once restricted to those who do not participate in employer retirement plans, for a time the law allowed anyone to make a tax deductible contribution to an IRA, although since 1986 upper-income taxpayers who are eligible for employer retirement plans may only make IRA contributions on a nondeductible basis. Withdrawals from an IRA are generally taxable when received.

Inheritance tax   Tax imposed on heirs on the privilege of inheriting cash or property. Several states impose inheritance taxes.

Installment method   Tax reporting that allows installment sale proceeds to be taxed as payments are received rather than in the year of the sale.

Integration   An income tax concept that would combine individual and corporate taxation, replacing the "double tax" on corporate profits with a single tax. S corporations are already taxed in this manner. S corporations pay no tax, but shareholders are required to pay the tax on the corporation's profits, whether or not the shareholders have received any cash distributions. Proponents of integration argue that it would make the U.S. economy more competitive.

Inter vivos trust   A trust created during the lifetime of the individual establishing the trust.

Inventory   Goods held by a business for resale to customers. Sale of inventory produces ordinary income, not capital gain.

Itemized deductions   Deductions allowed when their total exceeds the standard deduction. Includes medical expenses, charitable contributions, state and local taxes, and casualty losses.

Joint return   Form 1040 filed by married couples. Although joint filing normally results in a lower tax, it can also produce a "marriage penalty." Accordingly, reform efforts are being directed at removing this penalty.

Kiddie tax   Children under age nineteen must pay tax on their "unearned" income over a minimal amount at their parent's marginal tax rate.

Lien   Legal claim by the government to property of a taxpayer for unpaid taxes.

Like-kind exchange   A transaction in which taxpayers are allowed to exchange similar properties without triggering immediate tax. Mostly used for real estate exchanges.

Limited liability company   A recently developed type of business entity similar in some respects to a partnership and in other respects to a corporation.

Long-term capital gain   The gain from selling capital assets held for more than 12 months and 1 day. Taxpayers benefit from the special low tax rate on these gains.

Marginal tax rate   The tax rate at which the taxpayer's next dollar of income will be taxed.

Marriage penalty   Anomaly whereby a married couple pays more in tax than would be the case if the couple were unmarried and filing separate returns. The problems has become more widespread since spouses' incomes have grown more nearly equal.

Modified Accelerated Cost Recovery System (MACRS)   Tax depreciation system that replaced ACRS in 1986.

Net operating loss   The economic loss from business. A net operating loss deduction may be carried to other tax years to create a tax refund.

Nonrefundable credit   A tax credit that can only result in a tax refund if the taxpayer has paid a tax.

Partnership   Two or more persons carrying on a business for profit. A partnership itself does not pay income taxes; rather, the partners report the income on their own tax returns and pay the tax.

Passive activity loss rules   A reform measure to combat tax shelters. Passive activity losses cannot offset investment income or earned income. A passive activity is an investment or business at which the taxpayer spends little or no time.

Personal holding company tax   A special penalty tax imposed on companies with few or no operating assets.

Poll tax   A flat tax imposed as a precondition to voting. Now unconstitutional in the United States.

Progressive tax   A tax rate system whereby the tax rate increases as income increases. It is thought to be "fair" because the well to do pay a higher percentage of the tax than the poor. The current income tax system utilizes progressive tax rates.

Regressive tax   A tax rate system in which poor taxpayers pay a higher percentage of their income than the rich. The Social Security tax is an example of a regressive tax.

Regulations   The Treasury issues tax regulations interpreting the federal tax code passed by Congress. Although regulations must be followed, they do not have the force of law normally.

Related taxpayers   The tax code contains several rules concerning transactions between related parties, such as husbands and wives. For example, a married couple cannot generate a tax loss by selling one another property at a loss.

Retail sales tax   A sales tax that applies only to the ultimate consumer of goods. Middlemen who resell products are eligible for a resale exemption from the tax.

Revenue neutrality   The concept that tax measures will bring in at least as much revenue as they lose.

Roth IRA   A special type of IRA (*see* IRA) that allows nondeductible contributions but provides that any withdrawals after 5 years will be tax-free.

S corporation   A small-business corporation that is taxed like a partnership. The corporation itself normally pays little or no tax; instead, the corporation's shareholders report the taxable income.

Self-employment income   Income earned by self-employed individuals that is subject to Social Security taxes. Self-employed individuals must make quarterly estimated tax payments of both income tax and self-employment tax.

Severance taxes   Taxes on natural resources like timber or gas and oil.

Sin tax   Excise tax on a "vice," such as alcohol or gambling.

Sixteenth Amendment   The amendment to the U.S. Constitution authorizing an income tax.

Standard deduction   The fixed amount an individual may elect to deduct on a form 1040. Individuals may choose to itemize deductions if they exceed the standard deduction.

Statute of limitations   Time within which a tax return may be amended (corrected) by the taxpayer or audited by the IRS. The statute of limitations for income tax purposes is normally three years. Violations of the law also have statutes of limitations.

Surviving spouse   A widow or widower who maintains a household for a dependent child. The surviving spouse is entitled to use the joint return in the year of the spouse's death and the following year.

Tariff   A federal tax on imports and occasionally exports. Used to raise funds but also to protect domestic industry.

Taxable income   Gross income less deductions and exemptions. Tax is calculated as a percentage of taxable income. Individuals normally use the tax tables for this purpose.

Tax base   The collective value or income subject to tax.

Tax Court   United States Tax Court is a specialized court hearing only tax controversies.

Tax expenditure   Tax revenue forgone by the Treasury by allowing taxpayers a deduction or tax credit.

Tax incentive   A feature in the tax system designed to encourage or discourage taxpayer action.

Tax incidence   The determination of the individual or entity that will actually pay a tax.

Tax rate   The percentage of tax applied to the tax base to calculate the amount of the tax. In the United States the income tax has several graduated (varying) tax rates that rise with the amount of the income to be taxed.

Tax shelter   An investment designed to postpone tax. Tax shelters often use borrowing to create larger tax benefits. The passive activity loss rules were enacted to curb the widespread use of tax shelters (see passive activity loss rules).

Tax treaty   A treaty between two or more countries harmonizing the tax treatment to their respective citizens. Commonly entered into to eliminate double taxation.

Tenancy by the entirety   A type of joint ownership between spouses allowed in a few states.

Tenancy in common   Ownership held by two or more parties.

Testamentary trust   A trust included in a will that operates after death.

Transfer tax   The U.S. estate tax and gift tax are transfer taxes that are imposed on the transfer of wealth. The estate tax is imposed on a decedent's estate, whereas the gift tax is imposed on the donor (maker) of the gift.

Trust   Fiduciary relationship over property in which the grantor contributes trust property to a trust to be administered by a trustee for the benefit of one or more beneficiaries.

United Savings Allowance (USA) tax   A proposed personal consumption tax that includes features of the present individual income tax.

User fee   A fee for using a government service. A bridge toll is a user fee rather than a tax.

Value-added tax (VAT)   A consumption tax used in Europe and other developed countries that imposes a business-level tax on the value added at each level of production. The VAT has been proposed as an alternative to the current U.S. income tax system.

Vertical equity   The concept that a tax system should more heavily tax the wealthy than the poor.

Wealth tax   A tax on property rather than income. Property taxes and death taxes are wealth taxes.

Withholding   A system of collecting taxes from the wages of employees. Employers send the withheld tax to the Treasury.

Index

About the Author

JAMES JOHN JURINSKI, author of *Religion in the Schools: A Reference Handbook*, is an attorney-at-law in Portland, Oregon, and an associate professor at the University of Portland. He is the author of several books and articles on taxes and legal topics.